D1299112

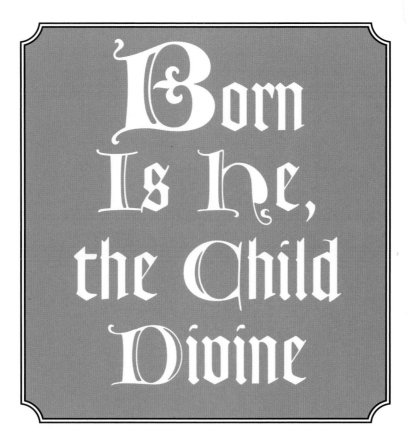

Born Is he, the Child Divine

Amy Gelber

MetroBooks

MetroBooks

Published in 1997 by Michael Friedman Publishing Group, Inc.
by arrangement with Todtri ProductionsLtd.

Copyright © 1997 by Todtri Productions Limited.

All rights reserved. No part of this publication may be reproduced, stored
in a retrieval system or transmitted in any form or by any means, electronic,
mechanical, photocopying, recording, or otherwise, without first obtaining written
permission of the copyright owner.

Library of Congress Cataloging-in-Publication Data available on request.

ISBN 1-56799-602-7

This book was designed and produced by Todtri Productions Limited
P.O. Box 572, New York, NY 10116-0572 FAX: (212) 279-1241

Author: Amy Gelber

Publisher: Robert M. Tod
Editorial Director: Elizabeth Loonan
Senior Editor: Cynthia Sternau
Project Editor: Ann Kirby
Photo Editor: Laura Wyss
Production Coordinator: Jay Weiser
Designer: Creative Studio Editions

Printed and bound in Singapore

For bulk purchases and special sales, please contact:
Friedman/Fairfax Publishers
Attention: Sales Department
15 West 26th Street
New York, NY 10010
212/685-6610 FAX 212/685-1307

Visit our website:
http://www.metrobooks.com

All pictures courtesy of Art Resource, New York, NY

Introduction

Like a medieval Book of Hours, or a Victorian album devoted to personal and spiritual memories, this book is a beautiful and inspiring combination of pictures and text, designed for quiet contemplation. The theme is the childhood of Christ, one that has moved countless artists and writers throughout the ages.

The works of art collected here cover the full range of Christian expression, from a Byzantine marble relief of Jesus lying on a rough-hewn manger, to an explosively colorful northern Renaissance altarpiece by Mathias Grüenwald, to a neo-primitive twentieth-century expressionist painting by Emil Nolde. Here are mosaics, paintings, and sculptures by the world's most famous artists, including Giotto, Fra Angelico, Botticelli, Dürer, da Vinci, Michelangelo, Raphael, Van Eyck, Rubens, Caravaggio, Rossetti, Chagall, and others.

Though few biblical passages detail Christ's childhood, the wealth of art devoted to it is overwhelming. Artists have not been embarrassed to portray the same themes time and time again, using traditional elements and compositions, even "borrowing" from others to an extent that might be considered plagiarism today. Some lovingly reworked a single theme, like Hans Memling, the late Gothic Flemish painter who obsessively recreated the Madonna and Child enthroned, flanked by angels.

While scenes of the Nativity and depictions of the Virgin and Child seem to have held sway in the popular imagination—judging by the number of masterpieces they have inspired—all the biblical events of Christ's early life are covered here, from the Annunciation to the Disputation with the Doctors (a rare glimpse of Christ as a twelve year-old). Included as well as are a host of apocryphal, traditional, or legendary themes not found in the Bible: the Holy Family resting during the flight into Egypt; scenes of the young Christ Child with his cousin, John the Baptist; the *Sacra Conversazione* , a grouping of Virgin and Child flanked by Saints that was popular in Renaissance times; the Holy Family at work in Joseph's carpentry shop; and various visions of the Madonna and Child, such as Caravaggio's *Madonna of Loreto*, in which two paupers witness their miraculous appearance in a slum doorway.

Each work has a brief caption identifying the piece and an art historical or thematic observation. Accompanying these images are quotations from prayers, sermons, carols, poems, hymns, and, of course, biblical passages. A nativity scene with a chorus of angels calls for the hosannas of a spirited carol; a stained-glass Madonna and Child is reflected in a prayer emphasizing the power of divine illumination; a contemplative, mysterious painting by da Vinci is offset with evocative quotes from the Psalms. These pages are, in essence, a collection of works of art—from paintings to poems—inspired by and paying tribute to the childhood of Christ.

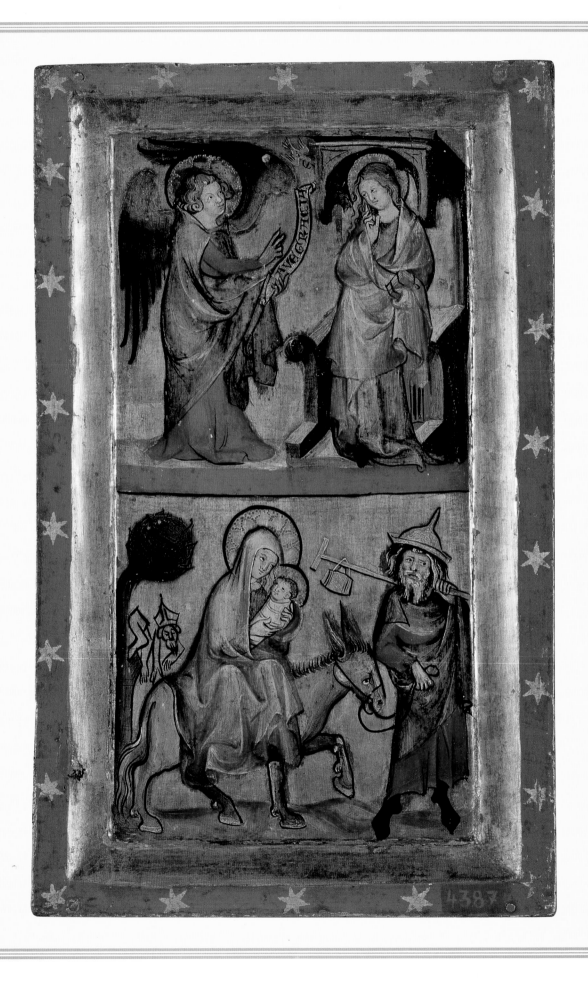

And the angel said unto her, Fear not, Mary: for thou hast found favor with God. And, behold, thou shalt conceive in thy womb, and bring forth a son, and shalt call his name JESUS. He shall be great, and shall be called the Son of the Highest; and the Lord God shall give unto him the throne of his father David: And he shall reign over the house of Jacob for ever; and of his kingdom there shall be no end.

—Luke 1:30–33.

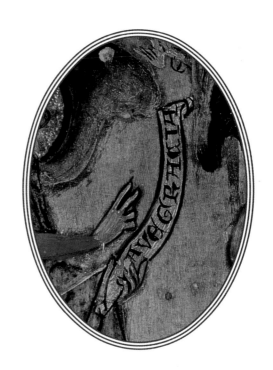

Annunciation and Flight into Egypt

Silesian master, c. 1370; tempera on panel, 17½ x 11¾ in (45 x 30 cm). National Museum, Warsaw.

This panel from the Clarissinnenaltar, the altar of the nuns of Saint Claraw in Wroclaw, Poland, depicts two distinct New Testament scenes. The top panel shows the Annunciation, when the Angel Gabriel appeared to Mary, and told her that she was to conceive the child Jesus by the Holy Spirit, traditionally represented as a dove. The bottom panel shows Joseph and Mary with the baby Jesus on their flight into Egypt.

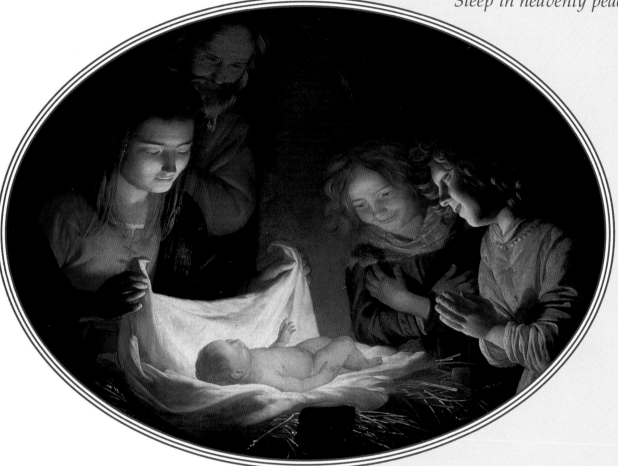

Silent night, holy night,
All is calm, all is bright,
Round yon virgin mother and child,
Holy infant so tender and mild,
Sleep in heavenly peace,
Sleep in heavenly peace.

Adoration of the Child

Gerrit van Honthorst, n.d.;
oil on canvas; 89¾ x 78 in.
(227.9 x 198.1 cm).
Uffizi, Florence.

Silent night, holy night,
Shepherds first saw the sight:
Glories streamed from heaven afar,
Heavenly hosts sing Alleluia:
Christ the Saviour is born,
Christ the Saviour is born!

—**Excerpt from Silent Night**
by Josef Mohr.

Holy Night

Gerard David, c. 1495; oil on panel; 22¼ x 16 in (57 x 41 cm). Kunsthistorisches Museum, Vienna.

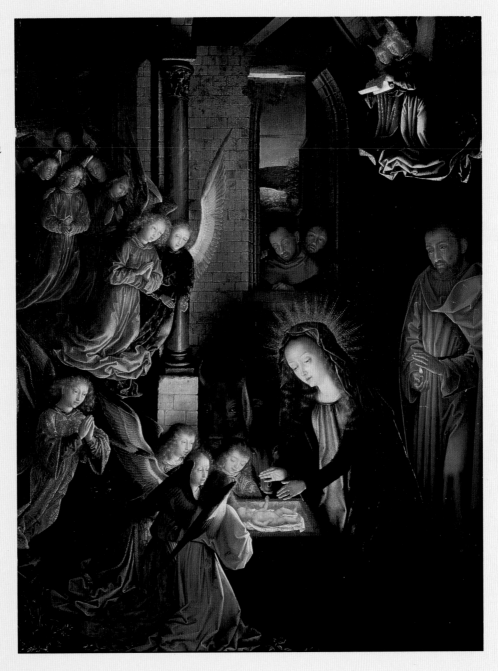

Gerard David's painting is a traditional rendition of the Birth of Jesus, with hovering angels and the Holy Ghost in the form of a dove. Honthorst takes a more intimate, realistic approach, emphasizing the humble beginnings of Jesus in details such as the straw sticking out beneath his swaddling clothes. Yet these paintings share a common use of light—flooding Jesus' and Mary's faces with heavenly illumination—to create a feeling of holiness and mystery.

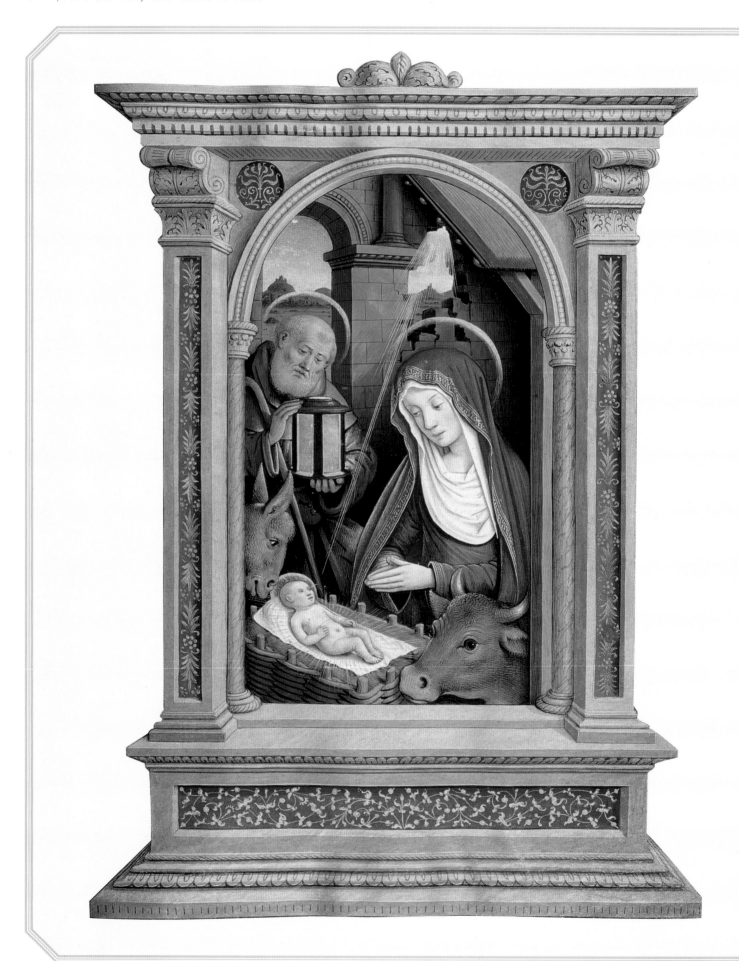

The people that walked in darkness have seen a great light: they that dwell in the land of the shadow of death, upon them hath the light shined. . . . For unto us a child is born, unto us a son is given: and the government shall be upon his shoulder: and his name shall be called Wonderful, Counselor, The Mighty God, The Everlasting Father, The Prince of Peace.

—Isaiah 9:2, 6.

The ox knoweth his owner, and the ass his master's crib.

—Isaiah 1:3.

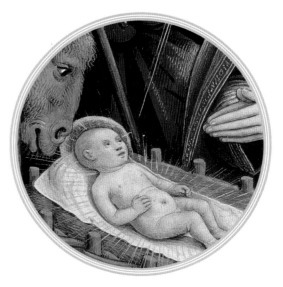

Nativity

Jean Bourdichon, c. 1515; illumination from Book of Hours. *The Pierpont Morgan Library, New York.*

Animals add a touching and often lighthearted note to many of the most pious artworks of the past. Here the wondrous, intent stare of the donkey is almost comical. The ox and the ass are traditionally portrayed in scenes of the Nativity on the basis of the biblical passage from this first chapter in Isaiah.

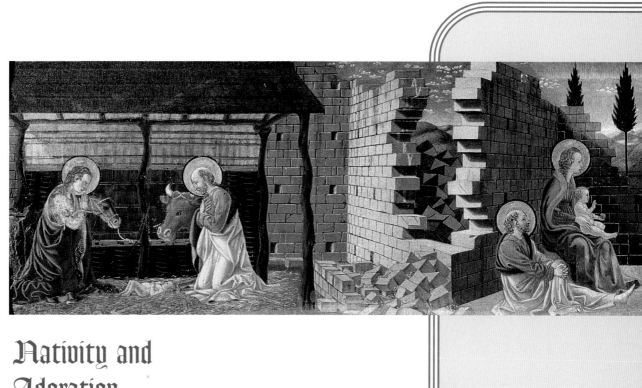

Nativity and Adoration of the Magi

*Giovanni di Francesco,
mid-fifteenth century;
oil on panel. Louvre, Paris.*

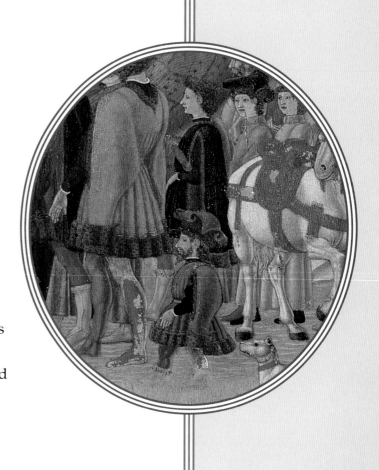

The Magi, offering gifts to the infant Jesus, have been portrayed in contemporary terms by this Italian Renaissance painter as a hunting party of nobles. Dwarves were often kept by rich aristocrats as court clowns or soothsayers. Note also the greyhounds in the foreground and the falcon held by one of the king's pages (at the end of the procession). Renaissance nobles often kept domestic falcons as trained hunting birds.

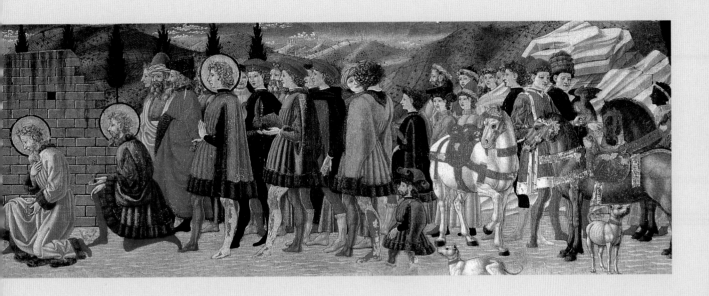

Three kings from Persian lands afar

To Jordan follow the pointing star;

And this the quest of the travellers three,

Where the new-born King of the Jews may be.

Full royal gifts they bear for the King;

Gold, incense, myrrh and their offering.

The star shines out with a stead-fast ray;

The kings to Bethlehem make their way,

And there in worship they bend the knee,

As Mary's child in her lap they see;

Their royal gifts they show to the King;

Gold, incense, myrrh are their offering.

—Excerpt from **The Three Kings**
by Peter Cornelius.

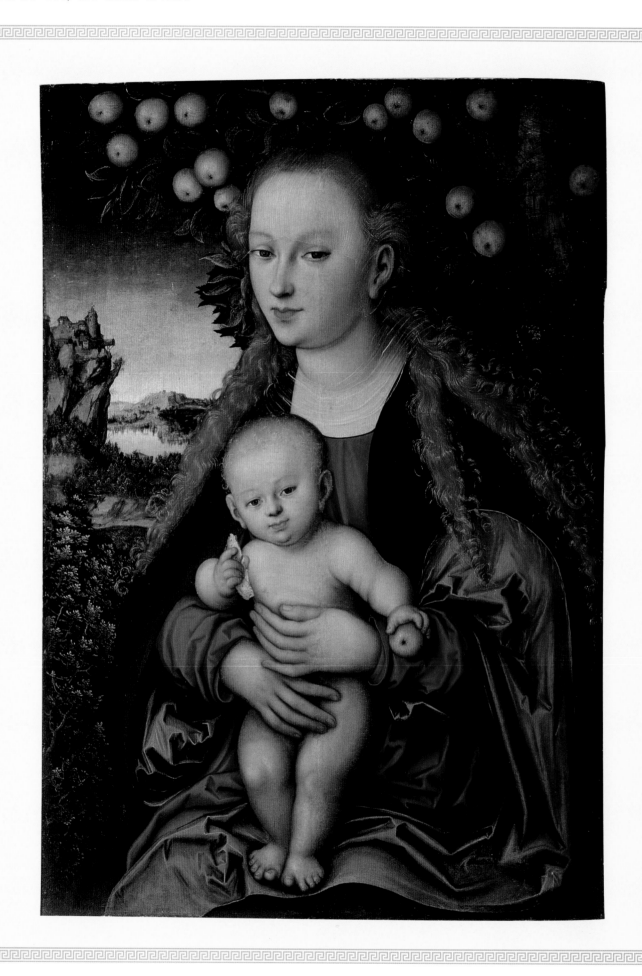

The tree of life my soul hath seen,

Laden with fruit and always green:

The tree of life my soul hath seen,

Laden with fruit and always green:

The trees of nature fruitless be

Compared with Christ the apple tree.

This fruit doth make my soul to thrive,

It keeps my dying faith alive:

This fruit doth make my soul to thrive,

It keeps my dying faith alive:

Which makes my soul in haste to be

With Jesus Christ the apple tree.

—Jesus Christ the Apple Tree
compiled by Joshua Smith.

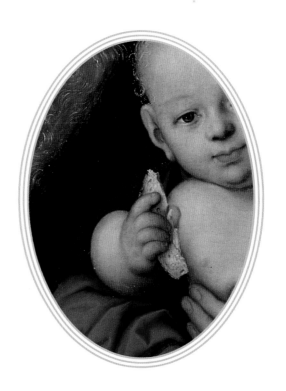

Madonna and Child Below the Apple Tree

Lucas Cranach the Elder, c. 1525; oil on canvas; 33¹⁵⁄₁₆ x 23 in. (87 x 59 cm). Hermitage, St. Petersburg.

When Adam and Eve ate the apple, mankind lost its immortality. The apples and apple tree in this painting allude to Jesus' role as the new Adam (and Mary's as the new Eve), because Christ restored our immortality. The bread in Christ's hand is yet another allusion to Christ's role as Saviour: bread is both the "staff of life" and the body of Christ in communion.

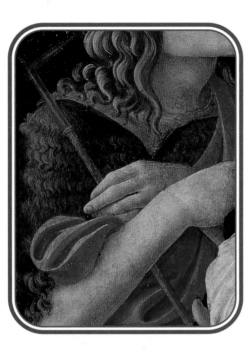

Madonna and Child with Saint John the Baptist

Sandro Botticelli, late fifteenth century; oil on panel; 36 x 26½ in. (91.4 x 67.3 cm). Louvre, Paris.

Though there is no biblical basis for such a scene, painters often depict an infant John the Baptist meeting with Mary and Jesus on their return from Egypt. Instead of the traditional landscape background, Botticelli has chosen to set his characters against a rose-filled hedge, a reference to Mary's chastity. John's reed cross emphasizes his mission as preacher as well as his rustic nature.

And thou, child, shalt be called the prophet of the Highest: for thou shalt go before the face of the Lord to prepare his ways; To give knowledge of salvation unto his people by the remission of their sins. . . . To give light to them that sit in darkness and in the shadow of death, to guide our feet into the way of peace.

—Luke 1:76–77, 79.

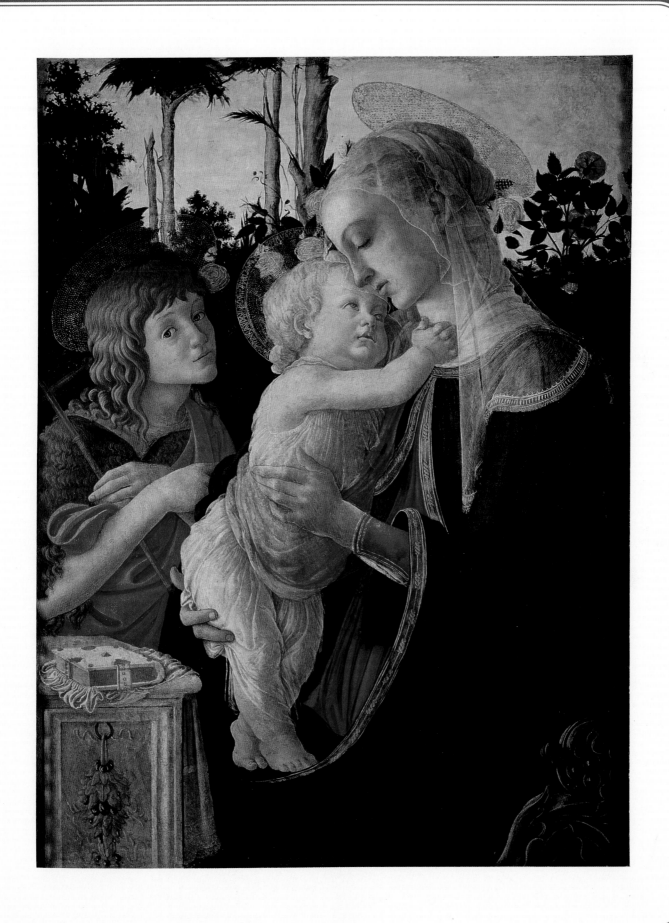

Thy brightness does consume all darkness,
transforms the gloomy night to light.
Lead us in Thy ways,
that Thy countenance
and glorious light
we may ever behold!

Enlighten, too, my dark thoughts,
illuminate my heart
throught the clear radiance of Thy beams.
Thy word shall be the brightest candle
to me in all my doings!
It shall prevent my soul embarking upon
aught evil.

—Excerpts from Christmas Oratorio
by Johann Sebastian Bach.

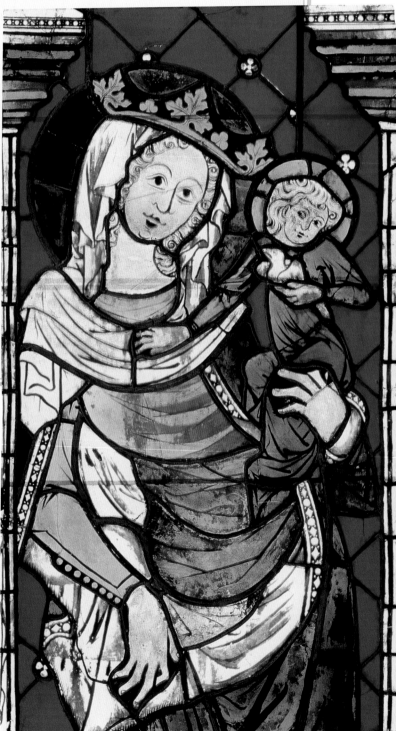

Madonna and Child

Unknown Vienna artist, c. 1300–10; Stained Glass; National Museum, Nuremburg.

Madonna and Child with Dove of Holy Spirit

Louniès Mentor, twentieth century; oil on panel. Milwaukee Art Museum, Wisconsin.

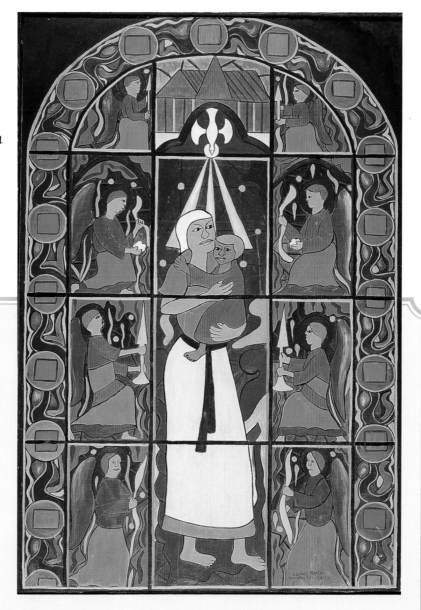

In medieval France, Abbot Suger started the craze for elaborate stained-glass windows to create an effect of miraculous, divine illumination inside churches and cathedrals. Gothic artists used tiny panes of colored glass, held in place by lead strips, to define geometric patterns, and even elaborate representational compositions. Here, a contemporary Haitian artist has harnessed the spiritual power of those stained-glass windows, using vibrant, sun-washed colors to recreate the feeling of transparency and brilliance. Painted bands, imitating lead strips, lend symmetry, strength, and clarity to the composition.

The Holy Family With Young St. John the Baptist

Michelangelo, c. 1504–7; oil on panel; 47¼ in. (120 cm) diameter. Uffizi, Florence.

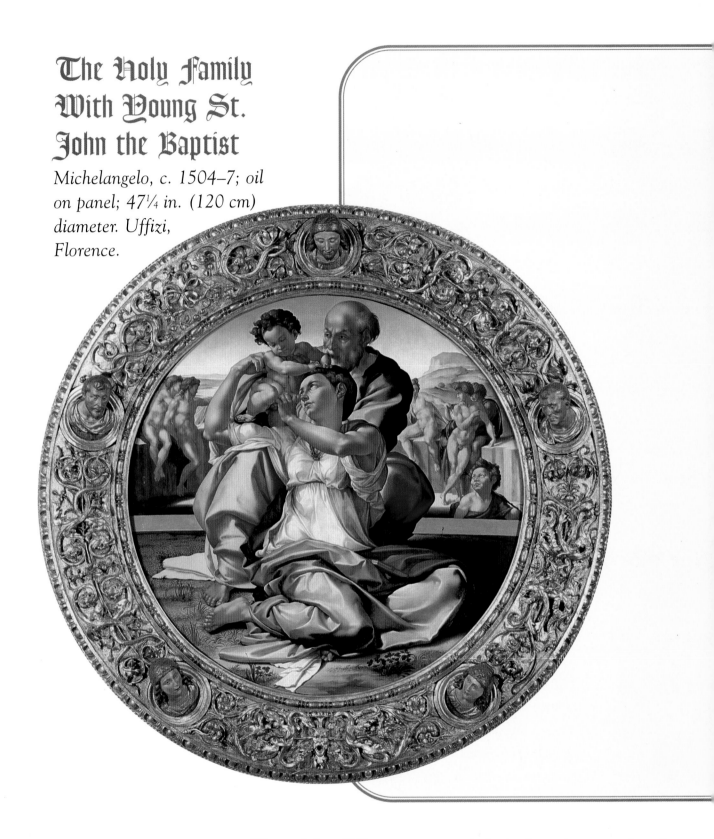

Though by different master artists, these two works of the high Italian Renaissance share a similar approach to this timeless subject. Rendered with great plasticity and anatomical correctness of form, Madonna and Child are tempered gently and evenly by the light of reason. Gone

You are love,

You are wisdom.

You are humility,

You are endurance.

You are rest,

You are peace.

You are joy and gladness.

You are justice and moderation.

You are all our riches,

And you suffice for us.

You are our faith,

Our great consolation.

You are our eternal life,

Great and wonderful Lord,

God almighty,

Merciful Saviour.

—Prayer of St. Francis of Assisi.

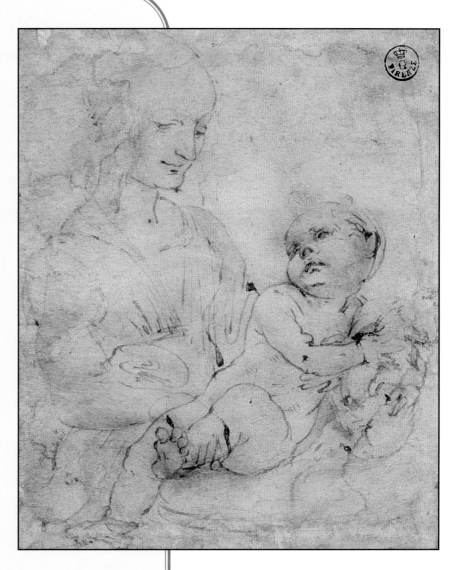

Madonna and Child

Leonardo da Vinci, n.d.; drawing. Gabinetto dei Disegni e delle Stampe, Florence.

are the halos and the dramatic light effects so often used to underscore the divine nature of this couple. The subject is the loving, human interaction of mother and child, and not the spiritual message they represent.

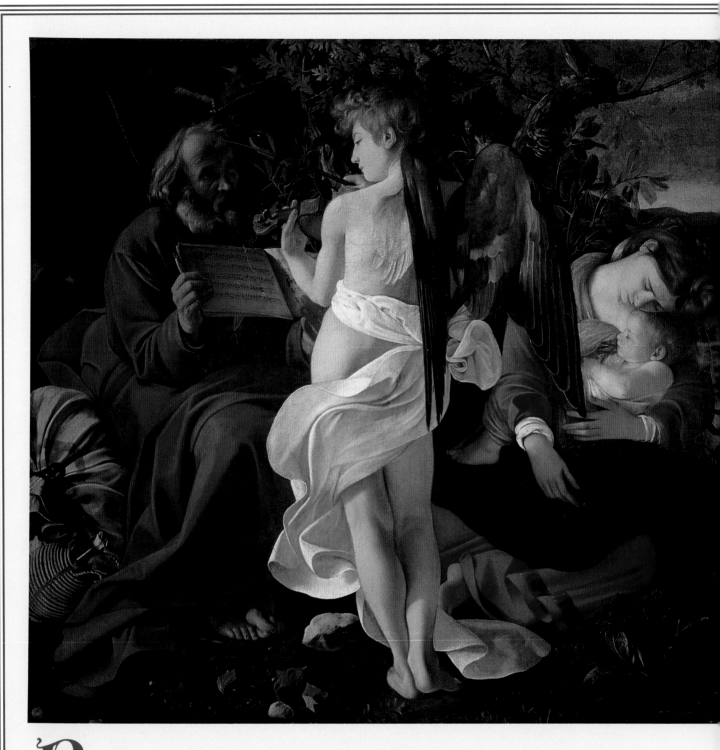

Behold, the angel of the Lord appeareth to Joseph in a dream, saying, Arise, and take the young child and his mother, and flee into Egypt, and be thou there until I bring thee word: for Herod will seek this young child to destroy him. When he arose, he took the young child and his mother by night, and departed into Egypt.

—**Matthew 2:13–14.**

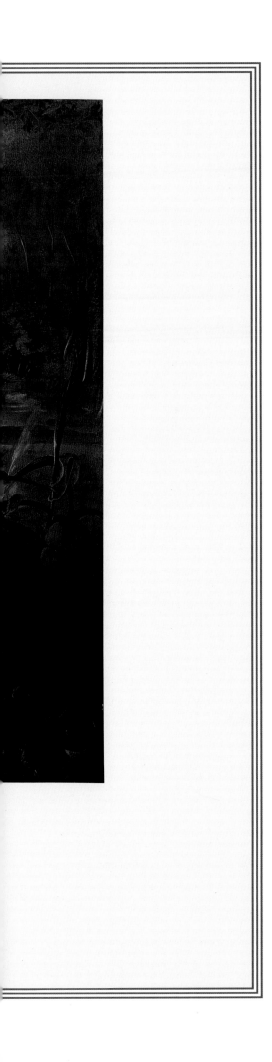

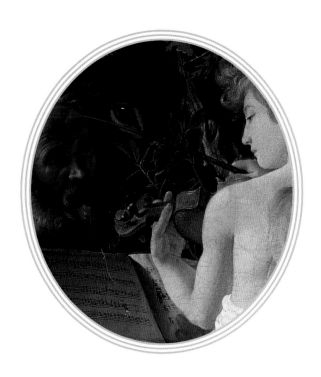

Rest on the Flight into Egypt

Caravaggio, c. 1596–97; oil on canvas;
51¼ x 63 in. (130.1 x 160 cm).
Galleria Doria Pamphili, Rome.

Caravaggio has taken a traditional subject and given it an astonishingly unconventional interpretation. Other paintings on this theme usually depict Mary at the center of a vast landscape, nursing her child; Joseph is often out of the picture. Here the center of the canvas is dominated by an angel's back, while Jesus and Mary are tucked into the left of the frame. And while angels are often associated with musical instruments, Caravaggio has Joseph acting as

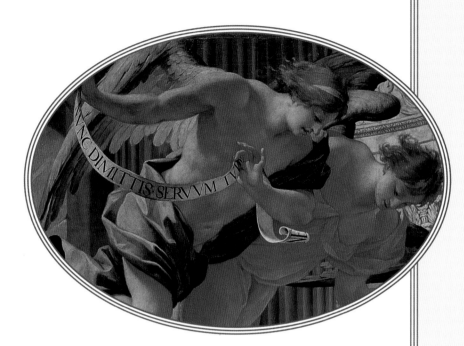

The Presentation of Christ in the Temple

Simon Vouet, 1640–41; oil on canvas;
12 ft. 9 in. x 8 ft. 1½ in.
(393 x 250 cm). Louvre, Paris.

Simon Vouet, a Baroque painter, was a great favorite at the French court for painting highly decorative, airy canvases on "Italian" themes (the Presentation in the Temple was a favorite of Italian Renaissance painters). Pretty pastel shades and the delicate lighting keep this scene from feeling crowded. Still, Vouet was guilty of some of the heavy-handedness associated with the Baroque: witness the massive scale of the figures in relation to their surroundings, and the all-too-corporeal angels hovering above. The banner in the angel's hand proclaims Simeon's plea to God.

And [Simeon] came by the Spirit into the temple: and when the parents brought in the child Jesus, to do for him after the custom of the law, Then took he him up in his arms and blessed God, and said, 'Lord, now lettest thou thy servant depart in peace, according to thy word: For mine eyes have seen thy salvation, A light to lighten the Gentiles, and the glory of thy people of Israel.'

—*Luke 2:27–32.*

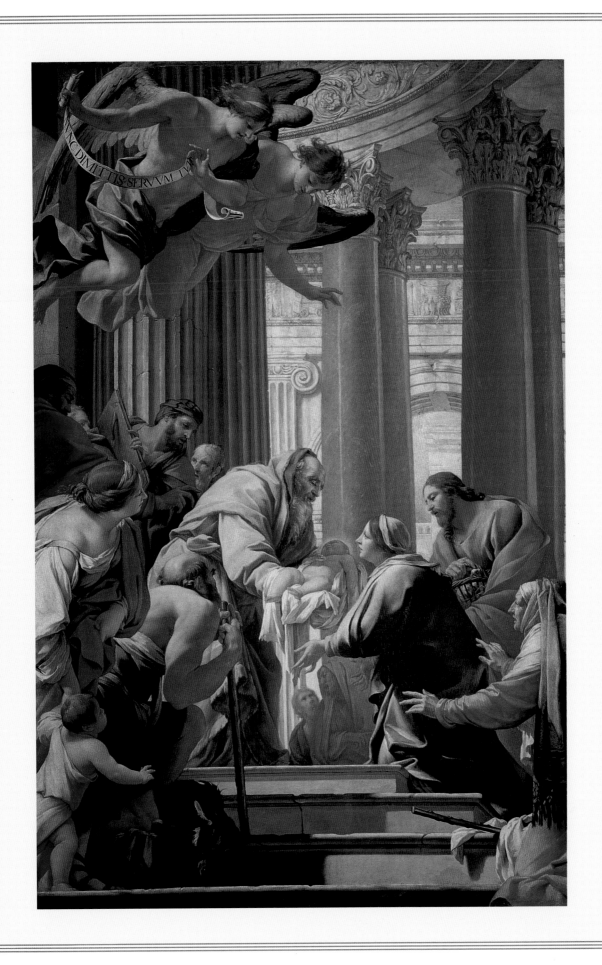

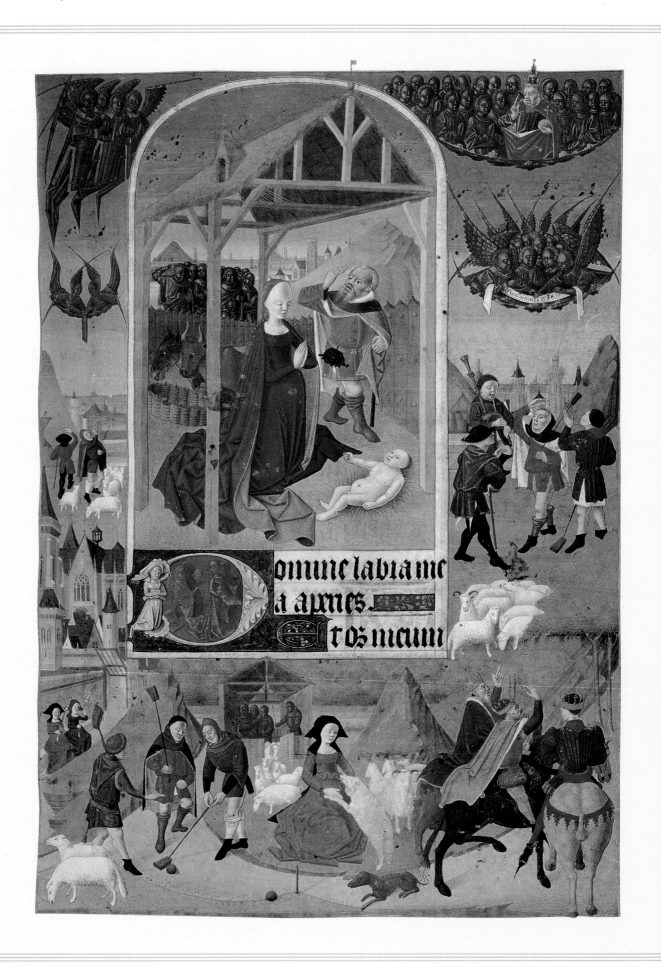

And there were in the same country shepherds abiding in the field, keeping watch over their flock by night. And lo, the angel of the Lord came upon them, and the glory of the Lord shone round about them: and they were afraid. And the angel said unto them, Fear not: for, behold, I bring you good tidings of great joy, which shall be to all people. For unto you is born this day in the city of David a Saviour, which is Christ the Lord.

—*Luke 2:8–11.*

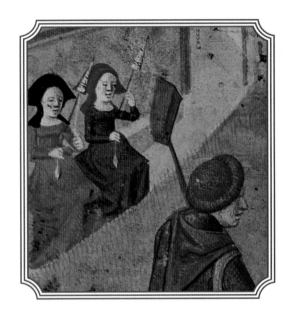

Nativity

Unknown artist, n.d.; illumination from Hours of the Duchess of Burgundy. *Musée Condé, Chantilly.*

This artist revels in portraying an entire courtly world, revealing an exquisite richness of detail, all in the tiny space of one manuscript page. From a devotional book of a rich noble, the artist has flattered his patron by setting the Nativity familiarly in her own environs. Among the lovingly rendered side scenes are images from everyday life of the times: three men play what appears to be a prototype for croquet, while two women are spinning by the castle wall.

The Birth of Christ

Unknown artist, early Christian or Byzantine; marble relief. Byzantine Museum, Athens.

This very early rendering of the Nativity contains only the most basic elements necessary: an infant in swaddling clothes lying in a manger with an ox and an ass looking on. The stark, altar-like quality of the infant's bed alludes to Christ's future sacrifice for mankind.

Great Lord and mighty King, beloved Saviour, oh, how little dost Thou esteem earthly pomp!
He who maintains the whole world, and did create its ornament and splendour, must sleep in a hard manger.

—Excerpt from Christmas Oratorio by Johann Sebastian Bach.

Ah, dearest Jesus, Holy Child,
*Make thee a bed, soft, undefiled,
Within my heart, that it may be
A quiet chamber kept for thee.*

—A Child's Prayer by Martin Luther.

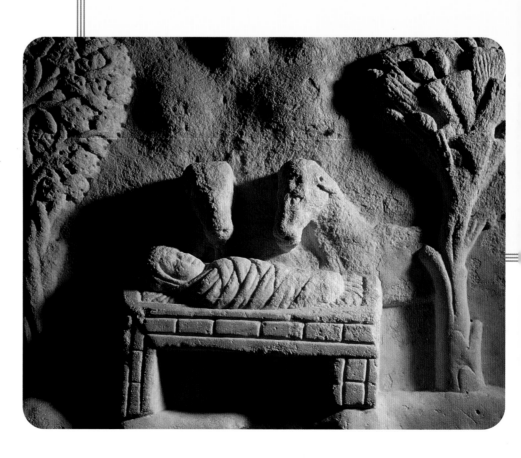

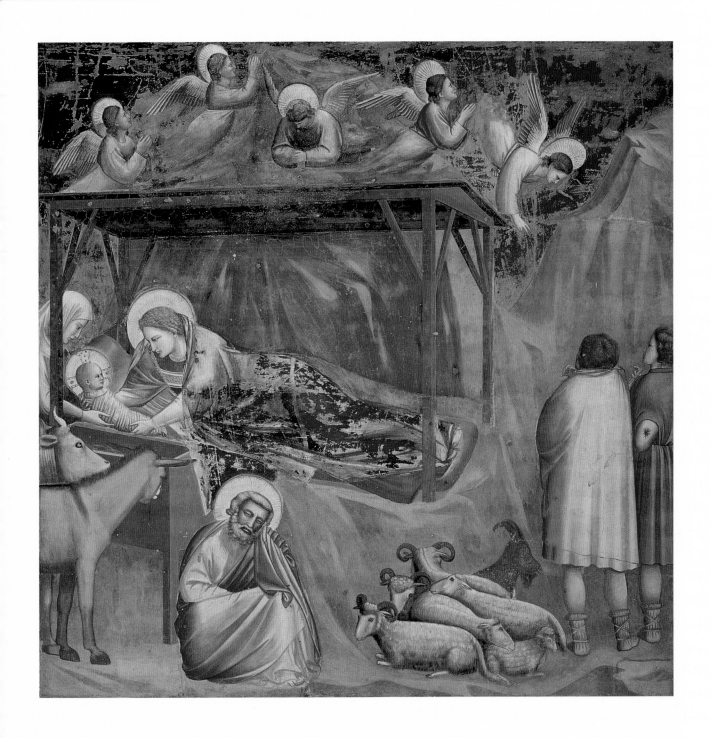

Nativity

Giotto, c. 1305–6; fresco. Scrovegni Chapel, Padua.

Giotto's work has a clarity of composition that retains some of the spiritual simplicity
of the marble relief. But the focus has shifted to a gentler, more loving message, as
Mary adoringly receives the infant Jesus from a midwife's hands.

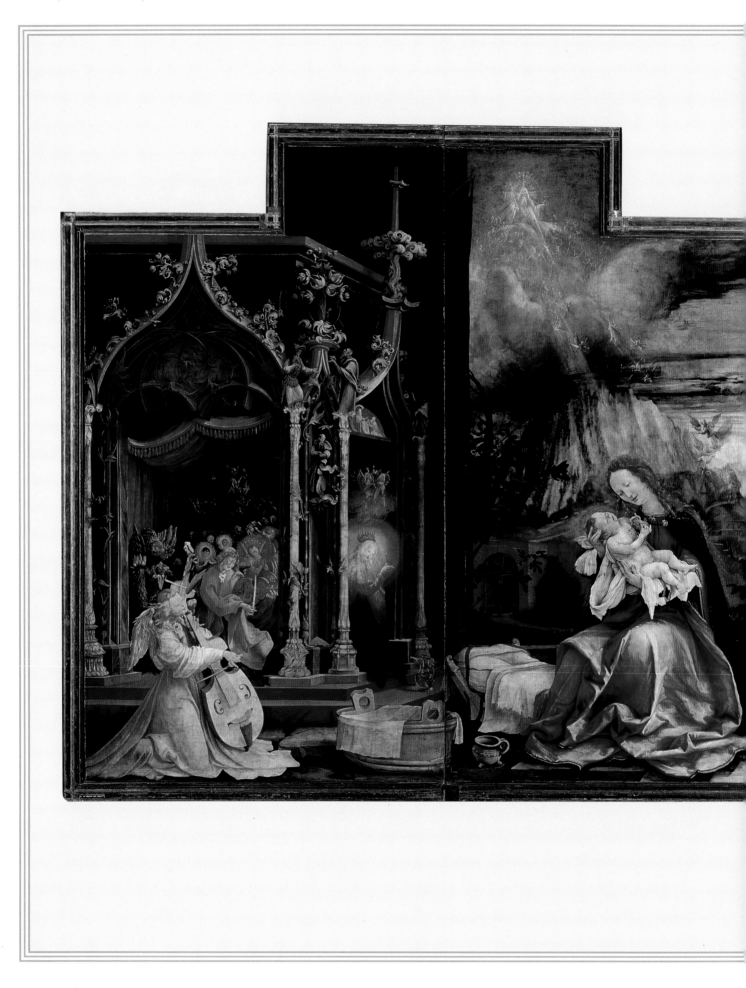

O Praise God in his holiness: praise him in the firmament of his power.

Praise him in his noble acts: praise him according to his excellent greatness.

Praise him in the sound of the trumpet: praise him upon the flute and harp.

Praise him in the cymbals and dances: praise him upon the strings and pipe.

Praise him upon the well-tuned cymbals: praise him upon the loud cymbals.

Let everything that hath breath: praise the Lord.

—**Psalms 150.**

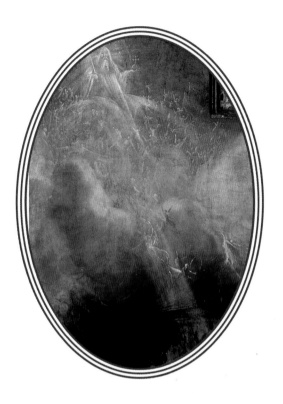

Concert of Angels for the Madonna and Child

Matthias Grünewald, c. 1510–15; central panel from the Isenheim Altarpiece; *8 ft. 10 in. x 11 ft 2½ in. (269.2 x 341.6 cm). Museé Unterlinden, Colmar.*

Matthias Grünewald was not greatly appreciated in his own time, only achieving fame during this century as the author of several important works. The *Isenheim Altarpiece* is his crowning achievement. Grünewald's trademark is his use of light and color to create an ecstatic atmosphere; here, the Heavenly Father appears as a glorious rainbow-colored cloud.

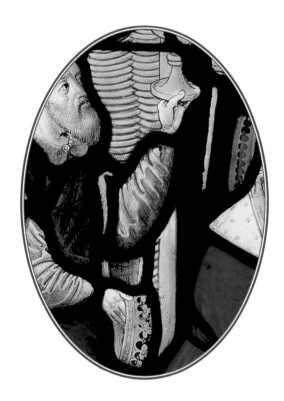

Adoration of the Magi

Unknown artist, late fifteenth century; stained glass. Cathedral, Bourges, France.

The three kings come to pay tribute to the newborn Saviour—doffing their worldly crowns in humble homage. The first king, kneeling before Christ, shows nothing but his bald pate. The second king, crown in hand, presents a golden vessel to Joseph, while the third is just about to remove his halo-like turban.

As with gladness men of old
Did the guiding star behold
So, most gracious God, may we
Evermore be led to thee.

As they offered gifts most rare
At that manger rude and bare,
So may we with holy joy,
Pure, and free from sin's alloy,
All our costliest treasures bring,
Christ, to thee our heavenly King.

In the heavenly country bright
Need they no created light;
Thou its light, its joy, its crown,
Thou its sun which does not go down.

—Excerpt from As With Gladness Men of Old by W. Chatterton Dix (1837–98).

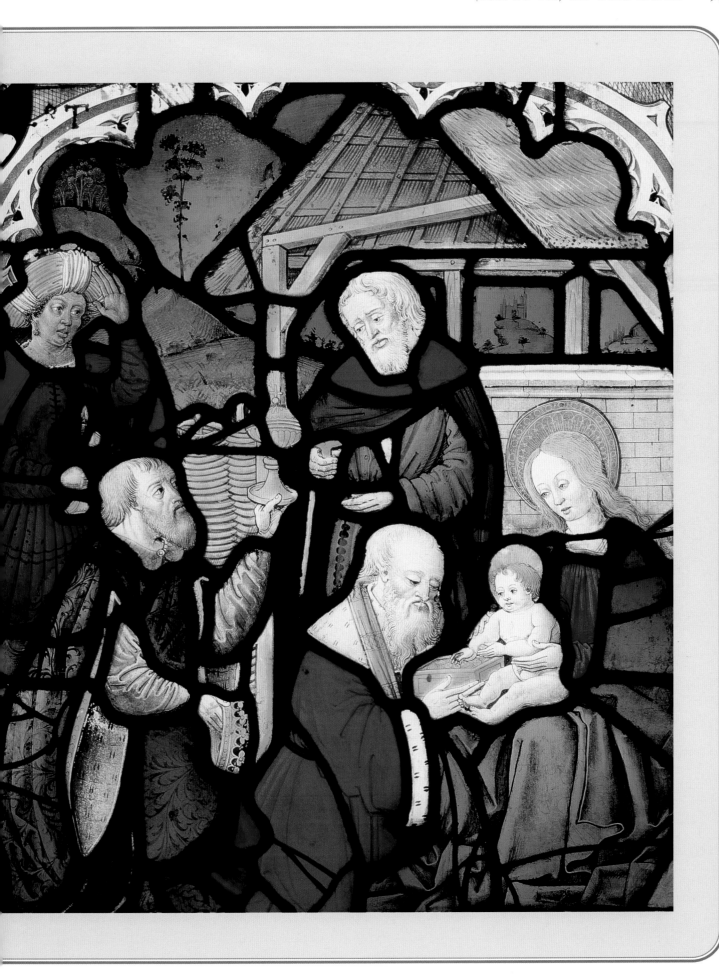

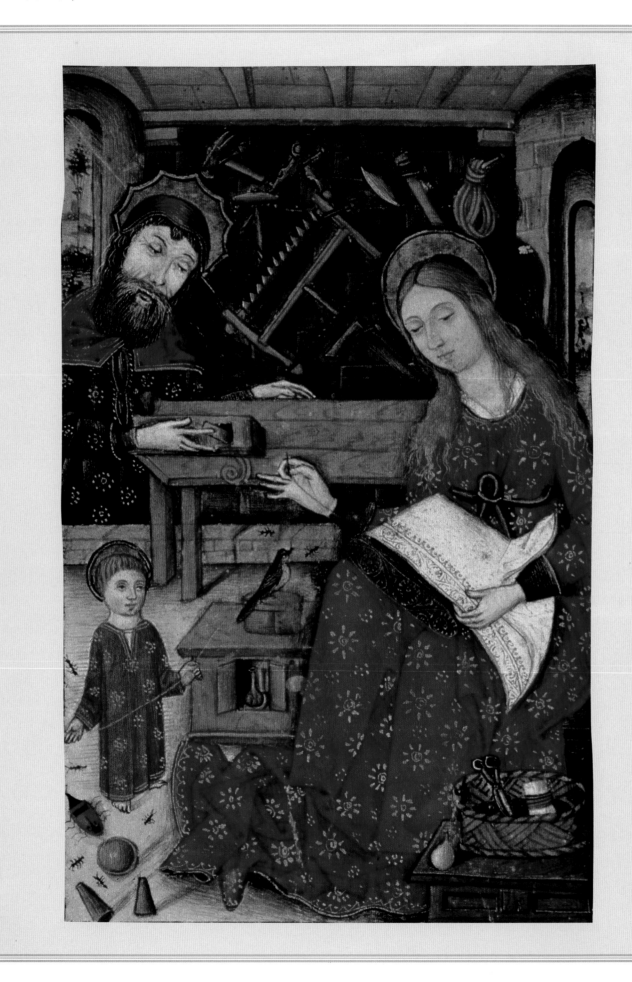

Come, my Way, my Truth, my Life:

Such a Way as gives us breath:

Such a Truth as ends all strife:

Such a Life as killeth death.

Come, my Light, my Feast, my Strength:

Such a Light, as shows a feast:

Such a Feast, as mends in length:

Such a Strength, as makes his guest.

Come, my Joy, my Love, my Heart:

Such a Joy, as none can move:

Such a Love, as none can part:

Such a Heart, as joys in love.

—George Herbert.

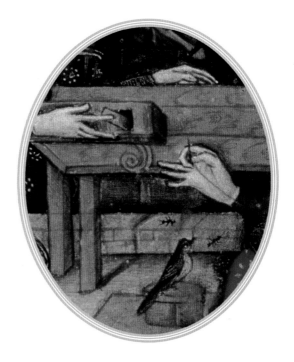

Holy Family in Joseph's Carpentry Shop

Unknown artist, late fifteenth century; illumination. British Library, London.

This warm scene is a touching, detailed portrait of a hardworking and close-knit family. Wood chips curl from beneath Joseph's lathe, Mary's embroidery is clearly detailed, and Jesus, tired perhaps from playing with the toys at his feet, holds a string tied to the sparrow perched on Mary's sewing box. As the humblest of God's creatures, the sparrow refers to Christ's material poverty; but this little bird also represents the human soul which Christ has come to save.

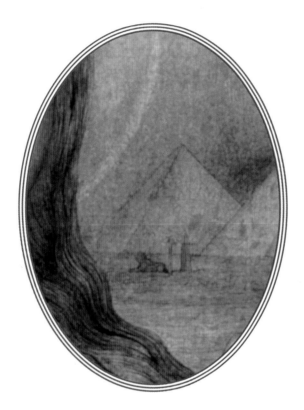

The Virgin and Child in Egypt

William Blake, 1810; tempera on canvas; 30 x 35 in. (76.2 x 88.9 cm). Victoria & Albert Museum. London.

William Blake, most famous for his poetry, but also a renowned artist and engraver, had a unique, visionary version of Christianity that incorporated much of ancient mythology as well as contemporary, Enlightenment ideals. Much of his prophetic work is destined to remain forever a mystery, like the Sphinx that sits in the background of this painting.

Sweet babe, in thy face
Holy image I can trace.
Sweet babe, once like thee,
Thy maker lay and wept for me,

Wept for me, for thee, for all,
When he was an infant small.
Thou his image ever see,
Heavenly face that smiles on thee,

Smiles on thee, on me, on all;
Who became an infant small.
Infant smiles are his own smiles;
Heaven & earth to peace beguiles.

—Excerpt from **A Cradle Song**
by **William Blake.**

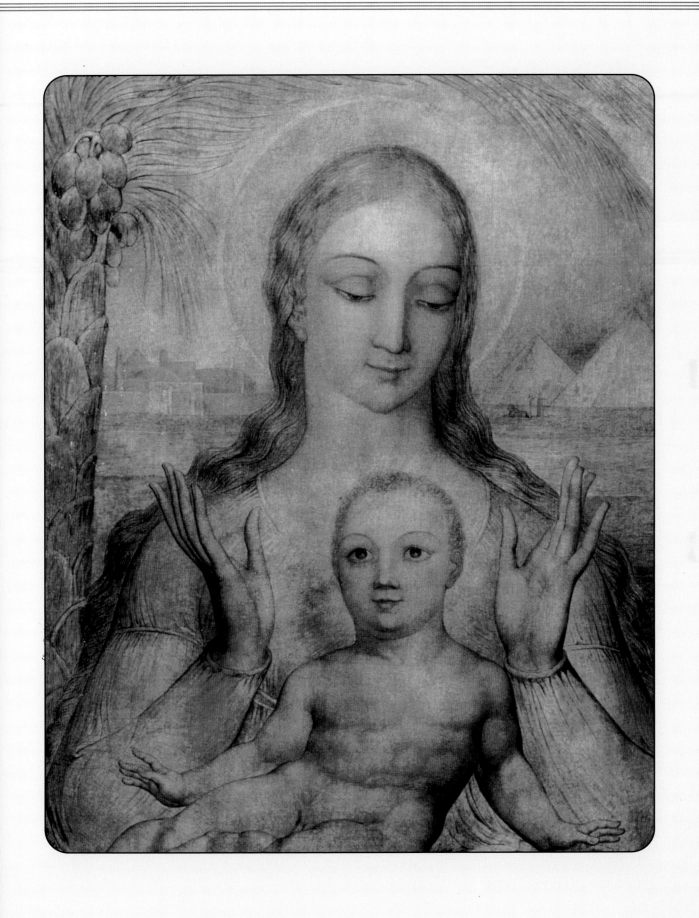

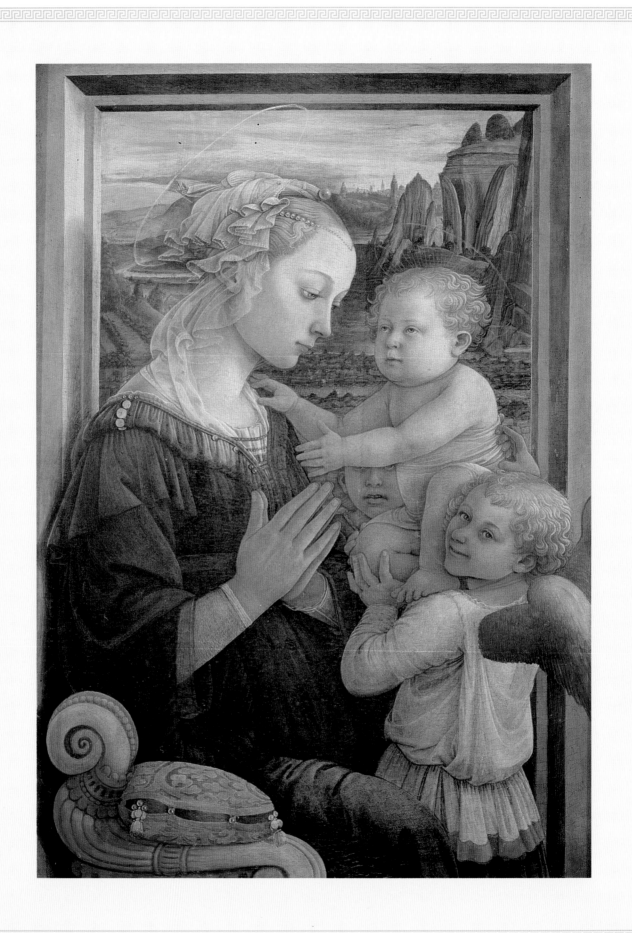

Jesus, the very thought of Thee
With sweetness fills my breast;
But sweeter far Thy face to see,
And in Thy presence rest.

No voice can sing, no heart can frame,
Or can the mem'ry find
A sweeter sound than Jesus' name,
O Saviour of mankind!

O Hope of ev'ry contrite heart!
O Joy of all the meek!
To those who fall, how kind thou art!
How good to those who seek!

But what to those who find?
Ah! this, no tongue or pen can show
The love of Jesus, what it is
None but His loved ones know.

—Jesus, the Very Thought of Thee
by Bernard of Clairvaux.

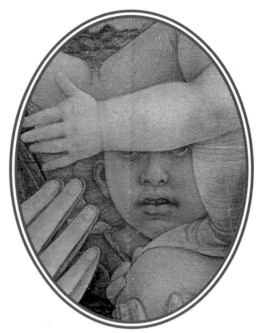

Madonna and Child With Angels

Fra Filippo Lippi, c. 1460; tempera on wood; 37⅜ x 24⅜ in. (94.9 x 61.9 cm). Uffizi, Florence.

Fra Filippo Lippi, a master artist in his own right, has perhaps been overshadowed by his famous student, Sandro Botticelli. It is easy to see similarities between the two, especially in terms of palette and their love of the fluid, linear patterns of hair and drapery. Fra ("brother") Filippo, a monk, threw off his vow of chastity to marry his model, a nun. He continued to paint his wife, and eventually his children, as models for religious subjects.

Make a joyful noise unto the Lord, all ye lands. Serve the Lord with gladness: come before his presence with singing. Know ye that the Lord he is God: it is he that hath made us, and not we ourselves; we are his people, and the sheep of his pasture. Enter into his gates with thanksgiving, and into his courts with praise: be thankful unto him, and bless his name. For the Lord is good; his mercy is everlasting; and his truth endureth to all generations.

—Psalms 100.

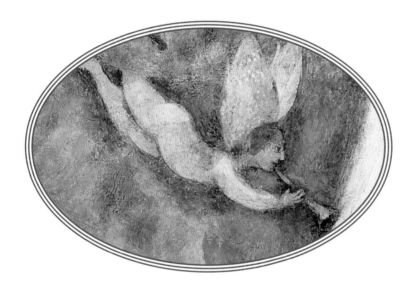

Madonna of the Village

Marc Chagall, 1930–42; oil on canvas, 39¾ x 38¼ in. (102 x 98 cm). Thyssen-Bornemisza Museum, Madrid.

Marc Chagall's work is full of complex, prophetic, dreamlike imagery that draws on a variety of sources. Many of the details here are not conventional in portraits of the Madonna and Child. Though white is the traditional symbol of purity and viginity, Mary is rarely depicted clothed entirely in white, as here. The traditional halo over Mary's head is replaced by a divine kiss. Other highly-charged symbols—such as the flying cow with the violin, and the single candle burning over the village—are distinct to Chagall's work.

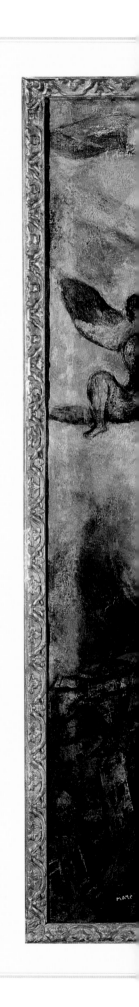

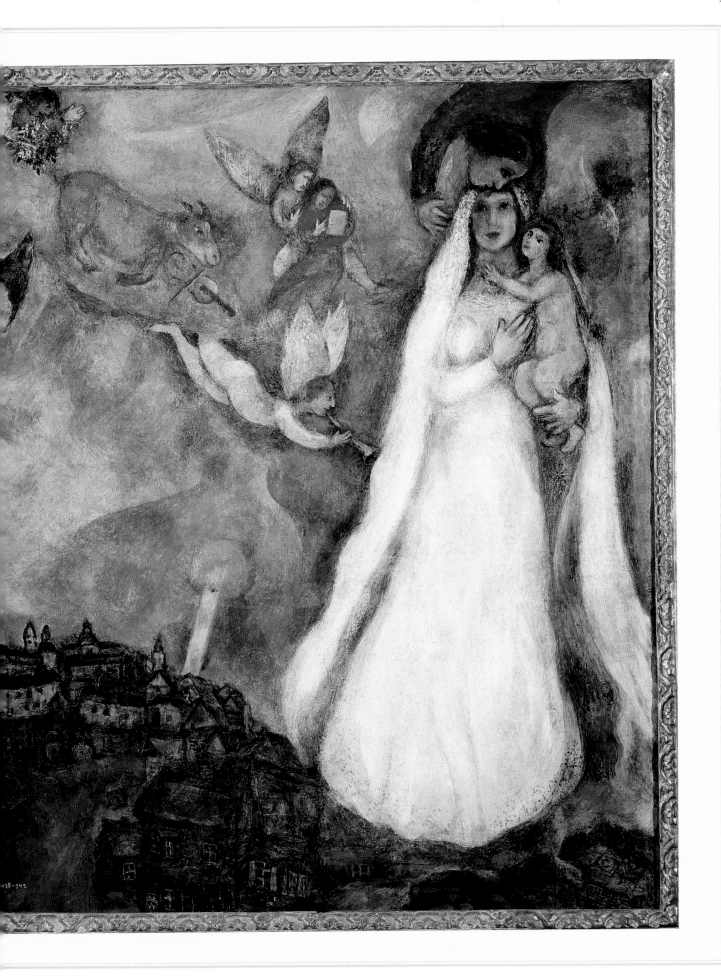

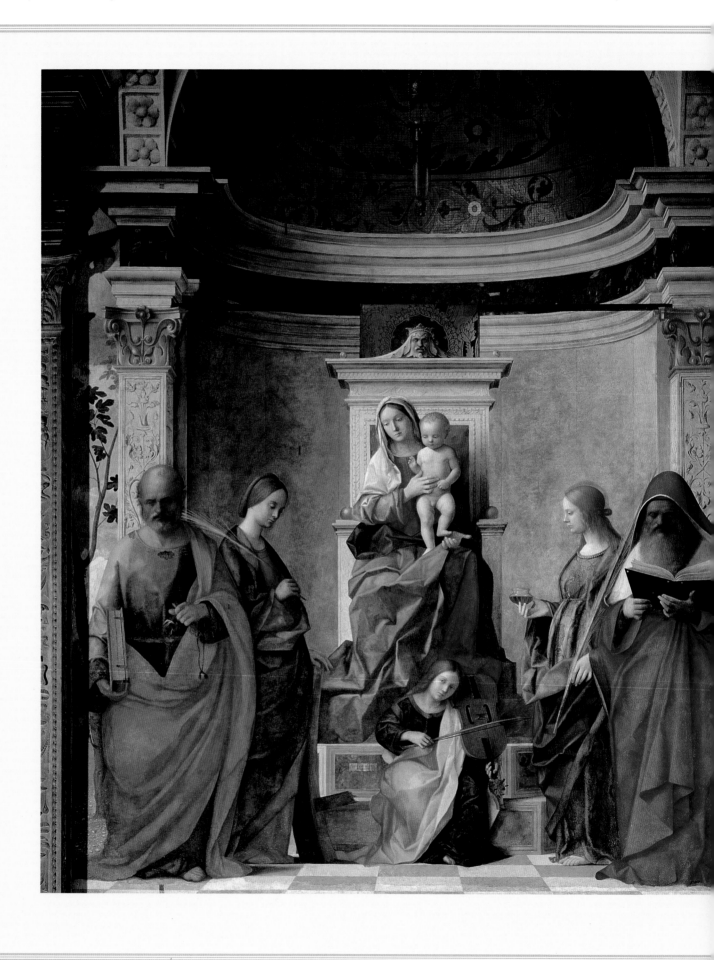

You take the pen,
and the lines dance.
You take the flute,
and the notes shimmer.
You take the brush,
and the colours sing.
So all things have
meaning and beauty
in that space beyond time
where you are.
How, then, can I hold
back anything from you?

—Dag Hammarskjöld.

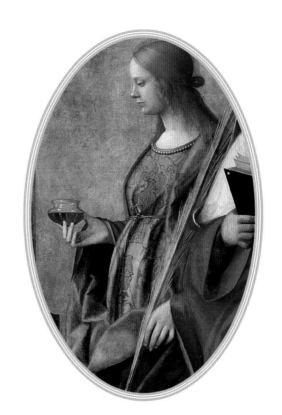

The Sacra Conversazione

Giovanni Bellini, 1505; oil on panel;
16 ft. 5½ in. x 7 ft, 9 in. (501.7 x
235.2 cm). San Zaccaria, Venice.

The *Sacra Conversazione* was a favorite scene of Renaissance painters. "Conversazione" does not mean conversation, but company, and such groupings include the Virgin and Child flanked on either side by saints, usually in an architectural setting. Typical of such scenes is a quiet, contemplative mood of communion that Giovanni Bellini has so perfectly captured by his delicate use of softly glowing colors and hazy light.

Jesus Among the Doctors

Giovanni Serondine, n.d.;
oil on canvas. Louvre, Paris.

The Bible contains few glimpses of Jesus' childhood, and this illuminating scene is the last. Vincenzo Campi emphasizes Jesus' spiritual authority by placing Him on a throne and has chosen a classical setting as most appropriate for a theme of intellectual disputation. By choosing a darker palette and a more contemporary setting, Serodine gives a rather worldly cast to the scene, as if Jesus were a sort of boy-prodigy among a wealthy congregation.

After three days they found him in the temple, sitting in the midst of the doctors, both hearing them, and asking them questions. And all that heard him were astonished at his understanding and answers. And when they saw him, they were amazed: and his mother said unto him, Son, why hast thou thus dealt with us? Behold, thy father and I have sought thee sorrowing. And he said unto them, How is it that ye sought me? Wist ye not that I must be about my Father's business?

—Luke 2:46–49.

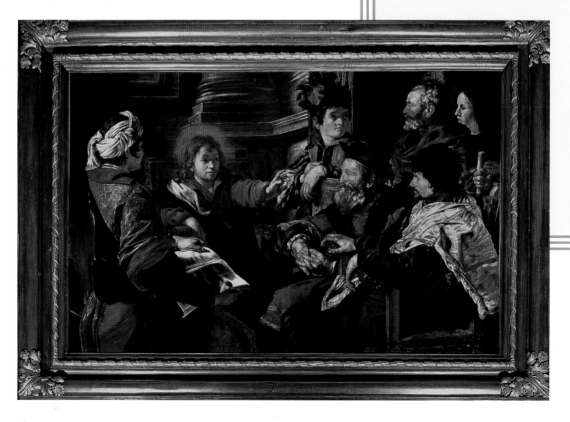

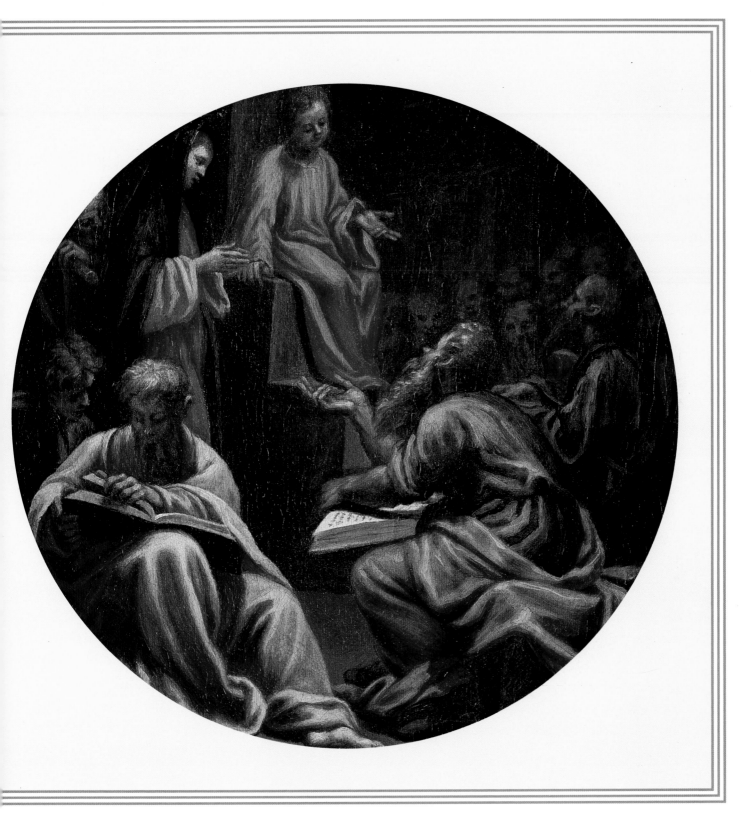

Christ Disputing Among the Doctors

Vincenzo Campi, late fifteenth century; tempera on panel.
San Bartolomeo, Busseto.

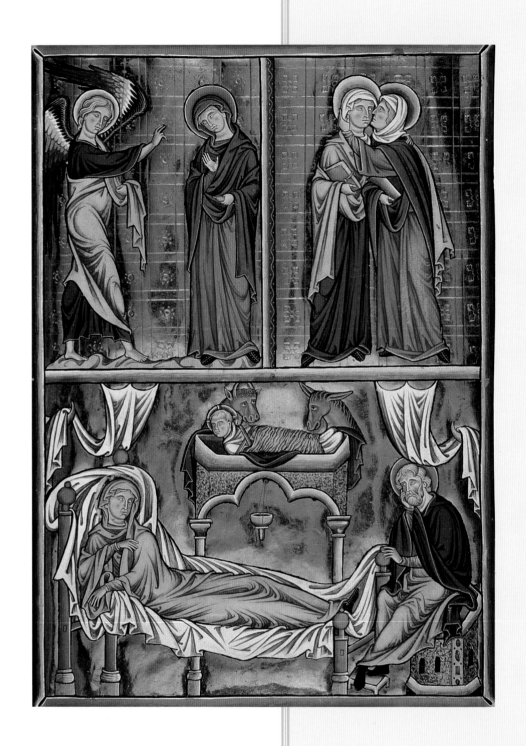

Annunciation/ Visitation/ Nativity

Unknown artist, c. 1210; illumination from the Ingeburg Psalter. *Musée Condé, Chantilly.*

In the Middle Ages, artists were more concerned with conveying spiritual and symbolic messages than they were with any sense of realism or aesthetic ideal. This manuscript page has been haphazardly divided in order to tell a sequential story; the figures appear disembodied because of the lack of perspective and strongly striated draperies that mask (rather than reveal) the forms beneath.

Therefore the Lord himself shall give you a sign; Behold, a virgin shall conceive, and bear a son, and shall call his name Immanuel, "God with us."

—Isaiah 7:14.

Madonna and Child

Deodato Orlandi,
fourteenth century;
oil on panel; 34⅜ x 16 in.
(88.2 x 41.2 cm).
Louvre, Paris.

In the medieval period religious painters moved from working mainly on manuscripts to different media, painting wooden panels, or using tempura on fresh plaster to create frescos. This early panel resembles the work of manuscript painters in its extensive use of gold leaf.

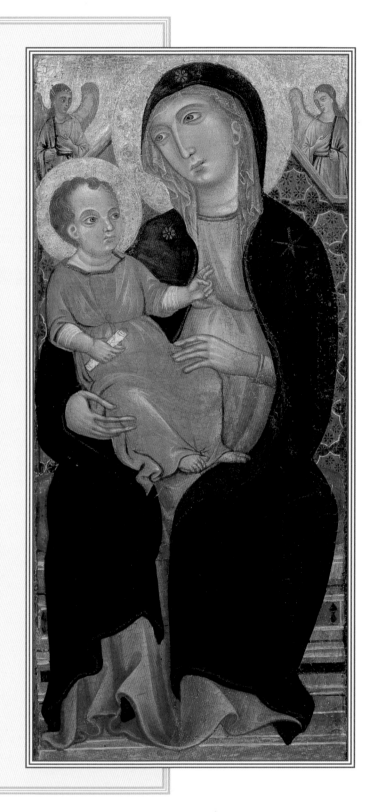

And Mary said, My soul doth magnify the Lord, And my spirit hath rejoiced in God my Saviour. For he hath regarded the low estate of his handmaiden: for, behold, from henceforth all generations shall call me blessed.

—Luke 2:46–49.

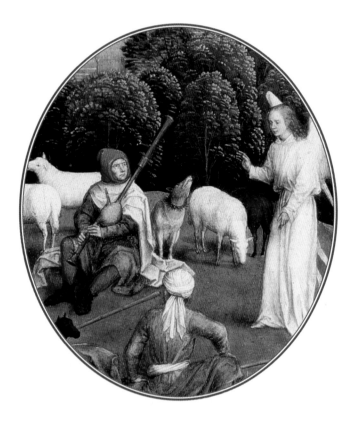

Nativity and Annunciation of the Shepherds

Hans Memling, c. 1480; detail from The Seven Joys of Mary; *oil on panel; 31 ⅞ x 74 ⅜ in. (80.9 x 188.9 cm). Alte Pinakothek, Munich.*

Northern Renaissance painters revel in elaborate detail, often creating intense microcosms, or, as here, opening up the scope of the artwork to reveal sweeping vistas crammed with information. The Annunciation to the Shepherds is a traditional adjunct to the Nativity scene.

Show your mercy to me, O Lord, to make my heart glad. Let me find you, for whom I long. I am the sheep that is gone astray; O good Shepherd, seek me out, and bring me home to your fold again. Deal favorably with me according to your good pleasure, that I may dwell in your house all the days of my life, and praise you for ever and ever with them that are there.

—Prayer of St. Jerome.

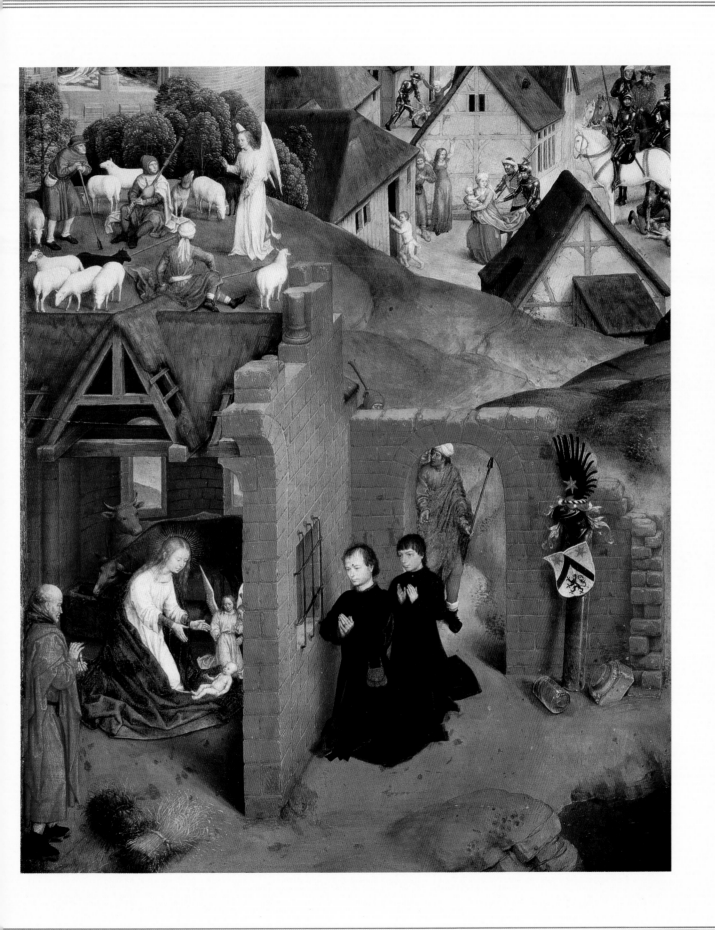

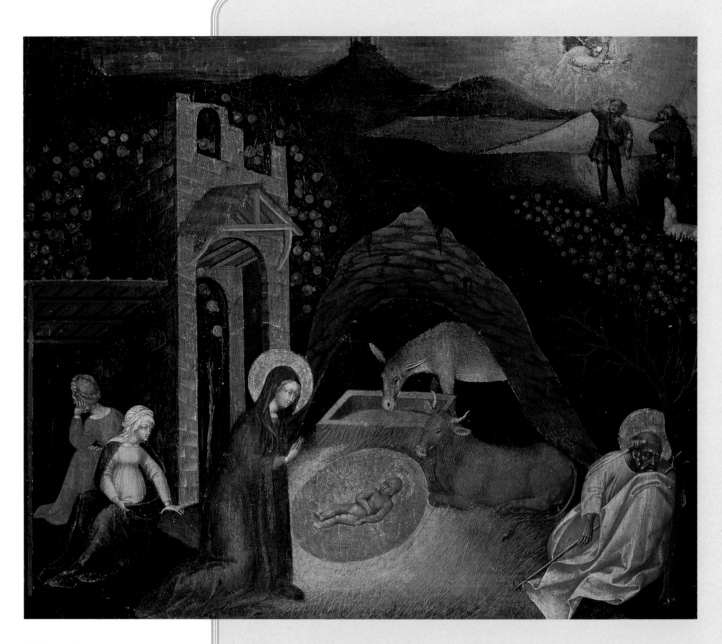

Nativity

*Giovanni di Paolo,
n.d.; oil on panel.
Pinacoteca, Vatican
Museums, Rome.*

Artists of earlier eras had a very different view about copying each other's work. Still, it's hard to see much difference in these two interpretations of the Nativity: a night scene lit from above left by the Star of Bethlehem with the Holy Ghost emanating from it; the dark hills with shepherds on them; the cave in which the ox and the ass are stalled in front of a manger; even the positions of the main characters, which have been copied exactly.

*S*hone to him the earth and sphere together,
God the Lord has opened the door;
Son of Mary Virgin, hasten thou to help me,
Thou Christ of hope, thou Door of joy,
Golden Sun of hill and mountain,
     All hail! Let there be joy!

—Gaelic Prayer.

Lock, my heart, this blessed wonder
fast within thy belief.
     Let this divine miracle of the divine works
     ever be the strength
     of thy weak faith!

—Excerpt from Christmas Oratorio
by Johann Sebastian Bach.

Nativity

Gentile da
Fabriano, 1423;
panel from the
Strozzi Altarpiece;
oil on panel;
12¼ x 29½ in.
(31.1 x 74.9 cm).
Uffizi, Florence.

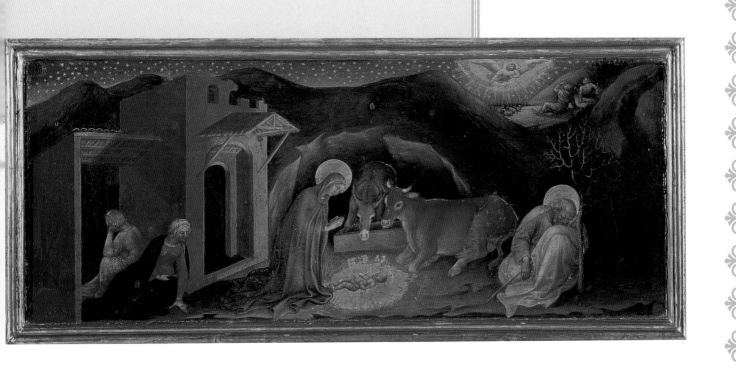

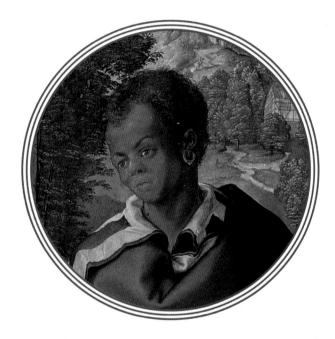

Adoration of the Magi

*Albrecht Dürer, 1504; oil on panel;
39 x 44 ¹⁄₁₆ in. (99 x 111.9 cm).
Uffizi, Florence.*

The Magi (or wise men) who came to
adore the Christ Child enjoyed a wild
popularity in early Christian tradition,
and apocryphal tales about them
abounded. They became the Three
Kings (because of the three presents),
named Balthasar, Melchior, and
Caspar. They were said to come from
Asia, Europe, and Africa and represented the three ages of man.
Accordingly, Dürer's African king
appears to be little more than a boy.

. . . And, lo, the
star, which they saw in
the east, went before
them, till it came and
stood over where the
young child was. When
they saw the star they
rejoiced with exceeding
great joy. And when
they were come into the
house, they saw the
young child with Mary
his mother, and fell
down, and worshipped
him: and when they had
opened their treasures,
they presented unto him
gifts; gold, and frankin-
cense, and myrrh.

—Matthew 2:9–11.

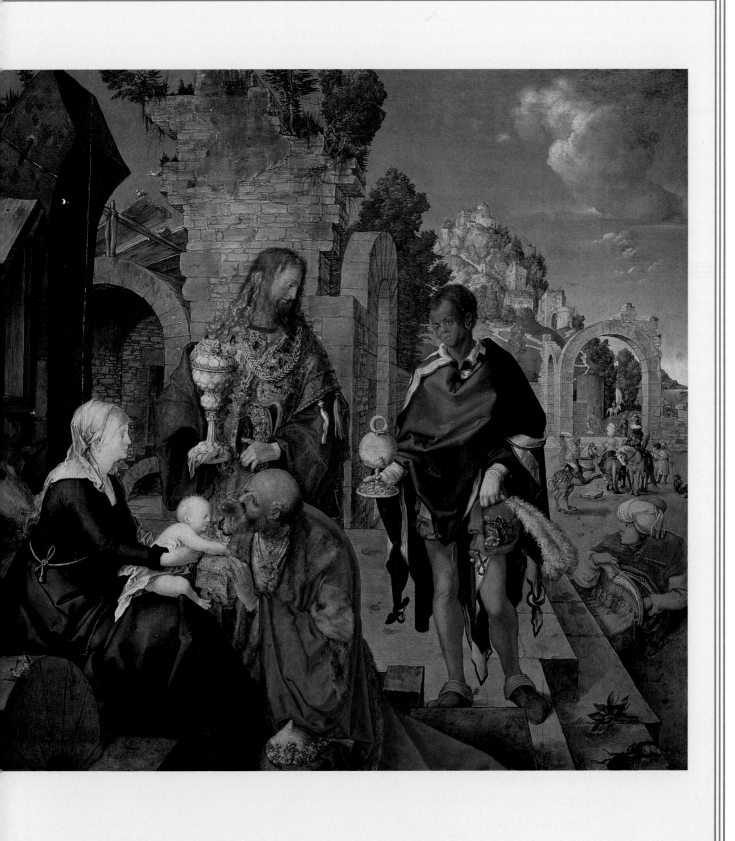

Christ in the House of His Parents

Sir John Everett Millais.
1850; oil on canvas;
34 x 55 in. (86.4 x 139.7 cm).
Tate Gallery, London.

This scene has been entirely re-interpreted: the setting is no longer a home, but a workshop with several others employed about the business. In fact, the casual reference to Christ coming to harm from the very tools of his humanly father's trade implied in the Master of Serrone's painting have become explicit here: Mary examines a stigmata on Christ's palm and there appears to be some blood on the board behind Him.

He came poor upon earth
Who can extol the love aright,
our Saviour cherishes for us,
for that he pities us,
yea, who is capable of comprehending,
how man's distress so moved him?
Make us rich in heaven,
The son of the All Highest comes into the world
because its salvation pleases Him so well,
and like unto His beloved angels,
that He will Himself be born as man.
Lord have mercy on us!

—Excerpt from **Christmas Oratorio**
by *Johann Sebastian Bach.*

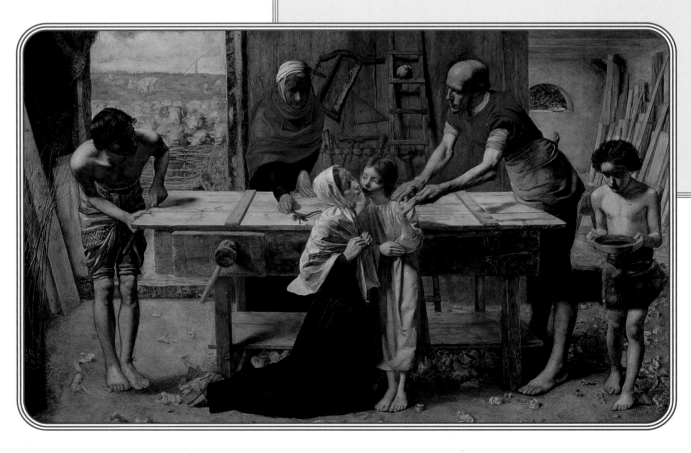

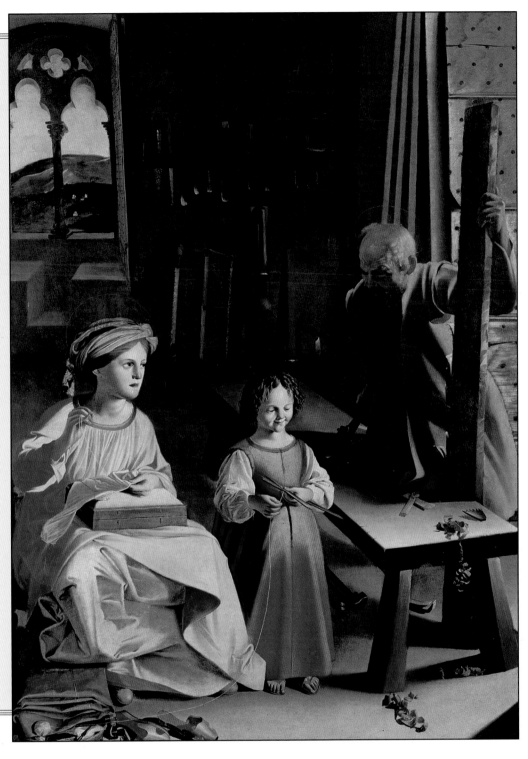

Joseph's Workshop

The Master of Serrone; n.d.; fresco. San Maria Assunta, Serrone.

Here are the customary elements of this often-painted scene: Joseph at his worktable, Mary with her needlework, and Jesus playing quietly. But the relationships among the family members is a far cry from the tender, loving-kindness of the medieval manuscript artists: Joseph appears to be chastising Jesus for childishly fashioning a cross out of wood scraps, while Mary looks on apprehensively.

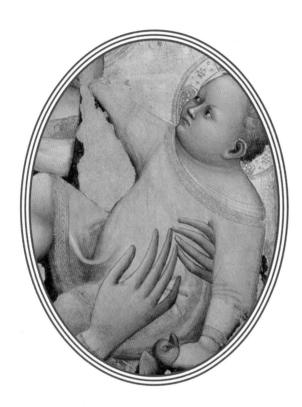

Polyptych with Madonna and Child and Saints

Giovanni di Nicola, n.d. National Gallery, Perugia.

In Christian symbolism, and, indeed, according to many of the world's cultures, birds are used to represent the human soul, or spirit. This Christ Child is keeping a very tight grasp indeed on the souls of humanity.

I will keep Thee diligently in my mind,
I will live
for Thee here,
I will depart with Thee hence.
With Thee will I soar at last,
filled with joy,
time without end,
there in the other life.

—**Excerpt from Christmas Oratorio**
by Johann Sebastian Bach.

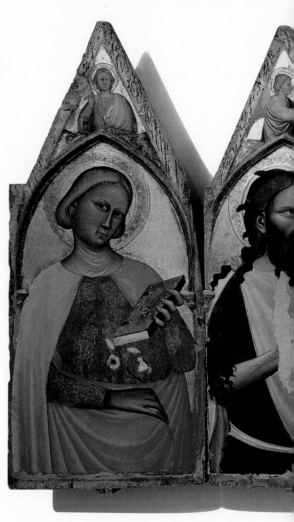

The Lord bless you and keep you;

The Lord make his face to shine upon you, and be gracious to you;

The Lord lift up his countenance upon you, and give you peace.

—Numbers 6:24–26.

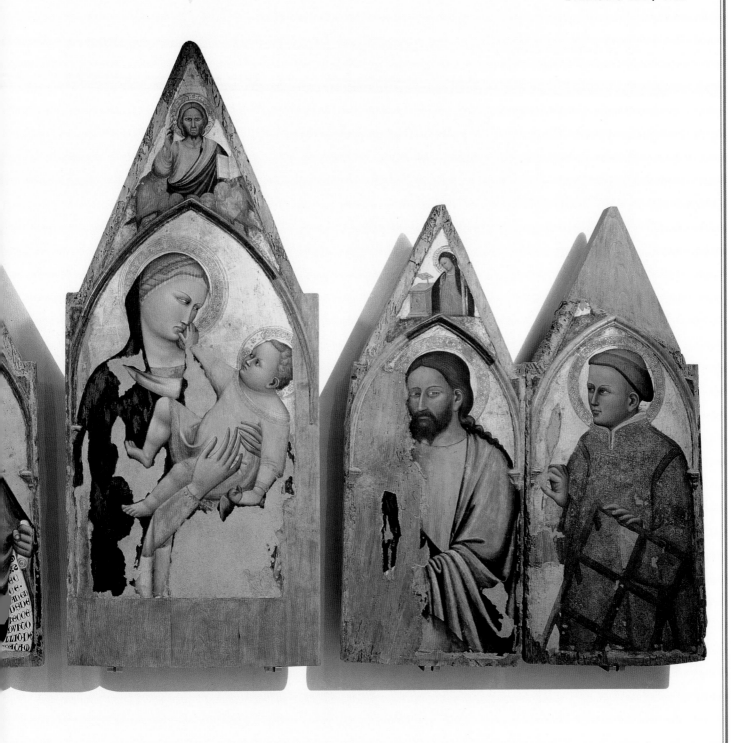

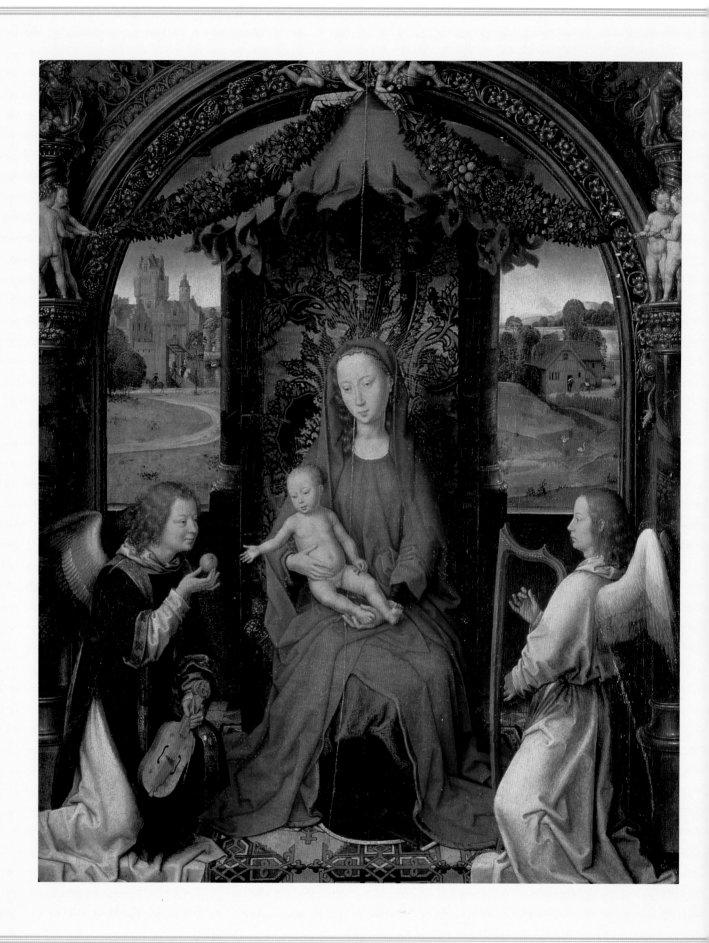

eep me as the apple of an eye: hide me under the shadow of thy wings.

—*Psalms 17:8.*

Rejoice, exult! Up, glorify the days,
praise what the All Highest this day has done!
Set aside fear, banish lamentation,
strike up a song full of joy and mirth!
Serve the All Highest with glorious choirs!
Let us worship the name of the Lord!

—**Excerpt from Christmas Oratorio**
by Johann Sebastian Bach.

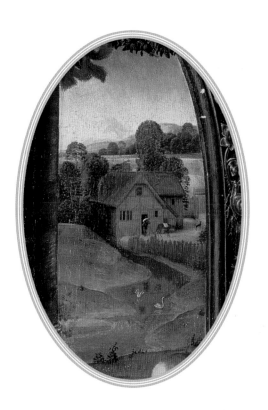

Madonna and Child with Two Angels

Hans Memling, late fifteenth century; oil on panel; 22⁷/₁₆ x 16⁹/₁₆ in. (57 x 42 cm).

Hans Memling's work has been called both the epitome of Flemish expression and a "Late Gothic Dream." This is one of many similar paintings in which Memling obsessively interchanged many of the same elements, using and reusing the same composition, models, tapestries, even background landscapes. Particular to Memling's work are his sadly sweet Madonnas and a pervading sense of serenity and calm.

Madonna and Child with Five Angels

(Madonna of the Magnificat)

Sandro Botticelli, 1481–5; tempera on panel; 46 ⁷⁄₁₆ in. (118 cm) diameter. Uffizi, Florence.

Come then, Thy name alone shall be in my heart!
So will I call Thee, filled with delight,
when heart and bosom do burn for love of Thee.
But, Best Beloved, tell me:
how shall I extol Thee? How shall I thank Thee?

Jesus, my joy and bliss,
my hope, treasure and lot,
my Redeemer, defense and Salvation,
Shepherd and King, light and sun!
Oh, how shall I worthily,
praise Thee, My Lord Jesus?

—**Excerpt from Christmas Oratorio**
by Johann Sebastian Bach.

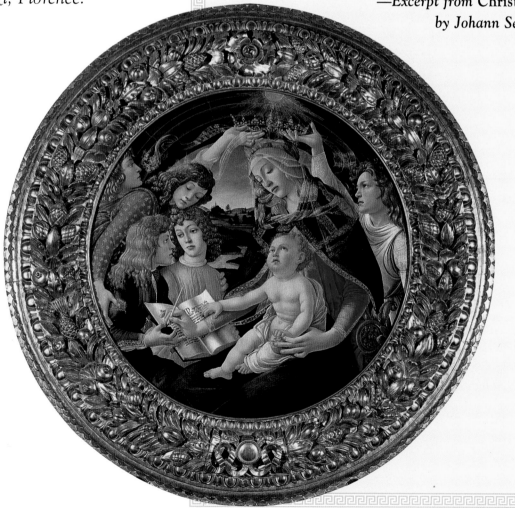

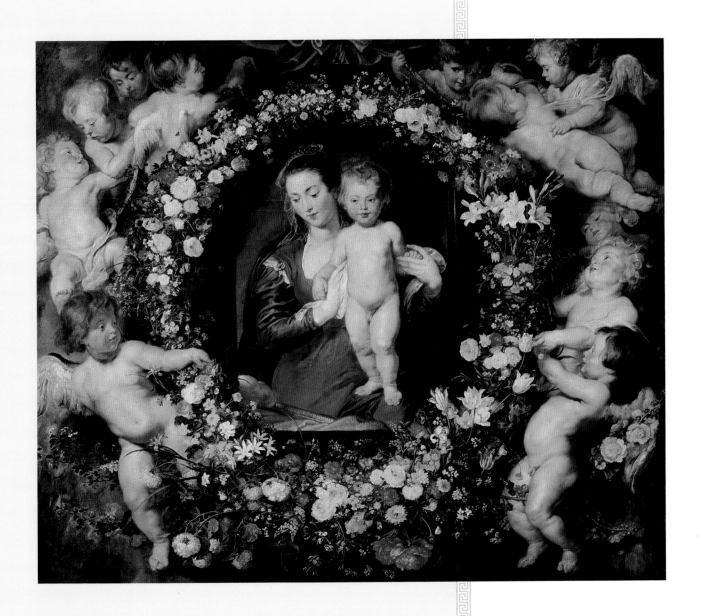

Although these paintings were produced two centuries apart, they use similar circular compositions to convey a sense of blissful jubilation and triumph at the coming of the Lord. Despite the many non-conventional details in these works, note that Mary still wears the colors most generally associated with her in her role of Madonna: a red robe, representing blood and symbolizing emotionalism, and a blue mantle, representing the sky and symbolizing her heavenly love.

Virgin and Child Inside a Garland of Flowers

Peter Paul Rubens, c. 1618–20; oil on panel; 72⅞ x 82⅝ in. (185.1 x 209.9 cm). Alte Pinakothek, Munich.

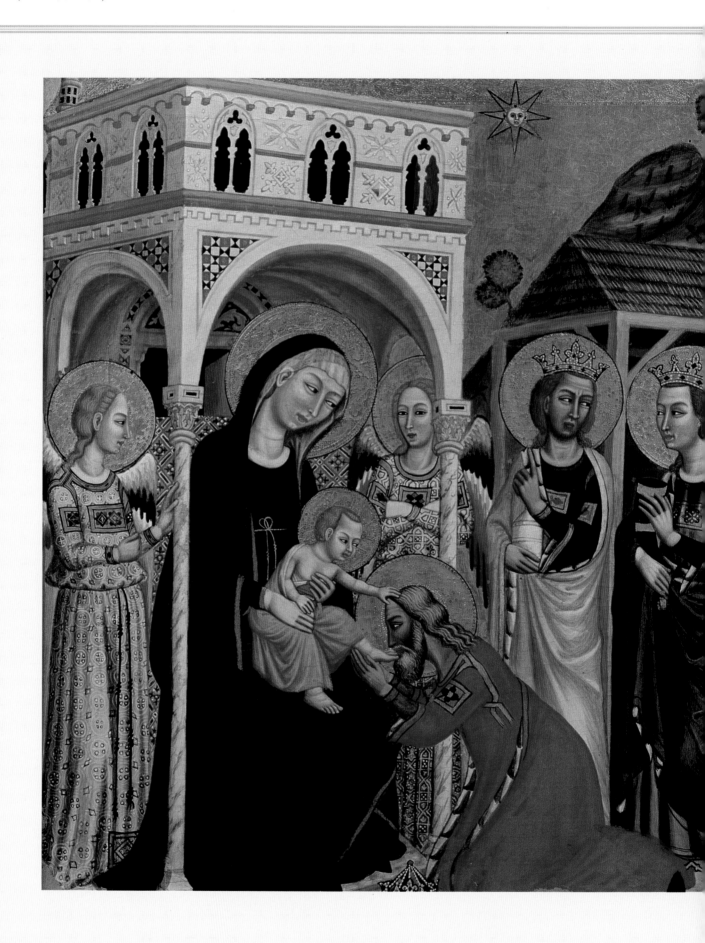

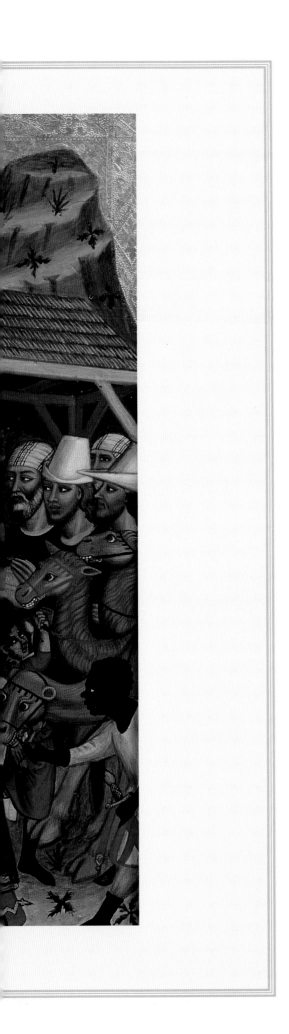

$\mathcal{W}$e three kings of Orient are;
Bearing gifts we traverse afar
Field and fountain, moor and mountain,
Following yonder star:

O star of wonder, star of night,
Star with royal beauty bright,
Westward leading, still proceeding,
Guide us to thy perfect light.

—Excerpt from Kings of Orient
by J.H. Hopkins.

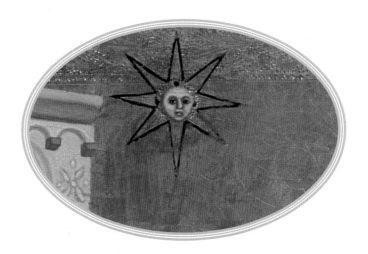

Adoration of the Magi

Master of Paciano, fourteenth century; oil on panel. National Gallery, Perugia.

The gifts presented to Jesus by the Three Kings symbolize His status: gold His kingship; frankincense His divinity; and myrrh His future suffering. Often the Star of Bethlehem is represented as a glowing cloud, representing God the Father, with the one or more doves (symbolizing the Holy Spirit) descending from it. This quaint little star with a face is a more primitive version.

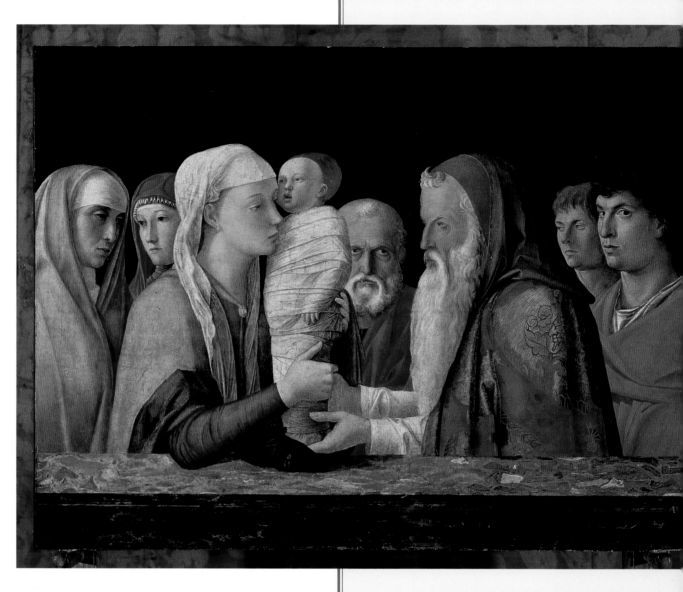

Presentation of Christ in the Temple

Giovanni Bellini, c. 1465; oil on panel;
29 $^{15}/_{16}$ x 35 $^{13}/_{16}$ in. (76 x 35.8 cm).
Museo Querini Stampilia, Venice.

Artists frequently portrayed classic biblical scenes in contemporary, familiar settings. Here, the infant Jesus, swaddled in a snug white bunting, was brought to the temple for presentation by his parents in accordance with Mosaic law. Although both works depict a pre-Christian, Jewish rite, details such as the ecclesiastical vestments worn by Simeon and the white garments worn by the Baby Jesus create a scene that closely resembles a Christian baptism.

Come, thou long expected Jesus, born to set thy
people free;
From our fears and sins release us; let us find our
rest in thee.
Israel's strength and consolation, hope of all the
earth thou art;
Dear Desire of every nation, joy of every longing
heart.
Born thy people to deliver, born a child and yet
a king.
Born to reign in us forever, now thy gracious
kingdom bring,
By thine own eternal Spirit, rule in all our
hearts alone;
By thine all sufficient merit,
raise us to thy glorious throne.

—Excerpt from **The Prayers
of Charles Wesley.**

Presentation
of Christ in
the Temple

*Fra Angelico, historiated
initial "S" from Missal,
c. 1430; illumination.
Museo di San Marco,
Florence.*

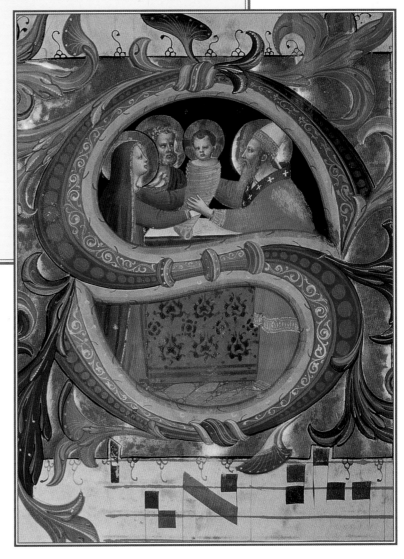

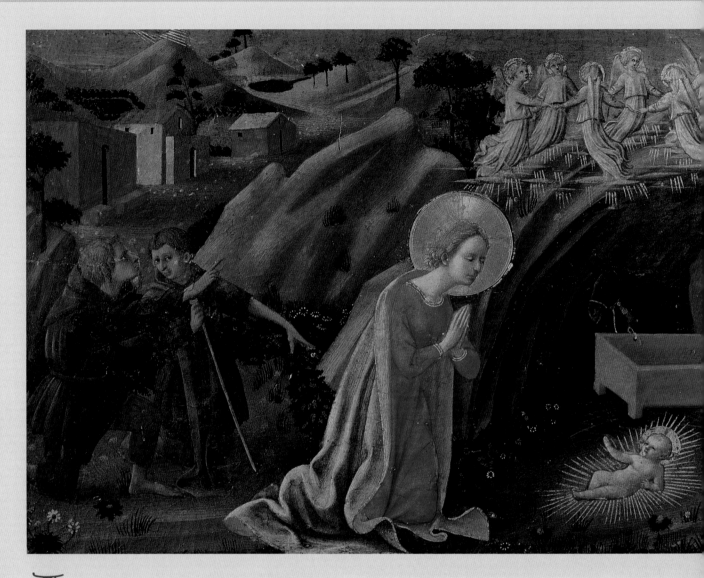

It came upon the midnight clear,
That glorious song of old,
From angels bending near the earth
To touch their harps of gold:

'Peace on the earth, good-will to men,
From heav'n's all-gracious King!'
The world in solemn stillness lay
To hear the angels sing

For lo! the days are hastening on,
By prophets foretold, When,
with the ever circling years
Comes round the age of gold;

When peace shall o'er all the earth
Its ancient splendours fling,
And the whole world give back the song
Which now the angels sing.

—It Came Upon the Midnight Clear, lyrics by E.H. Sears (1810–76)

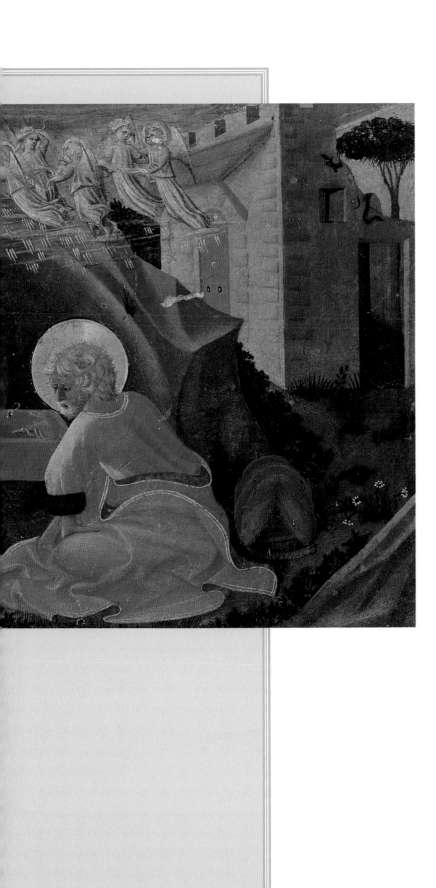

Birth of Christ

Agnolo Gaddi, fourteenth century; fresco. Duomo, Prato.

Agnolo Gaddi's Nativity keeps the focus specifically on the divinity of Christ. Gone is the focal light from the Star of Bethlehem, which has been reduced to a few streaks of light in the corner of the painting. The bed of straw that Jesus traditionally lies on has been replaced by an aureole—a field of radiance which surrounds his whole body and which is symbolic of the highest divinity. The cruciform halo Jesus wears is also specific to him alone and refers to his sacrifice for mankind on the cross. The angels that hover above have come to sing Christ's praises, while the blackbird and the snake, symbols of Satan, slink away over a ruined stone wall.

Then, spoke Jesus again unto them, saying, I am the light of the world: he that followeth me shall not walk in darkness, but shall have the light of life.

—John 8:12.

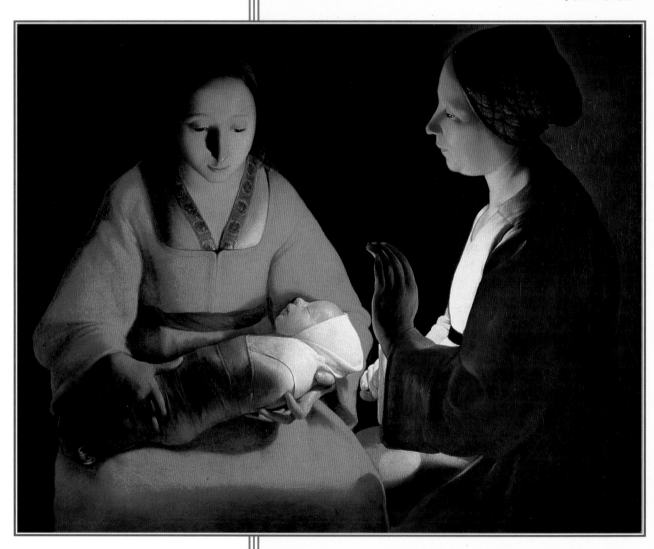

The Nativity

Georges de La Tour, c. 1645; oil on canvas; 29¹³⁄₁₆ x 35¹³⁄₁₆ in. (76 x 91 cm). Musée des Beaux-Arts, Rennes.

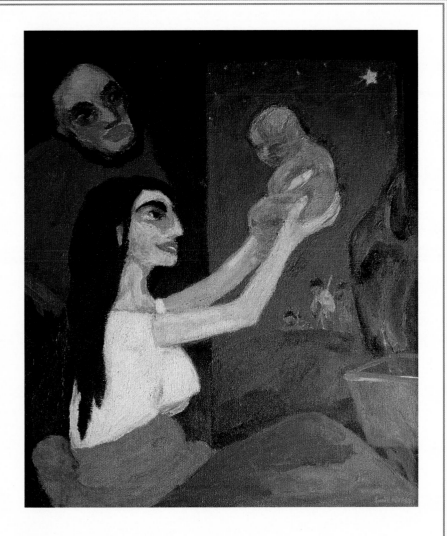

O Splendor of God's glory bright,

O thou that bringest light from light

O Light of Light, light's living spring,

O Day, all days illumining;

O thou true Sun, on us thy glance

Let fall in royal radiance,

The Spirit's sanctifying beam

Upon our earthly senses stream.

—**Hymn by Saint Ambrose,
Bishop of Milan.**

The Birth of Christ

*Emil Nolde,
1911–12; left wing
detail,* Life of Christ
*triptych.
Ada and Emil Nolde
Collection, Seebuell.*

Light is a powerful
Christian symbol of
divinity. In scenes of the
Nativity, Jesus and Mary
are customarily bathed
in the light from the Star
of Bethlehem, their faces
wrapped in the glow of
halos. These two paint-
ings show a different
approach: Georges de La
Tour uses a candle,
screened by a hand, to
cast an intimate, tender
glow over the infant
Jesus, while Emil Nolde
highlights the Virgin
Mary with a bright com-
plexion and white shift.

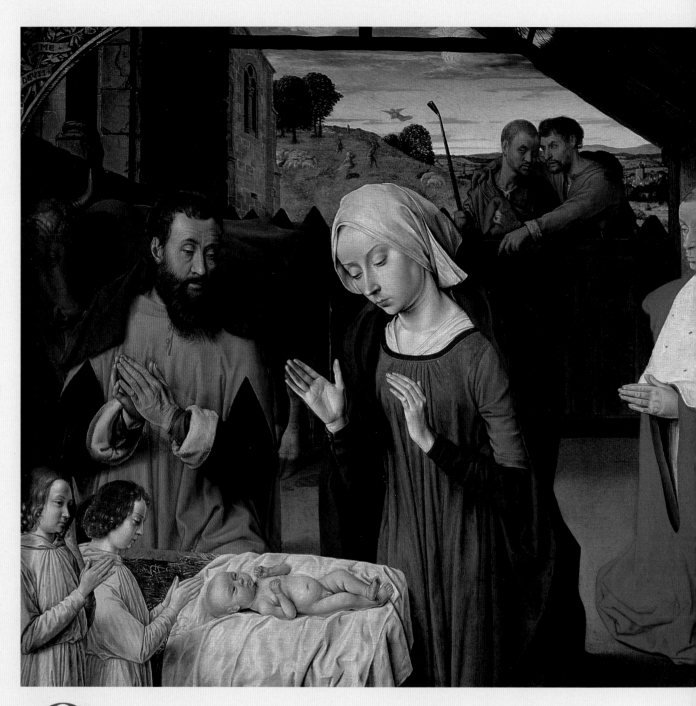

O morning stars, together
Proclaim the holy birth,
And praises sing to God the King,
And peace to men on Earth;

For Christ is born of Mary;
And, gathered all above,
While mortals sleep, the angels keep
Their watch of wond'ring love.

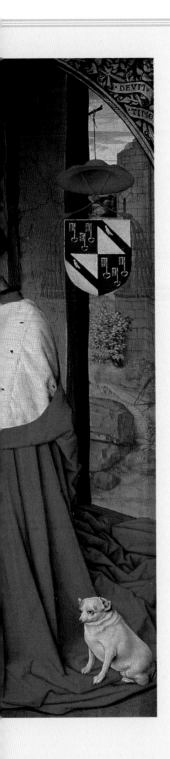

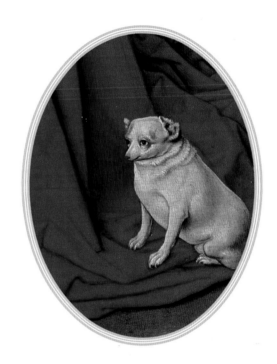

Adoration of the Child

*Jean Hey (Master of Moulins),
c. 1480; oil on panel; 21⅝ x 28 in.
(54.9 x 71.1 cm). Museé Rolin, Autun.*

"Art for art's sake" is a fairly modern
idea. In the Middle Ages, artists were
commissioned by important churchmen
or nobles to paint specific scenes. Artists,
in turn, often flattered their patrons by
including some reminder of them in their
works. Here the donor, Cardinal Jean
Rolin, appears at the Nativity richly
dressed in his robes of office. While dogs
represent watchfulness and fidelity in
Christian art, the dog sitting on the cardinal's robe may be his own.

*How silently, how silently,
The wondrous gift is giv'n!
So God imparts to human hearts
The blessings of His heav'n.*

**—O Little Town of Bethlehem
by Phillips Brooks.**

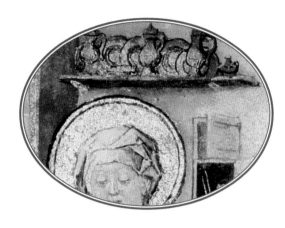

The Holy Family at Work

Master of Catherine of Cleves, c. 1440; illumination from Book of Hours of Catherine of Cleves. *The Pierpont Morgan Library, New York.*

Scenes of the Holy Family at work are most touchingly rendered by medieval miniaturists, as in this illumination. Each detail of the tidy abode of the Holy Family is lovingly rendered, such as the neatly stacked plates on the shelf above Mary's head. It is interesting to note that the infant walker is not a modern invention.

Lord, make me an instrument of your peace.

Where there is hatred, let me sow love,

Where there is injury, pardon;

Where there is doubt, faith;

Where there is despair, hope;

Where there is darkness, light;

Where there is sadness, joy.

O divine Master, Grant that I may not so much seek

To be consoled, as to console,

To be understood, as to understand,

To be loved, as to love,

For it is in giving that we receive;

It is in pardoning that we are pardoned;

It is in dying that we are born to eternal life.

—*Prayer of St. Francis of Assis*

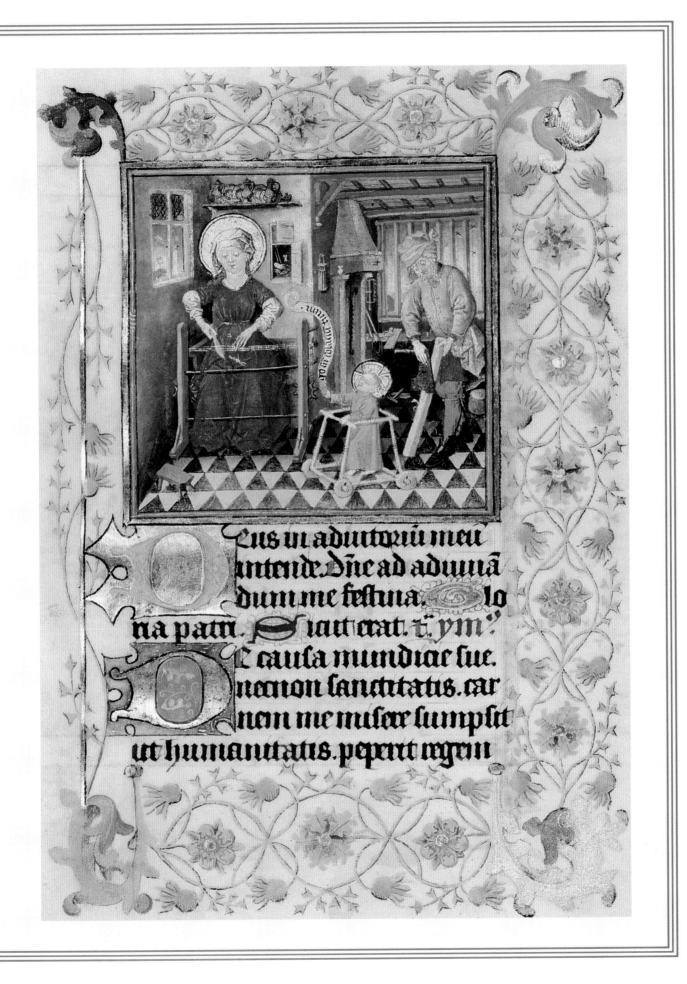

eus in adiutoriū meū
intende. Dñe ad adiuuā
dum me festina. Glo
na patri. Sicut erat. t̄ ym̄.
E causa mūdiciae sue.
necnon sanctitatis. car
nem me miserē sumpsit
ut humanitatis. peperit virgin

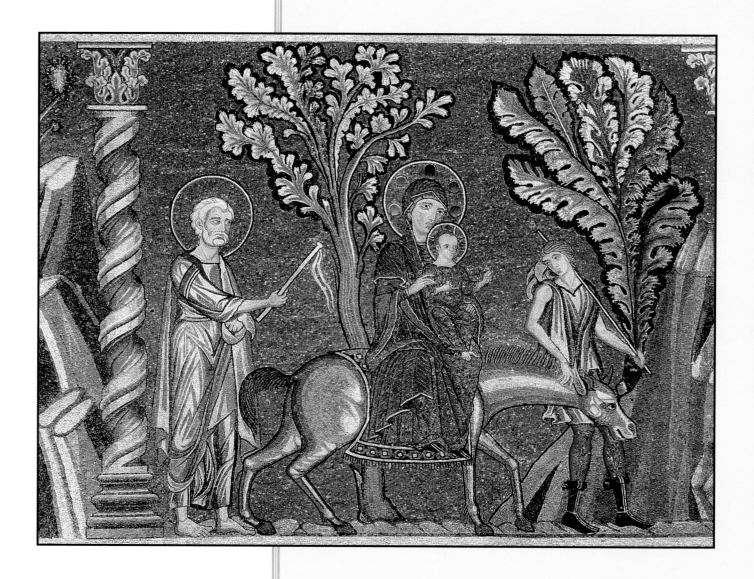

Flight into Egypt

Unknown artist, twelfth century; mosaic. Baptistery, Florence.

While Early Christian artwork focuses on a spiritual and often chastizing message, later works are increasingly expressive of a loving God, human emotions, and the artist's own aesthetic ideals. This mosaic conveys an overall sense of banishment: the Holy Family travels alone with a sullen-looking donkey that Joseph has to goad along. In the fresco, the Holy Family has become part of a protective procession full of human interaction.

nd when they were departed, behold, the angel of the Lord appeareth to Joseph in a dream, saying, Arise and take the young child and his mother, and flee into Egypt, and be thou there until I bring thee word: for Herod will seek the young child to destroy him. When he arose, he took the young child and his mother by night, and departed into Egypt: And was there until the death of Herod: that it might be fulfilled which was spoken of the Lord by the prophet, saying, Out of Egypt have I called my son.

—Matthew 2:13–15.

Flight into Egypt

Giotto, c. 1300; fresco. Scrovegni Chapel, Padua.

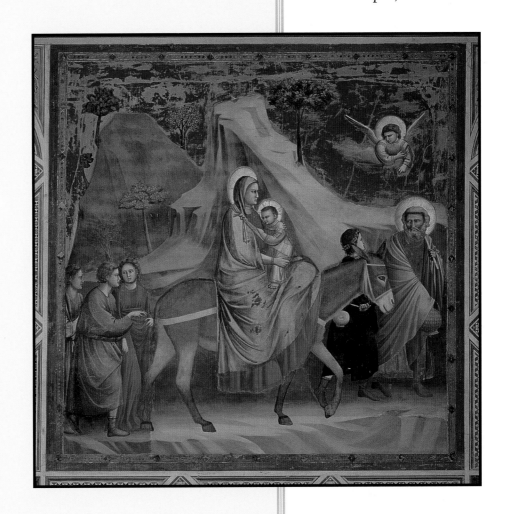

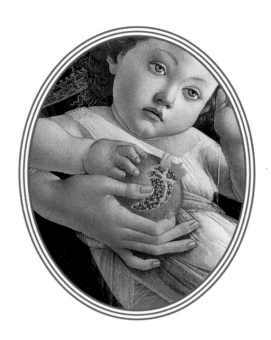

Madonna of the Pomegranate

Sandro Botticelli, 1487; tempera on panel; 56½ in. (143.5 cm) diameter. Uffizi, Florence.

Sandro Botticelli's rendering of Madonna and Child, both with expressions of such tender melancholy and limpid grace, is unsurpassed for its beauty. Garlands of roses, held by the angels on either side of the Madonna, are associated with Mary, who has been called the "rose without thorns" because she was free from sin. The pomegranate in Christ's hand has triple significance: it represents the immortality of Christ, the fertility of the Virgin, and the foundation of the Church.

Almighty God, who has given us thy only-begotten Son to take our nature upon His. . . . Grant that we . . . made thy children by adoption and grace, may daily be renewed by the Holy Spirit; through the same our Lord Jesus Christ, who liveth and reigneth with thee and the same Spirit, ever one God, world without end.

—**Book of Common Prayer.**

Grant us, O Lord, not to mind earthly things, but to love things heavenly; and even now, while we are placed among things that are passing away, to cleave to those that shall abide; through Jesus Christ our Lord.

—*Excerpt of a prayer from the* Leonine Sacramentary.

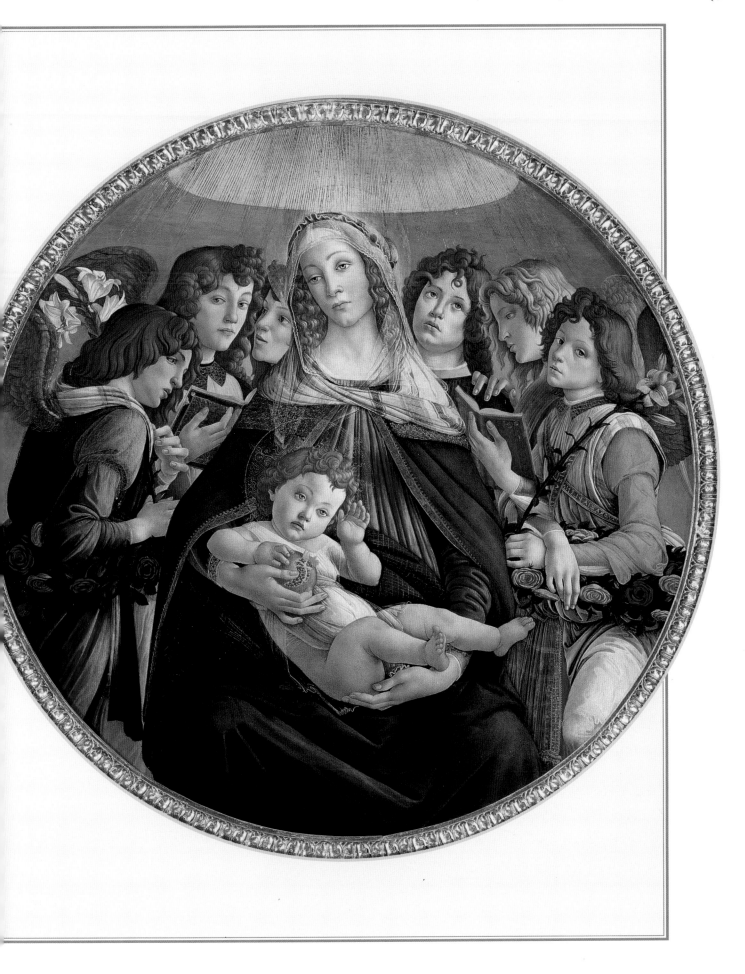

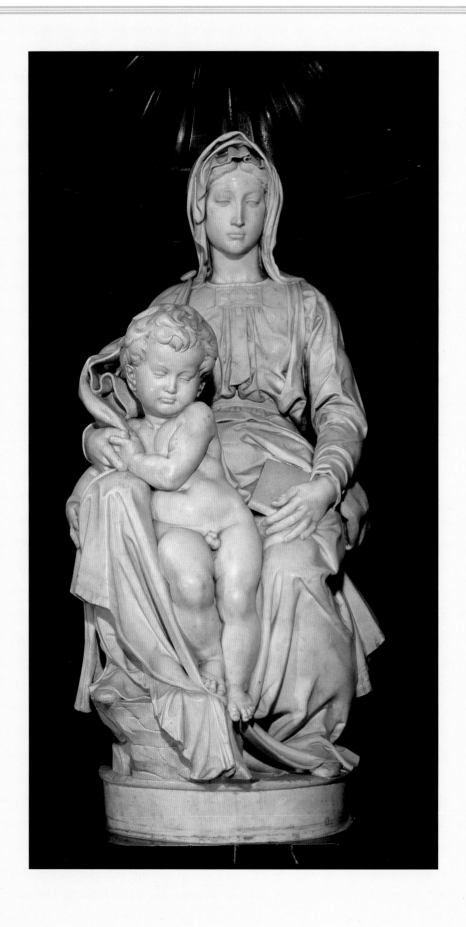

O Virgin of virgins, how shall this be? for neither before thee was any seen like thee, nor shall there be after. Daughters of Jerusalem, why do you marvel at me? The thing which you behold is a divine mystery.

—Excerpt from **The Greater Antiphons Vespers, Western Rite.**

Bruges Madonna

Michelangelo, 1503–4; marble sculpture; 43 in. (109.2 cm) high. Cathedral of Notre Dame, Paris.

Father in heaven! When the thought of thee wakes in our hearts let it not awaken a frightened bird that flies about in dismay, but like a child waking from its sleep with a heavenly smile.

—Søren Aabye
Kierkegaard, 1813–55.

These two sculptures highlight the differing concerns of the Renaissance and Gothic artist. The ivory sculpture is more of an icon than it is a representation of human form: smaller than life size, the crowned Madonna sways backward in an unrealistic, attenuated pose, while the Christ Child she holds looks more like a miniature adult perched magically on Mary's forearm, rather than a baby snuggling in his mother's arms. Michelangelo's life-sized group is shorn of any trappings of divinity, and emphasizes the human, physical relationship as the child holds his mother's hand and half-nestles, half-slides down his mother's lap.

Virgin and Child

Unknown artist, n.d.; ivory. Sainte Chapelle, Paris.

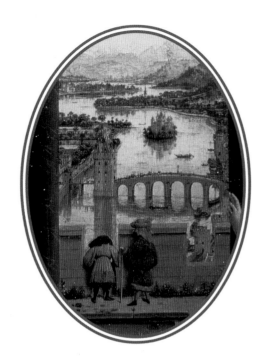

Madonna of Chancellor Rolin

Jan van Eyck, c. 1435; oil on panel; 26 x 24⅜ in. (66 x 71.9 cm). Louvre, Paris.

Jan van Eyck's masterpiece is a wonderful example of the style of the early Northern Renaissance with its obsessive attention to detail and rich appointments: note the heavy, brocaded velvets, mosaic floors, jeweled crown, and window opening onto a vast miniature landscape. This signature piece combines realistic effects with impossible perspectives and symbolic details, creating a vertiginous, mysterious atmosphere that suits religious subjects particularly well. Peacocks, whose flesh is said never to decay, are symbols of Christ's immortality.

O Lord, thou greatest and most true light, whence this light of the day and of the sun doth spring! O Light, which knowest no night nor evening, but art always a mid-day most clear and fair, without whom all is most dark, darkness, by whom all be most resplendent! Grant that I may walk in thy ways, and that nothing else may be light and pleasant unto me. Lighten mine eyes, O Lord, that I sleep not in death . . .

—*John Bradford.*

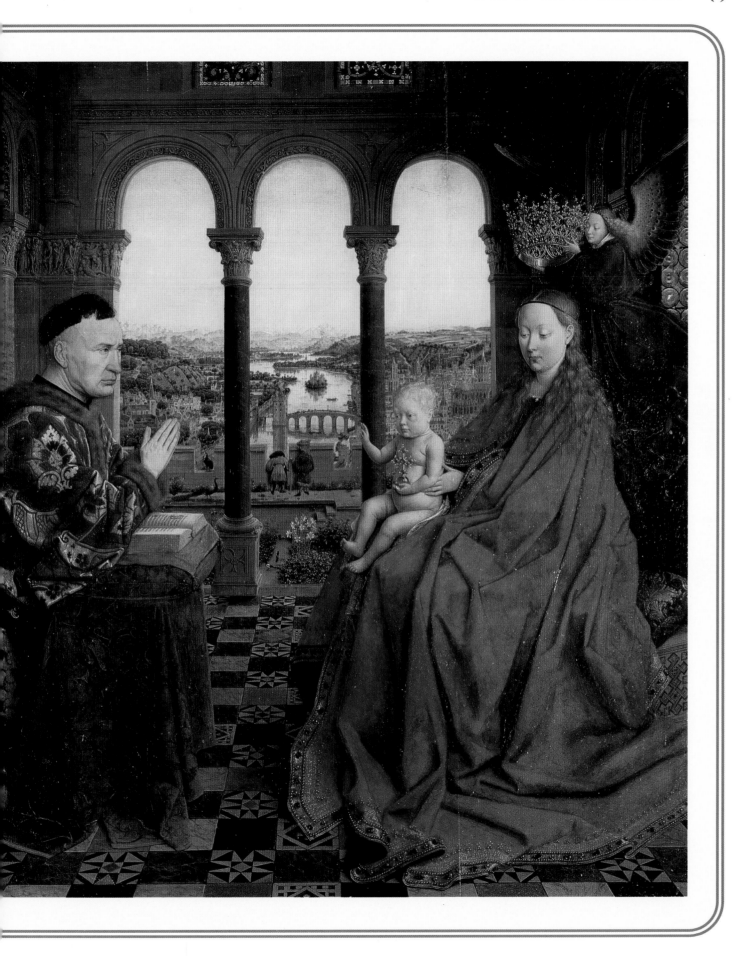

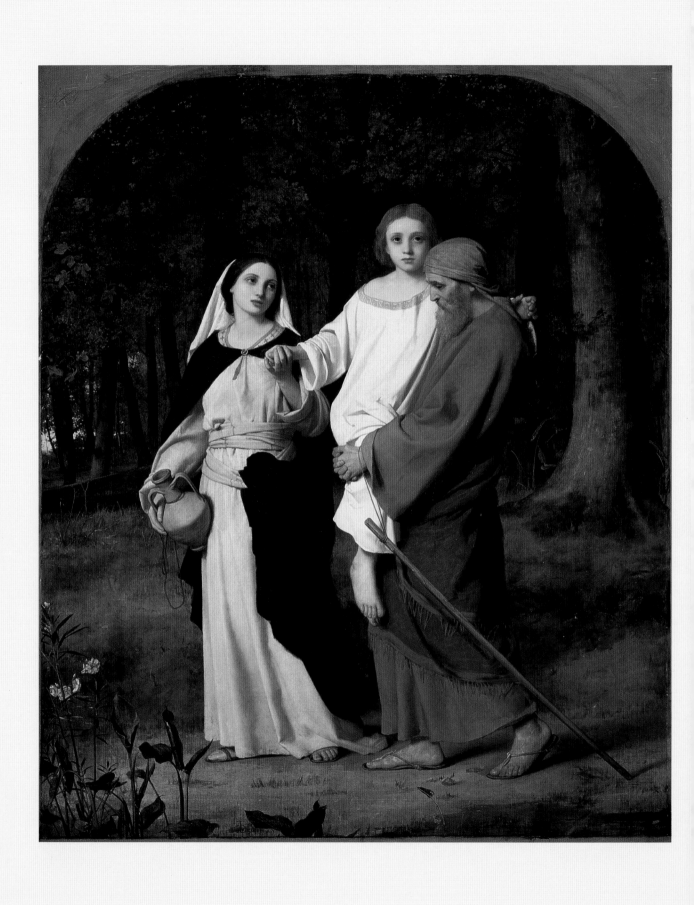

But when Herod was dead, behold, an angel of the Lord appeareth in a dream to Joseph in Egypt, saying, Arise and take the young child and His mother, and go into the land of Israel: for they are dead which sought the young child's life. And he arose, and took the young child and His mother, and came into the land of Israel.

—**Matthew 2:19–21.**

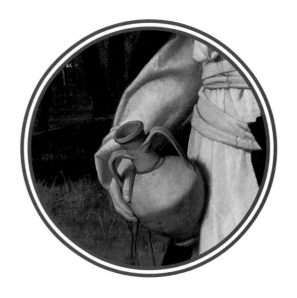

Jesus Returning to Nazareth with His Parents

William Dobson, early seventeenth century; oil on panel. Tate Gallery, London.

Though there are countless portraits of Jesus as a baby, as a toddler, and as a man, in this study He appears to be nine or ten years old. Indeed, Jesus appears too old for Joseph to carry Him on what must have been a long journey. The closeness of the family is apparent as they are all bound by touch, and one has the feeling they need to stick together on their travels through a gloomy landscape that arches over them ominously.

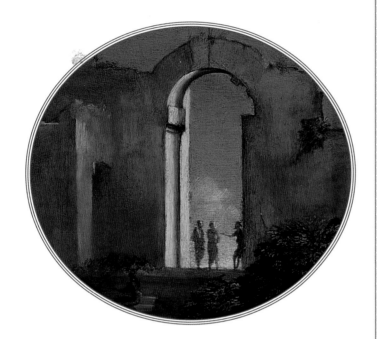

The Virgin with the Blue Diadem

Raphael, early sixteenth century; oil on panel; 27 x 19¼ in. (68.6 x 48.9 cm). Louvre, Paris.

The child John the Baptist—characteristically dressed in a rustic animal-skin tunic and holding a reed cross—and the Virgin Mary adore the sleeping infant Jesus. Raphael displays a Renaissance interest in classicism by setting his scene among Roman ruins, though these buildings would have been new in Christ's day.

O God of love, who has given a new commandment through your only begotten Son, that we should love one another, even as you did love us, the unworthy and the wandering, and gave your beloved Son for our life and salvation; we pray you, Lord, give to us, your servants, in all time of our life on the earth, a mind forgetful of past ill-will, a pure conscience and sincere thoughts, and a heart to love our brethren; for the sake of Jesus Christ, your Son, our Lord and only Saviour.

—Coptic Liturgy of St. Cyril.

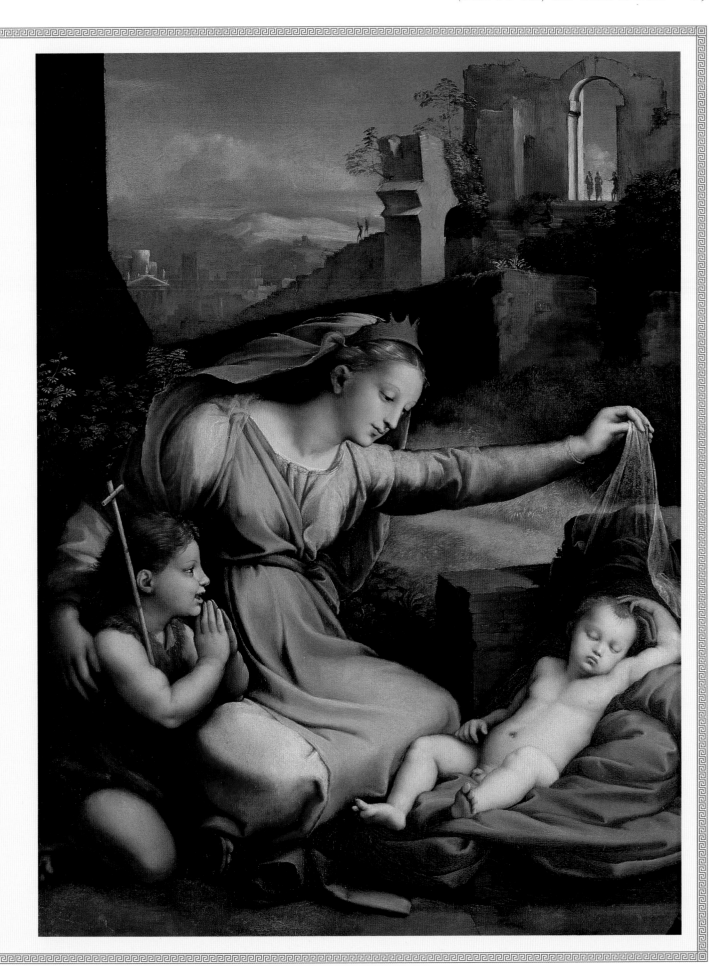

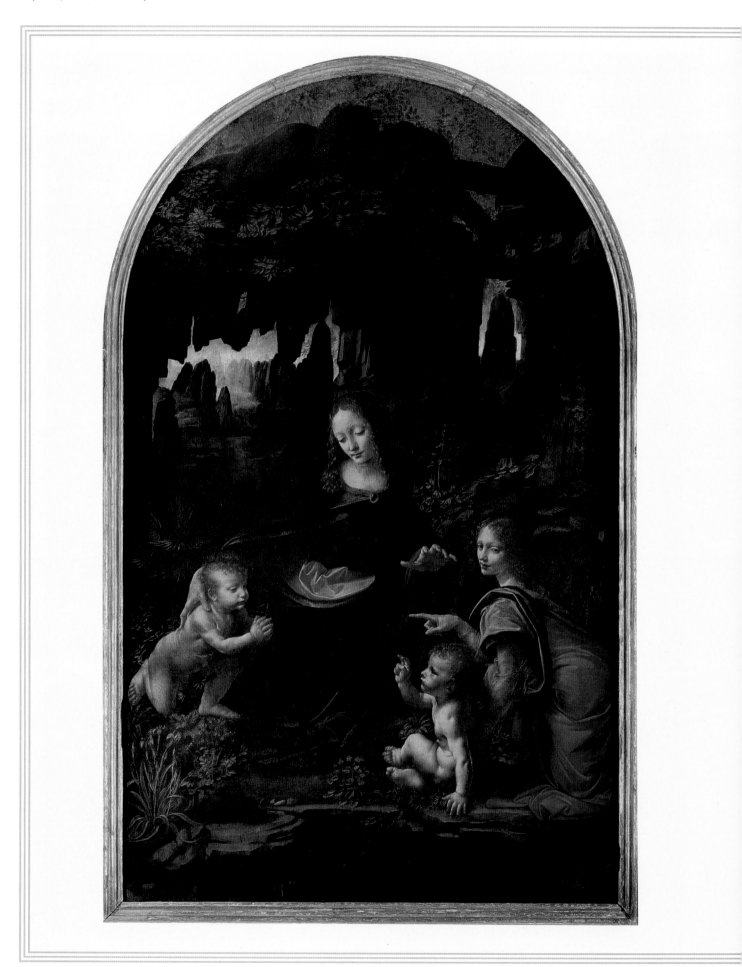

For with thee is the fountain of life: in thy light shall we see light. O continue thy loving-kindness unto them that know thee; and thy righteousness to the upright in heart.

—Psalms 36:9–10.

As a hart longs for flowing streams, so longs my soul for thee, O God. My soul thirsts for God, for the living God.

—Psalms 42:102.

...All my fresh springs shall be in thee.

—Psalms 87:7.

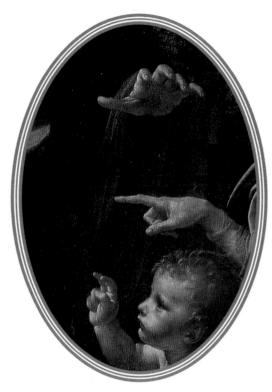

Virgin of the Rocks

Leonardo da Vinci, c. 1485; oil on panel; 75 x 43½ in. (190.5 x 110.5 cm). Louvre, Paris.

Leonardo da Vinci uses a shading technique called *sfumato* (literally "gone up in smoke") to create a mysterious, dream-like air in his portrayal of the meeting of the infants John and Jesus. The symbolic meaning is similarly hazy. Departing from convention, the figures are grouped about a pool in a dark, rocky grotto. Perhaps the meaning can be found in the hand gestures, which link these four figures in sacred communion.

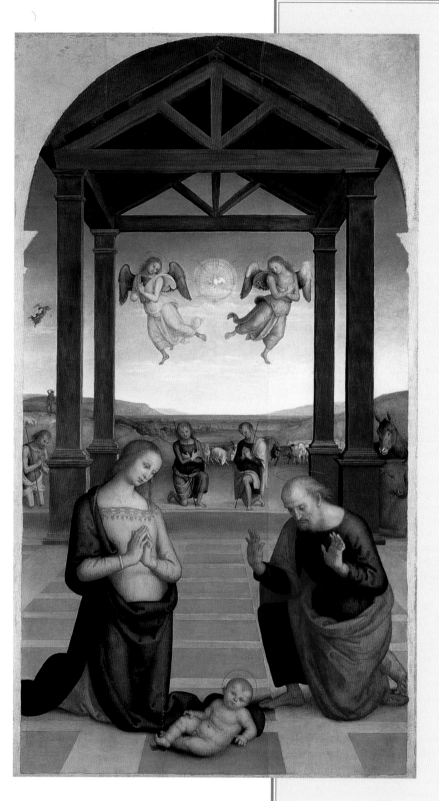

hark! *the herald-angels sing*

Glory to the new-born King;

Peace on earth and mercy mild,

God and sinners reconciled;

Joyful all ye nations rise,

Join the triumph of the skies,

With th'angelic host proclaim,

Christ is born in Bethlehem.

—Charles Wesley.

Nativity

Pietro Perugino, 1506–10; detail from the polyptych of St. Augustine. National Gallery, Perugia.

The fresco retains a feeling of the Gothic past with its nighttime setting, celestial lighting, and pious group of haloed forms around the infant Jesus on a bed of straw. Pietro Perugino, rejecting much of the standard religious

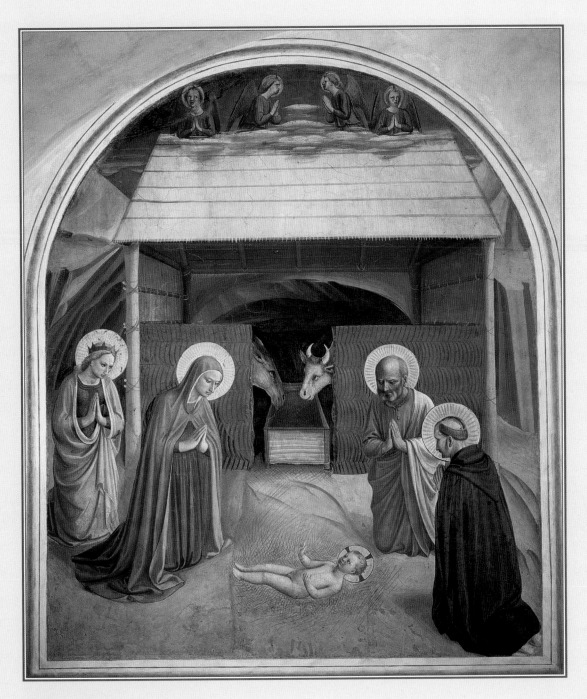

Nativity

Master of Cell 2, c. 1450; fresco;
7 ft. 4 in. x 5 ft. 1¾ in. (189 x 157 cm). Convent of San Marco, Florence.

fare for an architectonic calm, looks ahead to a humanistic
future: the divine Infant lies on a tessellated marble floor,
in broad daylight, with a refined-looking wooden shelter
in the background that bears little resemblance to a stable.

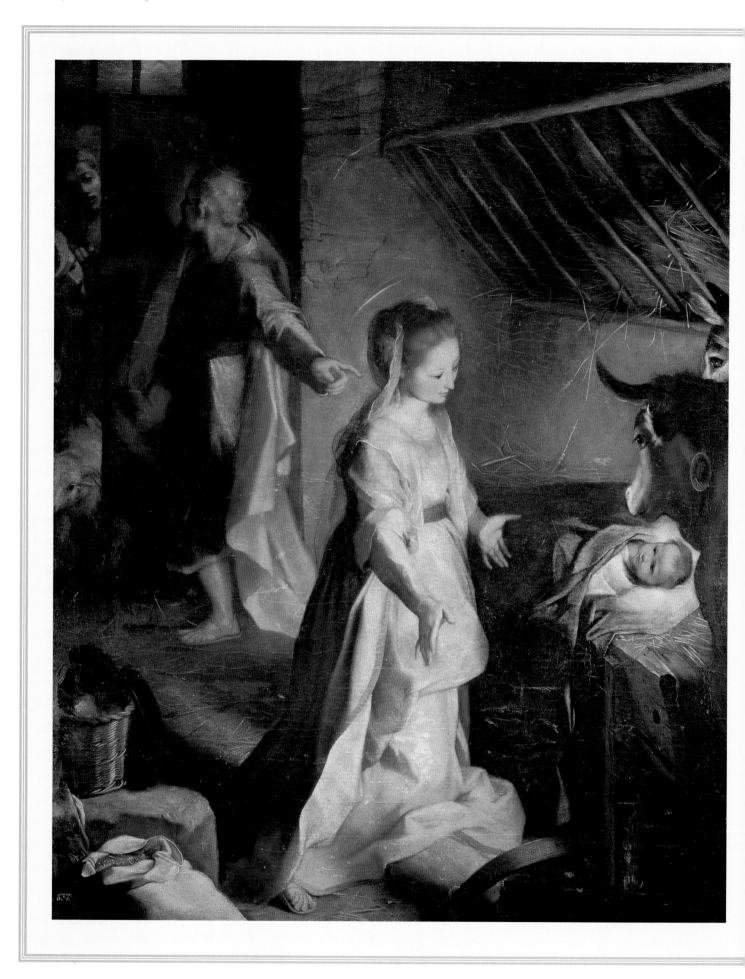

nd so it was, that, while they were there, the days were accomplished that she should be delivered. And she brought forth her firstborn son, and wrapped him in swaddling clothes, and laid him in a manger; because there was no room for them in the inn.

—Luke. 2:6–7.

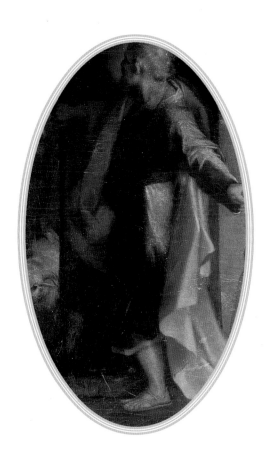

The Nativity

Frederico Barocci, c. 1580; oil on canvas; 53 x 41 in. (134.6 x 104.1 cm). Prado, Madrid.

Frederico Barocci was a popular painter of the Counter-Reformation, which strove for a new piety in religious works that would be easily understandable to ordinary people and avoided obscure or apocryphal references or symbols. This sweetly humble Nativity, in muted tones flooded with a serene golden light, is a perfect example. Gone are the angels, the halos, and the complex symbolic references that crowd earlier works.

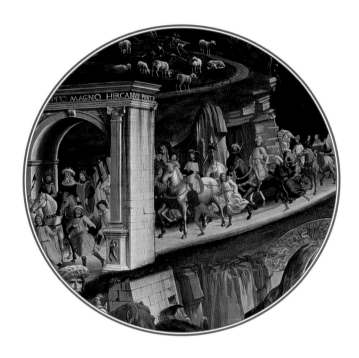

Adoration of the Shepherds

Domenico Ghirlandaio, fifteenth century; oil on panel. San Trinita, Florence.

The landscape, with its procession winding along the hills into the far distance, shows a genius for detail that is reminiscent of the Northern Renaissance. But Domenico Ghirlandaio is a true Italian, and has made the most glaring references to Roman history to prove it: the adoring crowd on the hill must pass through a triumphal arch; two Corinthian pillars, with no particular architectural function, are inserted in the foreground; and Jesus' humble manger has been transformed into a Roman sarcophagus, which displays a Sibylline prophesy concerning Christ's birth.

He shall feed his flock like a shepherd: he shall gather the lambs with his arm, and carry them in his bosom, and shall gently lead those that are with young.

—*Isaiah 40:11.*

Worthy is the Lamb who was slain, to receive power and wealth and wisdom and might and honour and glory and blessing! . . . To him who sits upon the throne and to the Lamb be blessing and honour and glory and might for ever and ever!

—**Revelation 5:12–13.**

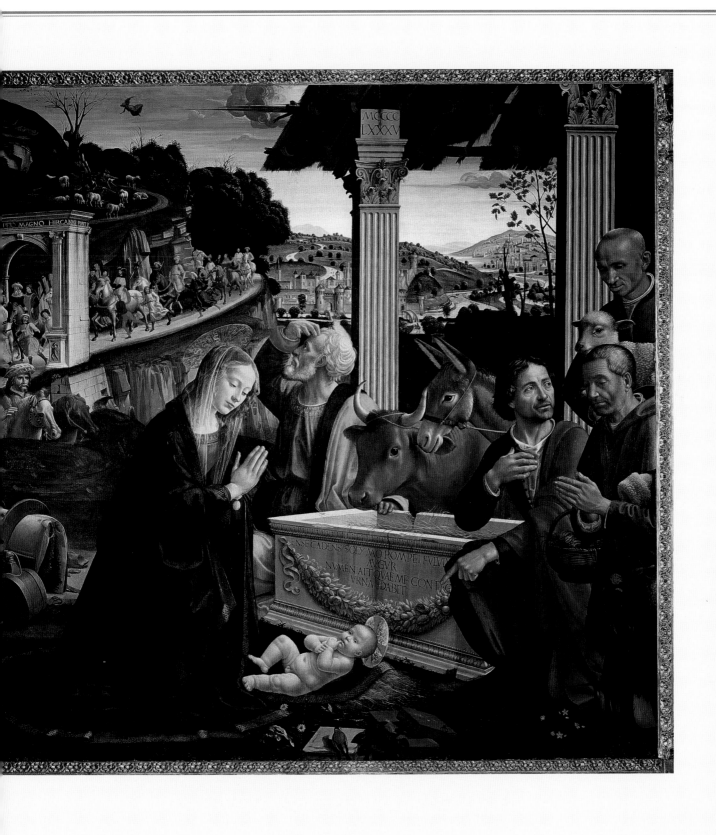

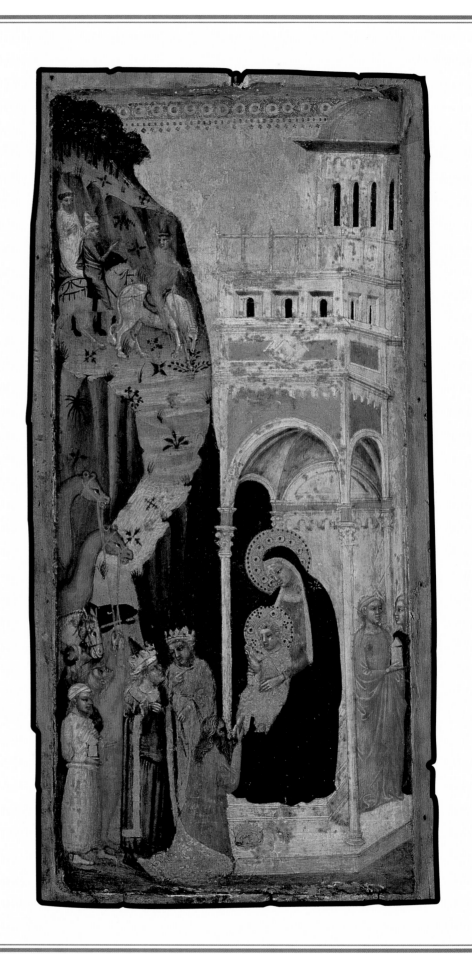

Where is he that is born King of the Jews?

Seek him in my bosom,

here He dwells for my delight, and His.

For we have seen his star in the east,

and are come to worship him.

Blessed be ye, that ye have seen that light,

it came to pass for your salvation.

My Saviour Thou, Thou art the light,

that should have shone upon the heathen, too

and they still do not know Thee,

when they already want to worship Thee.

How bright, how clear, beloved Jesus,

must Thy radiance be!

—Excerpt from Christmas Oratorio
by Johann Sebastian Bach.

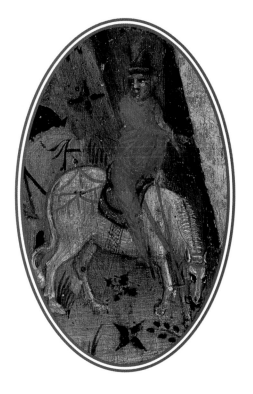

Adoration of the Magi

*Niccolo di Tommaso, n.d.;
oil on panel. Christie's,
London.*

Medieval artists, ignorant of the use of perspective, manipulated space differently to tell a story. It did not disturb the medieval viewer to see characters portrayed twice in the same frame, as here: the Three Kings can be seen on horseback in the upper left hand corner, still on the road, and lower left, their goal attained, adoring the Christ Child.

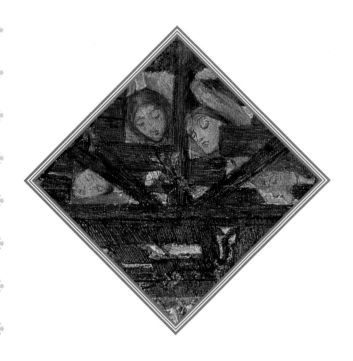

The Seed of David

*Dante Gabriel Rossetti, 1856;
oil on panel; central panel of a
triptych altarpiece. Tate Gallery,
London.*

Dante Gabriel Rossetti was one of
the founding members of the Pre-
Raphaelite Brotherhood, artists who
called for a return to the style and
spirit of the Italian masters of the
Quattrocento. The Pre-Raphaelites
espoused realism, the study of nature,
and social and spiritual purpose. Most
frequently they painted religious,
mythological, or medieval themes.
The commission for a Welsh altarpiece
was a perfect subject for Rossetti, who
conventionally selected a triptych format with a Nativity at its center. The
circle of love surrounding the infant
Jesus, however, is strictly Pre-
Raphaelite in its sensual warmth.

Born is He, the Child divine,
Oboes, bag-pipes, sound your greeting!
Born is He, the Child divine,
Pipe and voice in song combine.

During many thousand years,
Prophets wise foretold the story,
During many thousand years,
We did wait mid hopes and fears.

Oh how charming, oh how sweet,
Oh how lovely is this infant,
Oh how charming, oh how sweet,
In him all the graces meet.

—Traditional French Carol.

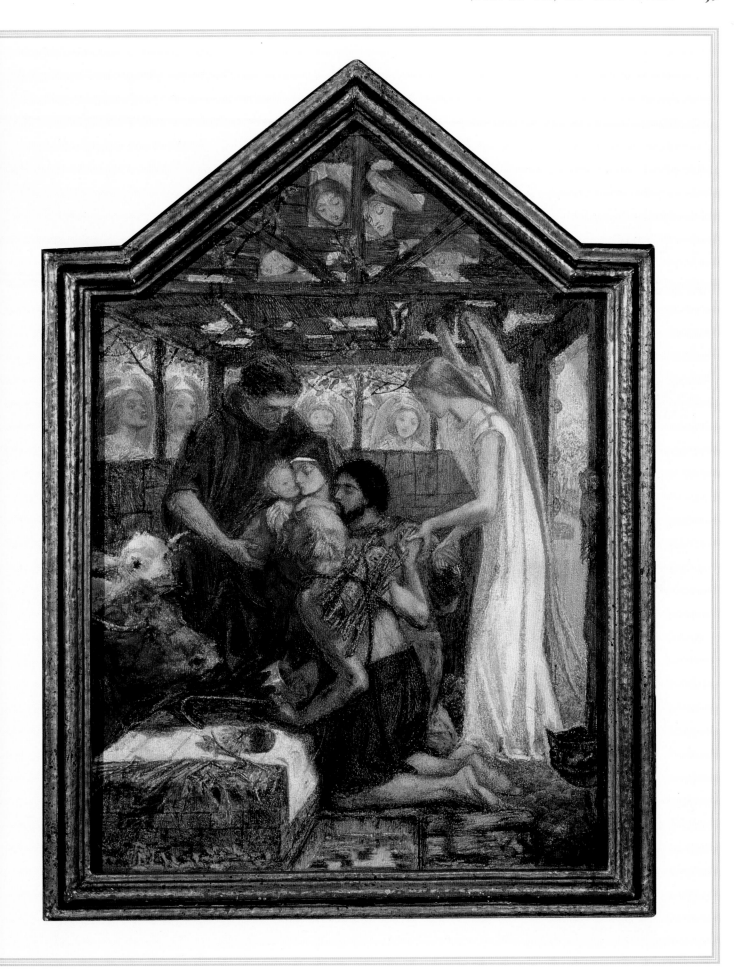

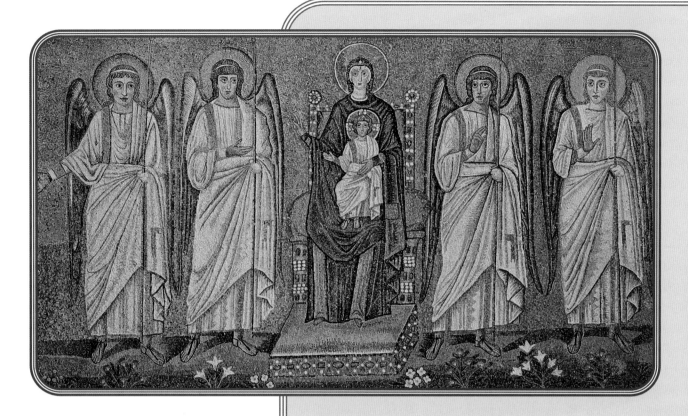

Madonna Enthroned With Four Angels

Unknown artist,
c. 500 AD; mosaic.
San Apollinare
Nuovo, Ravenna.

Temporal symbols of authority are put at the service of the church: brilliant gold, precious jewels, and princely purple are used to portray Mother and Child enthroned as the reigning monarchs in heaven. The symbolism here has a double meaning, for the gold and precious stones are also indicative of divine illumination.

ow beautiful upon the mountains are the feet of him that bringeth good tidings, that publisheth peace; that bringeth good tidings of good, that publisheth salvation; that saith unto Zion, Thy God reigneth!

—*Isaiah 52:7.*

Be thou my vision, O Lord of my heart;
Naught be all else to me, save that thou art,
Thou my best thought, by day or by night,
Waking or sleeping, thy presence my light.

—**Traditional Irish Prayer.**

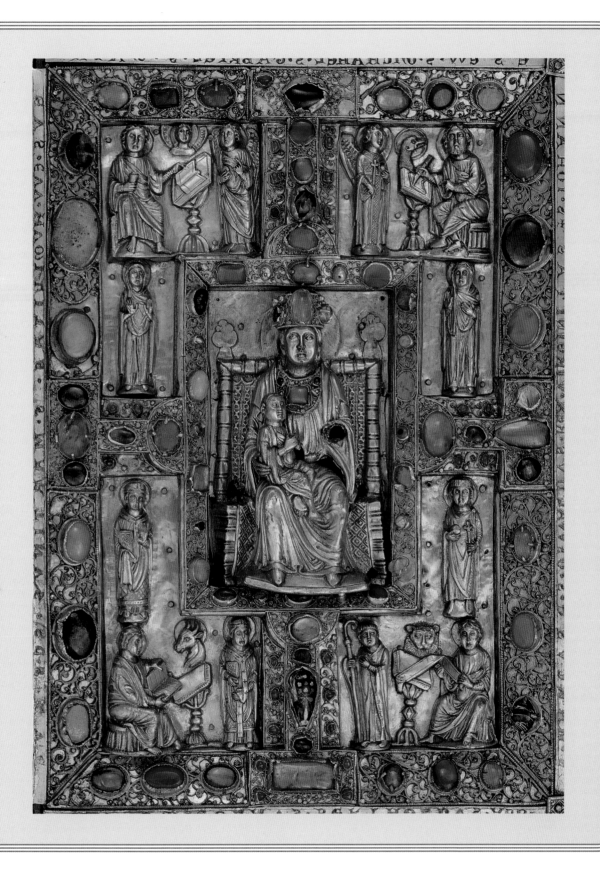

Virgin and Child With Evangelists and Saints

Unknown artist, c. 1200–1232; original front cover of a missal with silver gilt and jeweled plaque. Abbey of Weingarten, Germany.

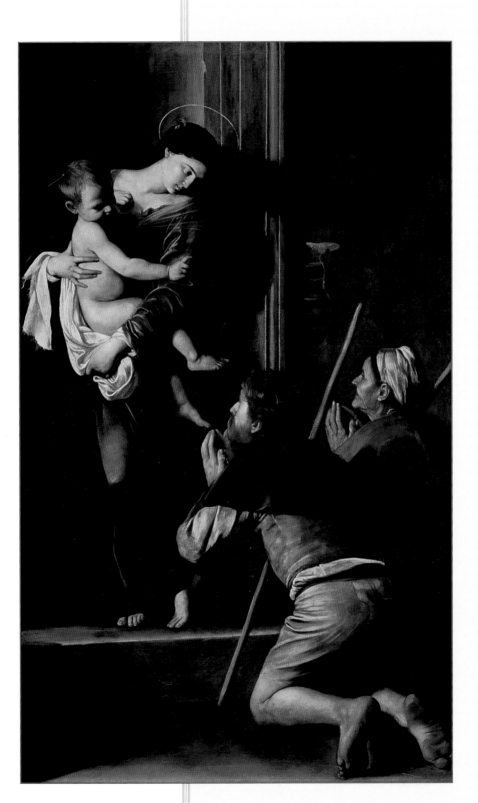

Madonna di Loreto

Caravaggio, 1603–4, oil on canvas, 8 ft. 8½ in. x 4 ft. 11 in. (265.4 x 149.9 cm). Cavelletti Chapel, San Agostino, Rome.

Two paupers in a dark street fall on their knees in rapturous prayer before a beatific vision of the Virgin and Child appearing in a doorway. Caravaggio paints realistic detail (the bricks showing through a patch of peeled plaster) and lifelike forms (Christ appears to be an extremely healthy two-year-old), but still manages to create an other-worldly scene with a night setting, dramatically lighting the figures from above.

ear us, O never-failing light, Lord our God, the fountain of light, the light of your angels, principalities, powers, and of all intelligent beings; who has created the light of your saints. May our souls be lamps of yours, kindled and illuminated by you. May they shine and burn with the truth, and never go out in darkness and ashes. May the gloom of sins be cleared away, and the light of perpetual faith abide with us.

—Excerpt from Mozarabic Liturgies.

The Virgin

Master of Vysehrad, fourteenth century; tempera on wood. Monastery Saint George, Prague.

Raying halos and Mary's blue garments placed against a blue sky transfigure Virgin and Child into a celestial couple, stars of divine illumination in the night sky.

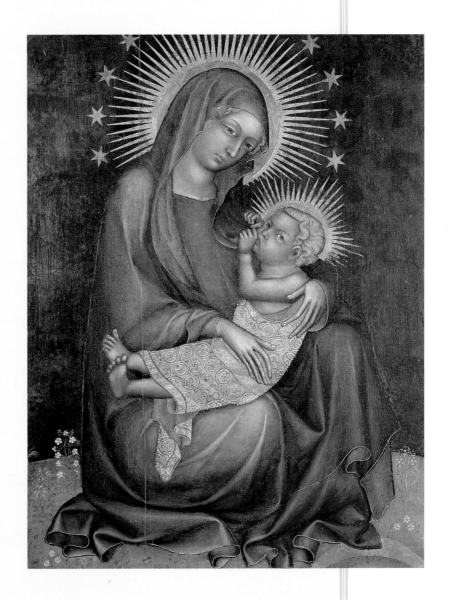

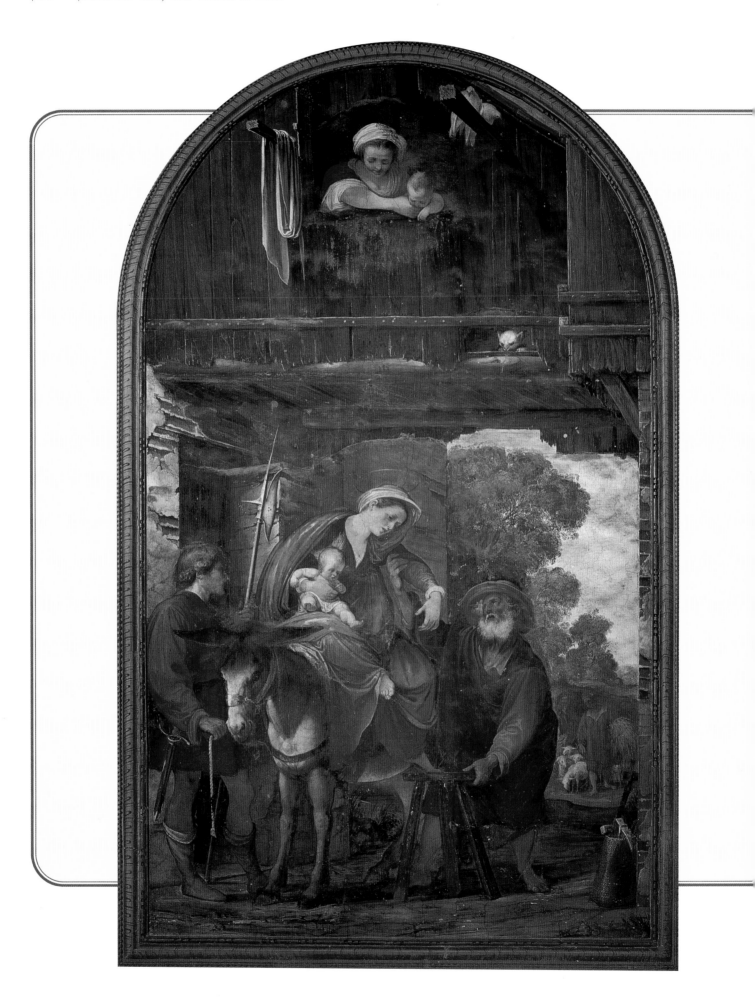

*T*hanks be to you, our Lord Jesus Christ,

for all the benefits that you have given us,

for all the pains and insults that you have borne

for us.

Most merciful Redeemer, Friend, and Brother,

may we know you more clearly,

love you more dearly,

and follow you more nearly,

day by day.

—Prayer of St. Richard.

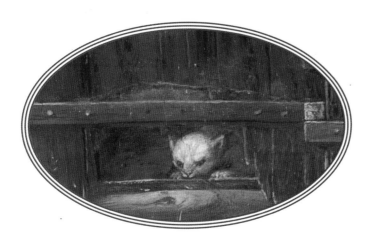

Rest on the Flight into Egypt

Giovanni da San Giovanni, early seventeenth century; fresco.
Chapel of the Accademia, Florence.

An unusual setting for this theme, the Holy Family is not shown resting by the side of a road, but being welcomed at a rustic farm house. It's interesting that instead of divine guidance from above, there is human and animal interest. As Joseph helps Mary dismount, two doves sitting on a rafter, a mother and child at a loft window, and a cat peeking through a hole all look on.

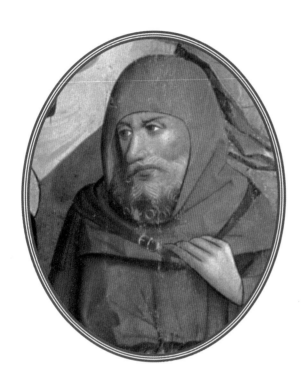

Flight to Egypt

Unknown artist, fifteenth century; Poland.

Joseph is cast in the role of adoring caretaker to his two heavenly charges. Mary, riding on the donkey, appears completely absorbed as she enfolds her infant in her dark blue robe with embroidered golden bands, while Joseph, without a halo, and wearing an unadorned red travelling outfit, looks anxiously up at his family as he walks alongside.

O *Jesus, king most wonderful,*
Thou conqueror renowned,
thou sweetness most ineffable,
In whom all joys are found!

When once thou visitest the heart,
Then truth begins to shine;
Then earthly vanities depart;
Then kindles love divine.

—**Latin Prayer.**

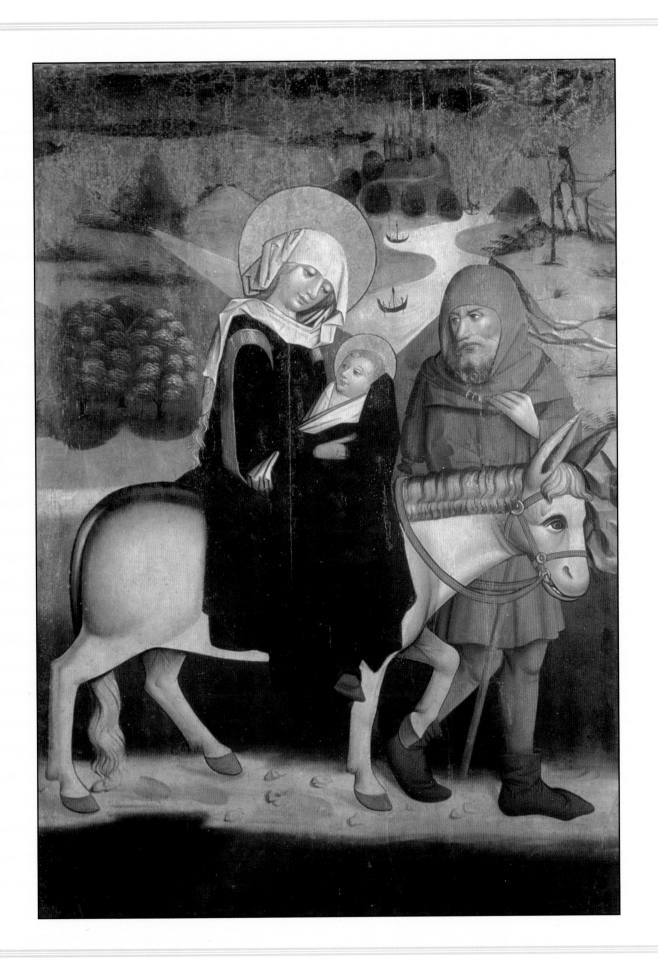

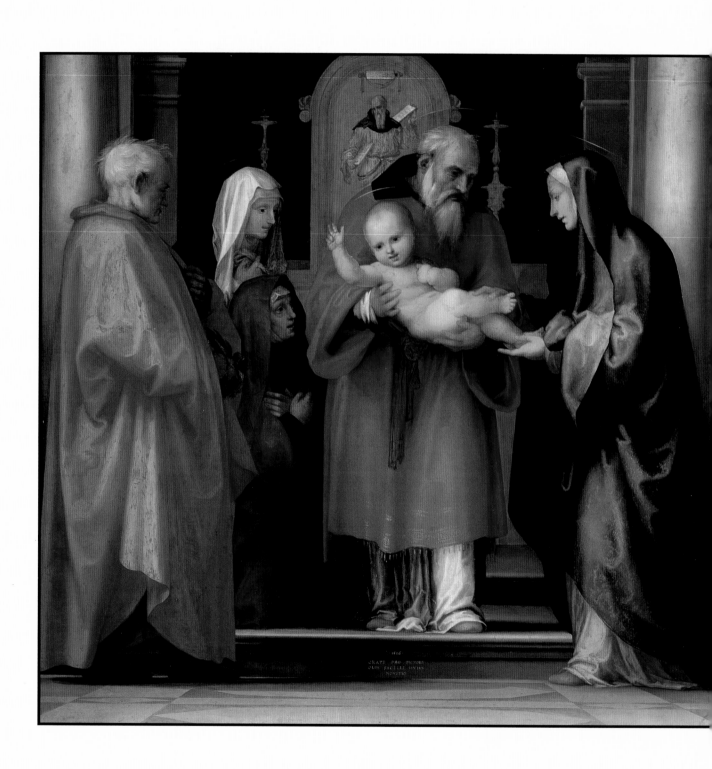

I thank thee, Father, Lord of heaven and earth, that thou hast hidden these things from the wise and understanding and revealed them to babes; yea, Father, for such was thy gracious will. All things have been delivered to me by my Father; and no one knows who the Son is except the Father, or who the Father is except the Son and anyone to whom the Son chooses to reveal him.

—Luke 10:21–22.

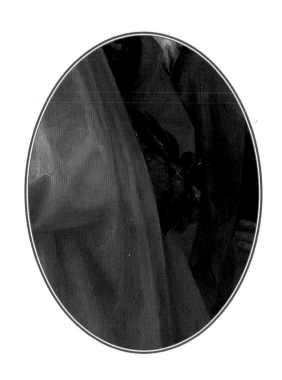

The Presentation of Jesus in the Temple

Fra Bartolomeo, 1516; oil on panel; 60½ x 62 in. (155 x 159 cm). Kunsthistorisches Museum, Vienna.

Although it looks as if Mary is handing her child to a priest for presentation, the central figure is actually Simeon, for whom it was foretold that he would not die until he saw the Messiah. The kneeling woman is Anna, a prophetess, who also recognized the divinity of Jesus. The brace of pigeons that Joseph holds beneath his cloak are for use in a ritual purification that Mary must undergo after having given birth.

The Adoration of the Shepherds

Philippe de Champaigne, c. 1628; oil on canvas;
87 x 63$\frac{1}{26}$ in. (233 x 163.2 cm). Wallace Collection, London.

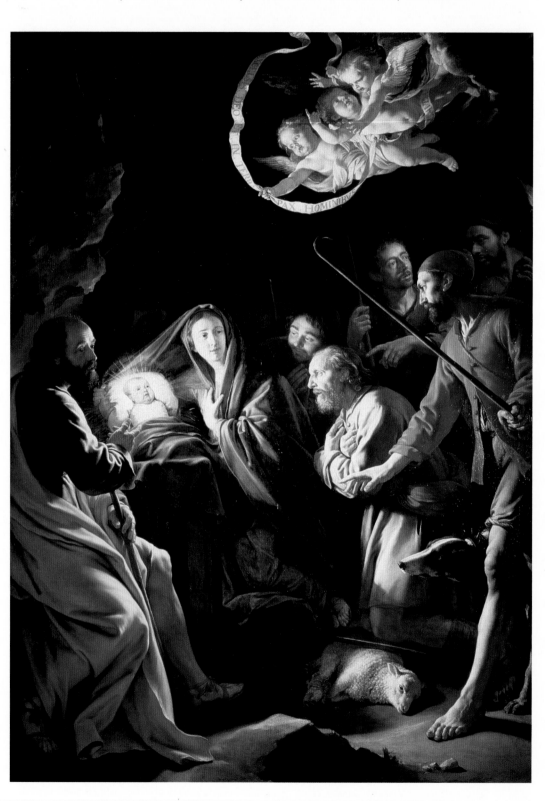

Look upon us, O Lord, and let all the darkness of our souls vanish before the beams of your brightness. Fill us with holy love, and open to us the treasures of your wisdom. All our desire is known unto you, therefore perfect what you have begun, and what your Spirit has awakened us to ask in prayer. We seek your face; turn your face unto us and show us your glory, then shall our longing be satisfied, and our peace shall be perfect; through Jesus Christ our Lord.

—Prayer of St. Augustine of Hippo.

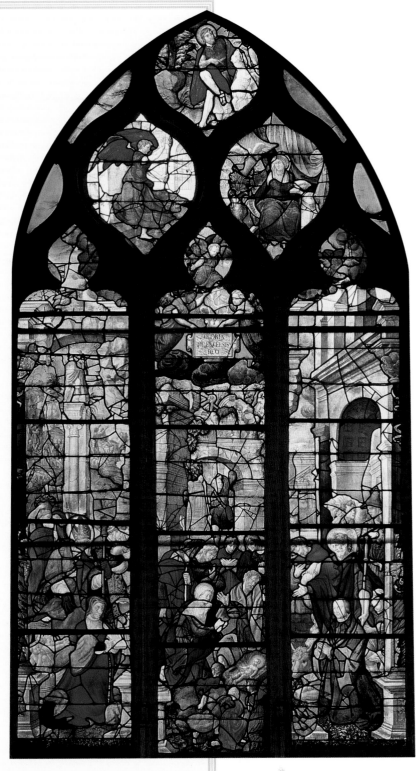

Stained glass was extensively used in medieval and Renaissance times to create a visionary, miraculous atmosphere within the Church. The light of God's divine illumination would bring Old and New Testament scenes to life. In a different way, but with the same spiritual intent, Philippe de Champaigne uses stark overhead lighting to dramatize his Nativity.

Nativity.

Unknown artist, sixteenth century; stained-glass window. Abbey Ste. Foy, Conques.

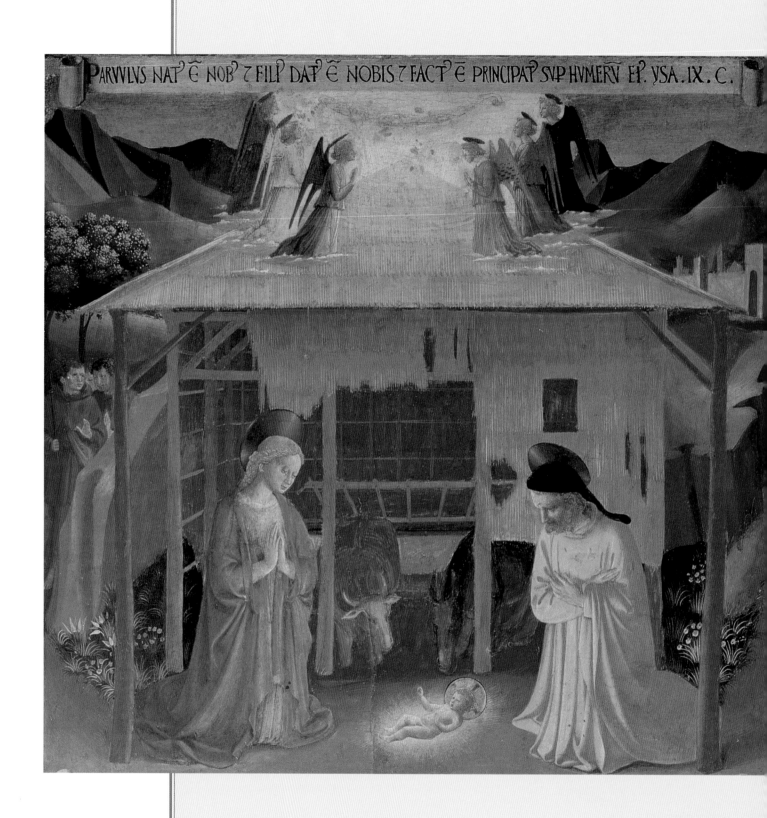

O thou that bringest good tidings to Zion, get thee up into the high mountain; O thou that bringest good tidings to Jerusalem, lift up thy voice with strength; lift it up, be not afraid; say unto the cities of Judah, Behold your God!

—Isaiah 40:9.

And this shall be a sign unto you; Ye shall find the babe wrapped in swaddling clothes, lying in a manger. And suddenly there was with the angel a multitude of the heavenly host praising God, and saying, Glory to God in the highest, and on Earth peace, good will toward men.

—Luke. 2:12–14.

Nativity

Fra Angelico, 1451–53; panel from the Annunziata Silver Chest; 15¼ x 15¼ in. (39 x 39 cm). Museo di San Marco, Florence.

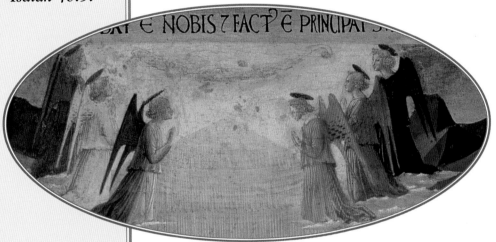

The *Annunziata Silver Chest* is the last work that can absolutely be attributed to Fra Angelico. The chest shows the full cycle of the life of Christ. The top and bottom of each panel has a scroll, the top containing a quotation from the Old Testament, the bottom a quotation from the New Testament. Here Angelico has chosen appropriate quotes from Isaiah, prophesying the coming of the Messiah, and from Luke, describing the birth of Christ.

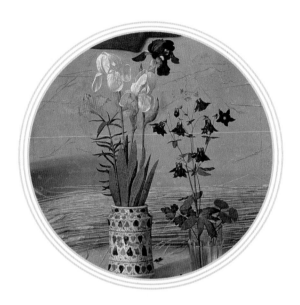

Nativity Scene with Adoration of the Shepherds

Hugo van der Goes, c. 1476; central panel from the Portinari Altarpiece; oil on panel; 8 ft. 3½ in. x 10 ft. (252.7 x 304.8 cm). Uffizi, Florence.

Van der Goes' mental instability may have had an effect on the strange, often totally obscure imagery in this Nativity scene. The angels are smaller in stature than the Holy Family, while the shepherds are another awkward fit—realistic to the point of homeliness—as they crowd in upon this other-worldly scene. While a lily and a clear glass vase both symbolize the purity of the Virgin, there are several other types of flowers and two types of vases here, the combined meaning of which is unclear.

See how the shepherds,
Summoned to his cradle,
Leaving their flocks, draw
nigh with lowly fear;
We too will thither
Bend our joyful steps

O come let us adore him,
O come let us adore him,
O come let us adore him,
Christ the Lord!

—**O Come, All Ye faithful**
lyrics by J.F. Wade.

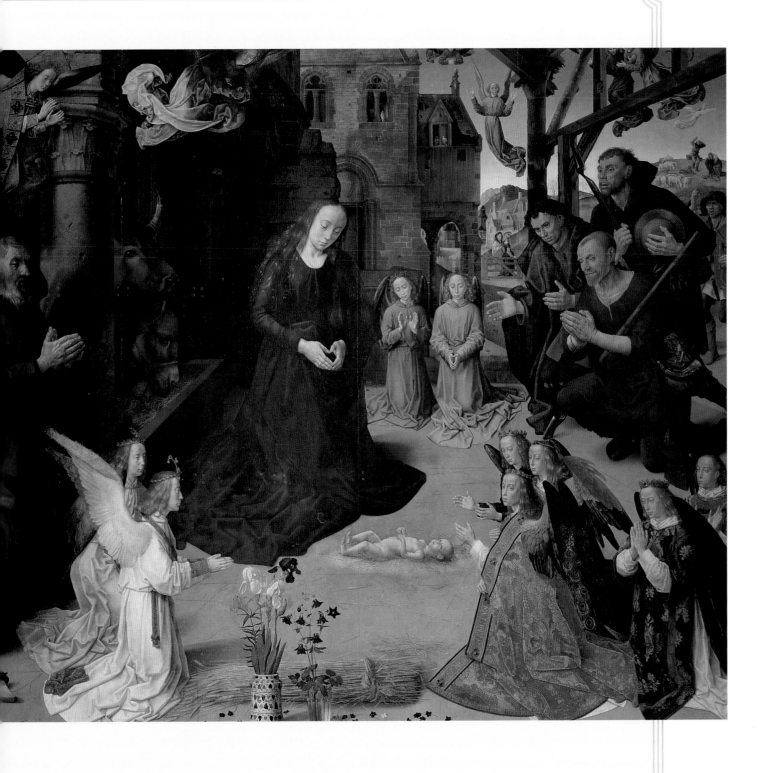

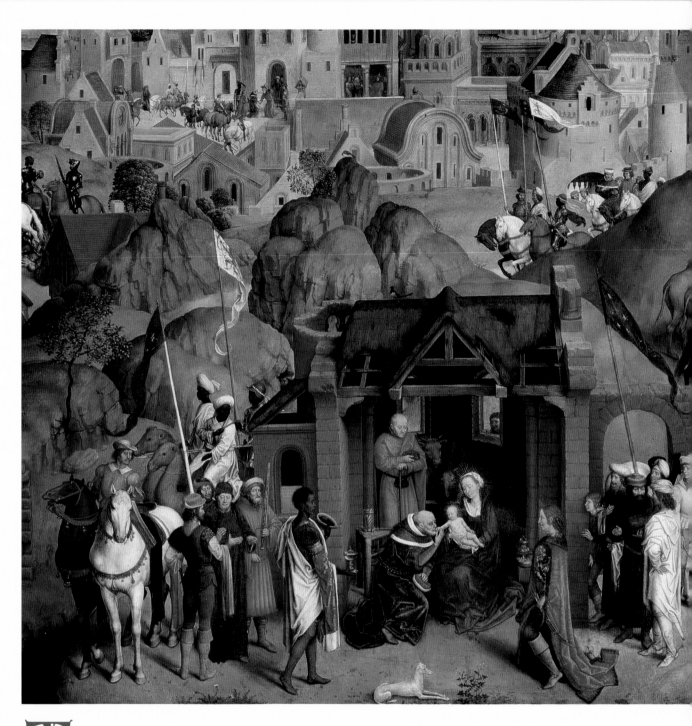

Take, O Lord, and receive my entire liberty, my memory, my understanding, and my whole will. All that I am, all that I have, you have given me and I will give it back again to you to be disposed of according to your good pleasure. Give me only your love and your grace; with you I am rich enough, nor do I ask for aught besides. Amen.

—Prayer of St. Ignatius of Loyola.

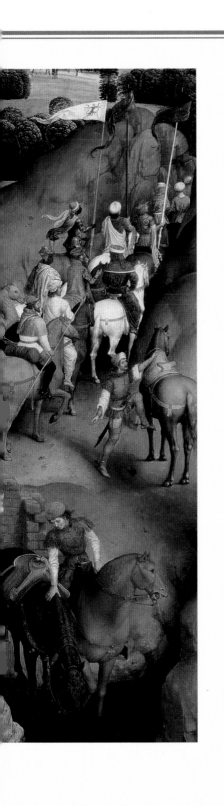

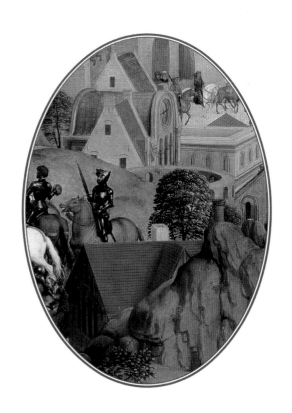

The Adoration of the Magi

Hans Memling, c. 1480; from
The Seven Joys of Mary; *oil on panel;*
31⅞ x 74⅜ in. (80.9 x 188.9 cm).
Alte Pinakothek, Munich.

The Adoration of the Magi has been transformed into a late Gothic pageant, replete with banners showing European and Asian coats-of-arms and knights in full armor against the backdrop of a medieval castle. The Massacre of the Innocents, occurring in the top left of the picture, is traditionally shown in conjunction with the arrival of the Three Kings.

Virgin of Loreto

Raphael, sixteenth century; oil on panel. Musée Condé, Chantilly.

A refined view of the Holy Family: the baby Jesus lies in a cloud of brilliant white linen and feather pillows, while a richly dressed Mary holds out a fine veil for Him to grasp at as Joseph looks on.

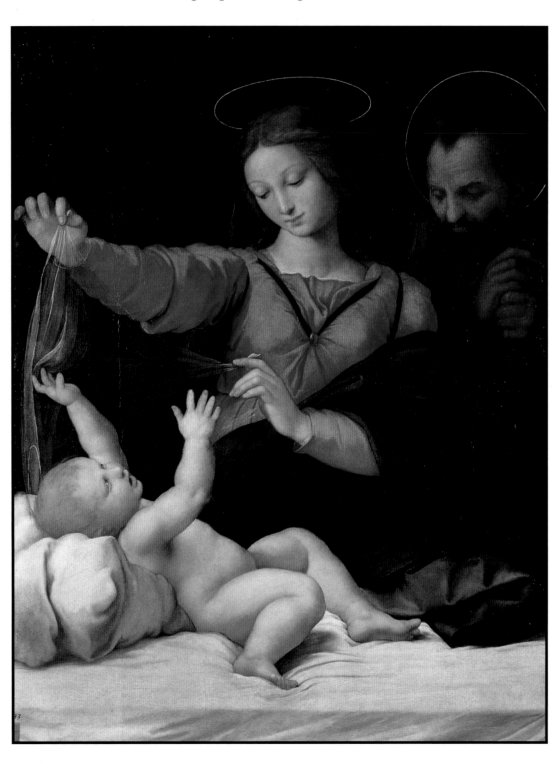

Behold, the angel of the Lord appeared unto him in a dream, saying, Joseph, thou son of David, fear not to take unto thee Mary thy wife: for that which is conceived in her is of the Holy Ghost. And she shall bring forth a son, and thou shalt call his name Jesus: for he shall save his people from their sins.

—Matthew 20–21.

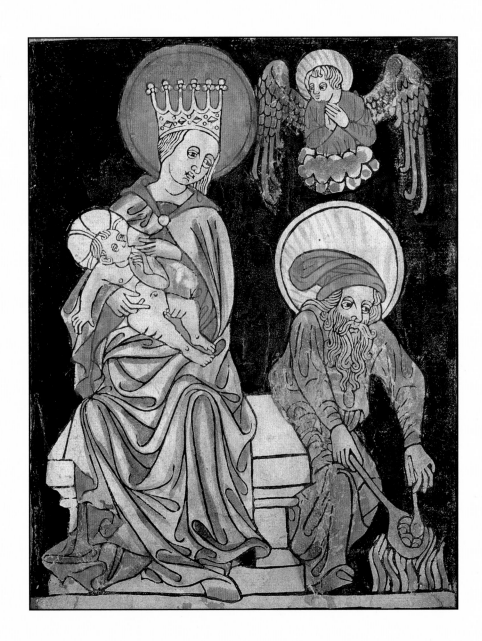

Holy Family

Unknown artist, n.d.; colored woodblock print.
Graphische Sammlung Albertina, Vienna.

Woodblock prints, crude but inexpensive to reproduce, often showed less refined images intended for popular consumption. Here the Holy Family is shown doing a most human thing (eating), with a humorous role-reversal as Joseph cooks for his family. Note the three different types of halos: Joseph's, a simple circle framing his face and cap; Mary's, a red circle that frames her more elaborate crown, and Jesus, with a cruciform nimbus that only He can wear.

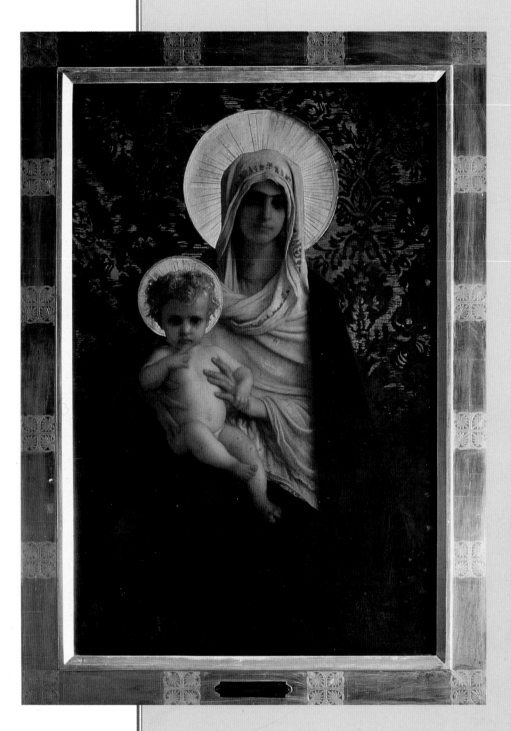

I have calmed and quieted my soul, like a child quieted at its mother's breast: like a child that is quieted is my soul.

—**Psalms 131:3.**

Madonna and Child

Antoine Auguste Ernest Hébert, 1872; oil on canvas. Church at la Tronche, France.

This pious French work, which harkens back to Gothic visions of the Madonna and Child in its vertical composition, extensive use of gold leaf, and its subtle distortion of perspective, has much in common with the work of the pre-Raphaelites from across the channel.

Love divine, all loves excelling,

Joy of heaven to earth come down,

Fix in us thy humble dwelling,

All thy faithful mercies crown.

Jesus, thou art all compassion, Pure, unbounded love thou art;

Visit us with thy salvation,

Enter every trembling heart.

—Excerpt from The Prayer of Charles Wesley.

Our Lady of Czestahowa (the "Black Madonna")

Unknown Siennese painter, c. 1375; tempera with chalk base on canvas and panel, 47⅝ x 32 in. (122.2 x 82.2 cm). Katowice, Poland.

Called the "Black Madonna" because the passage of time has darkened the image, this is perhaps one of the most famous representations of the Mother and Child due to the miraculous powers attributed to it. Indeed, the modern-day city of Katowice, near Czestahowa, grew mainly due to the traffic of pilgrims who came to see this holy work.

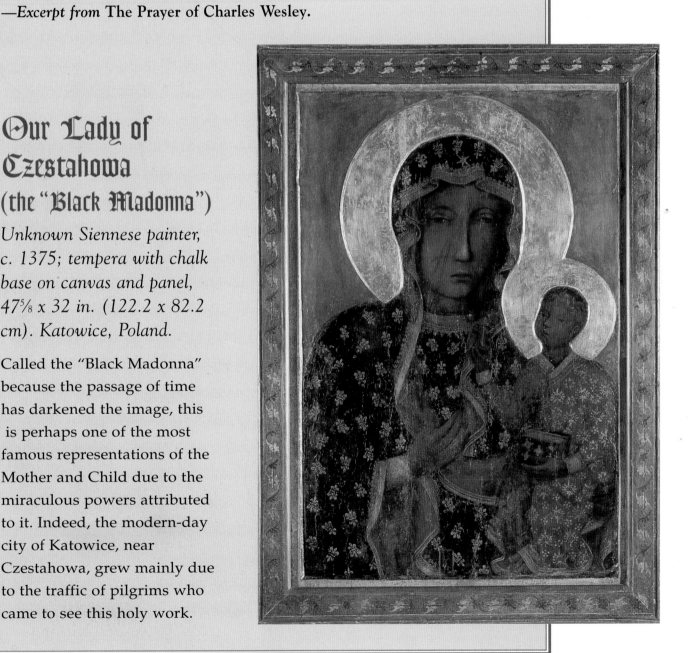

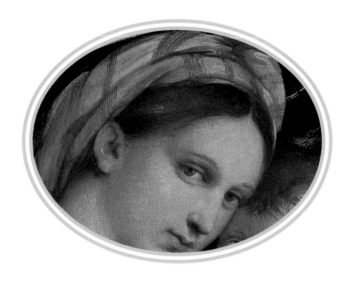

Madonna of the Chair

Raphael, c. 1513; oil on panel; 27$^{15}/_{16}$ in. (40.6 cm) diameter. Palazzo Pitti, Florence.

Raphael has given us a very secular Madonna and Child indeed: a softly fleshy infant of Rubenesque dimensions and a turbaned Madonna wearing a gorgeous Oriental costume. Still, this work has not wholly departed from the Gothic canon: Mary's halo, faint as it is, is in place over her turban, and the infant John the Baptist is shown in his customary pose, palms together in prayer with his trademark reed cross in the crook of his arm.

O Lord Jesus Christ, which art the sun of the world, evermore arising, and never going down, which by thy most wholesome appearing and sight dost bring forth, preserve, nourish and refresh all things, as well that are in heaven, as also that are on earth; we beseech thee and favourably to shine into our hearts, and the night and darkness of sins, and the mists and errors on every side are driven away, thou brightly shining within our hearts, we may all our life space go without stumbling or offence, and may decently and seemly walk, (as in the day time) being pure and clean from the works of darkness, and abounding in all good works which God hath prepared for us to walk in; which with the Father and with the Holy Ghost livest and reignest for ever and ever.

—Thomas Cranmer.

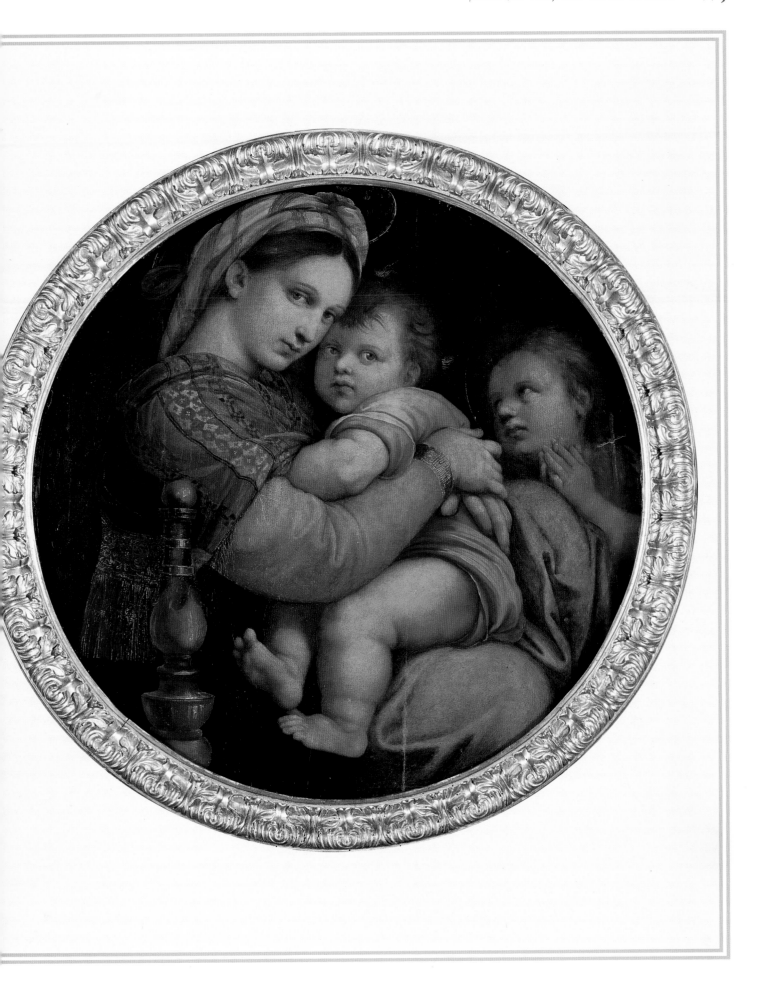

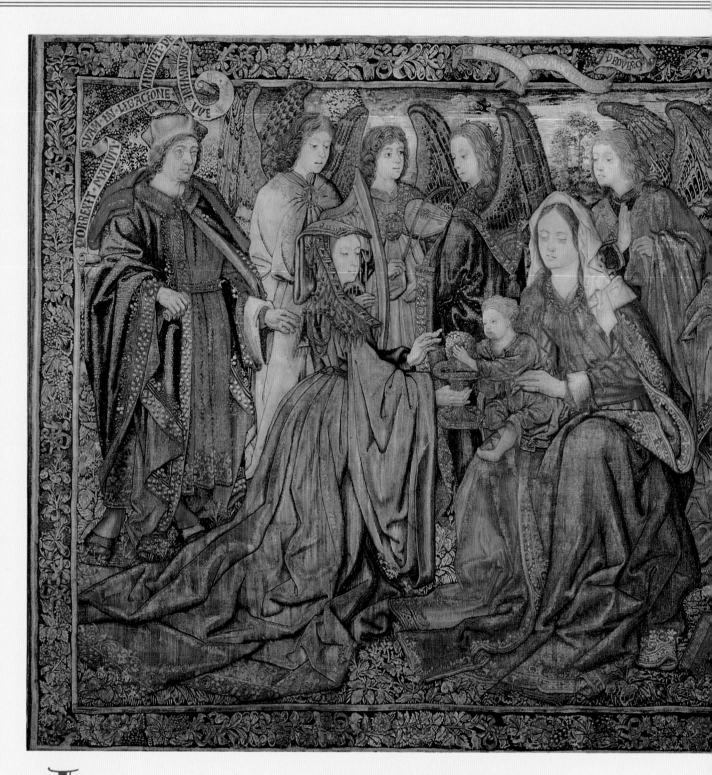

I am the true vine, and my Father is the husbandman . . . I am the vine, ye are the branches: He that abideth in me, and I in him, the same bringeth forth much fruit: for without me ye can do nothing . . . Herein is my Father glorified, that ye bear much fruit; so shall ye be my disciples.

—John 15:1, 5, 8.

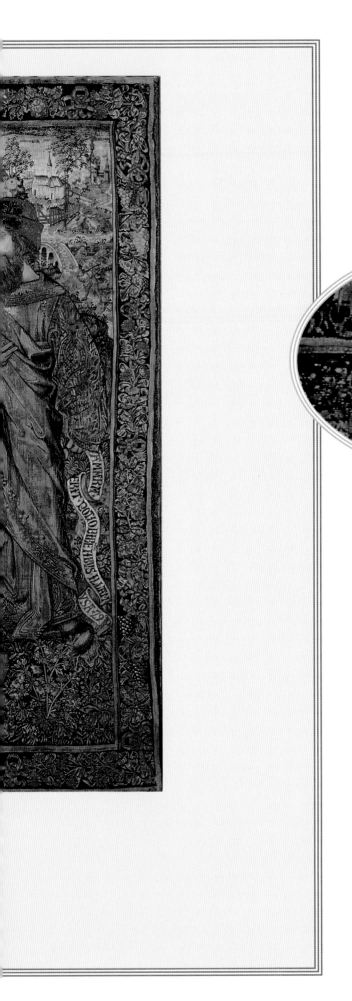

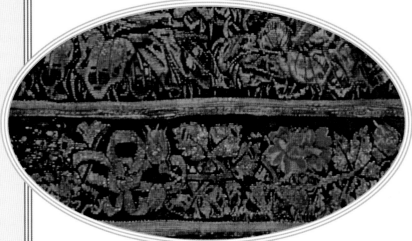

The Mystic Wine

Flanders, early sixteenth century; tapestry in wool and silk with silver and silver-gilt threads; 54¾ x 68⅛ in. (139 x 173 cm). Papal Apartment, Vatican City, Rome.

In an allegory of the Eucharist, the infant Jesus turns a bunch of grapes into wine (or blood), which a kneeling woman, representing the Church, gathers in a richly ornamented chalice. The grapevine, which appears in the border, is used in the Old Testament to describe the relationship of God to his people (whom He tends with the loving care of a farmer), and in the New Testament becomes the symbol of Jesus himself, as the intermediary between God and man.

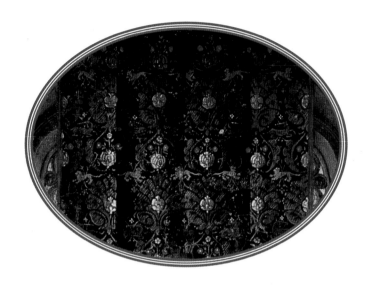

Enthronment of Saint Mary

Jan van Eyck, mid-fifteenth century; central panel of a triptych altar; oil on panel; 12⅞ x 10¾ in. (33.1 x 27.5 cm). Alte Meister, Dresden.

A sophisticated, worldly Madonna and Child rendered in van Eyck's classic mix of hyper-realism and complex symbolism. The Virgin has a crown (in lieu of a halo), but it has been reduced to the most delicate of jeweled Renaissance headbands. Behind the Madonna a richly detailed tapestry with princely and Christian motifs (the lions are popular both in heraldry, as a symbol of majesty and courage, and in religious art, as a symbol of Christ) gives the illusion of an enclosed garden, a reference to Mary's chastity.

O gladsome light, *O* grace of God the Father's face, th'eternal splendour wearing; celestial, holy, blest, our Saviour Jesus Christ, joyful in thine appearing.

Now, ere day fadeth quite, we see the evening light, our wonted hymn out-pouring; Father of might unknown, thee, his incarnate Son, and Holy Spirit adoring.

To thee of right belongs all praise of holy songs, O Son of God, Life-giver; thee, therefore, O Most High, the world doth glorify, and shall exalt forever.

—Nunc Dimittis, *Greek hymn.*

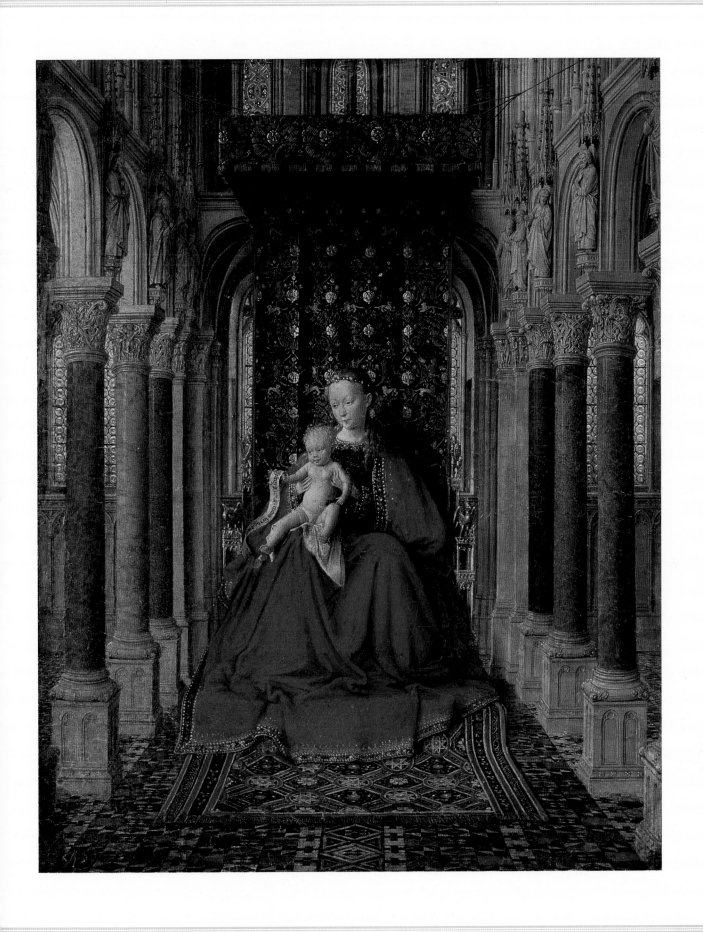

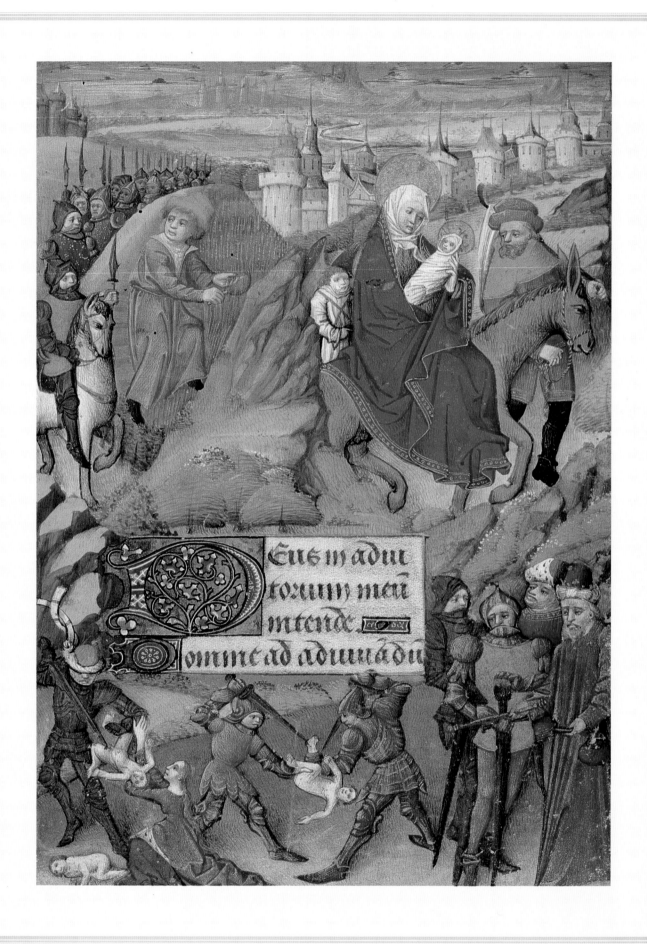

Jesus, our Master, do meet us while we walk in the way, and long to reach the Country; so that, following your light, we may keep the way of righteousness, and never wander away into the darkness of the world's night, while you, who are the way, the truth, and the life, are shining within us; for your own name's sake.

—Excerpt from the Mozarabic Liturgies.

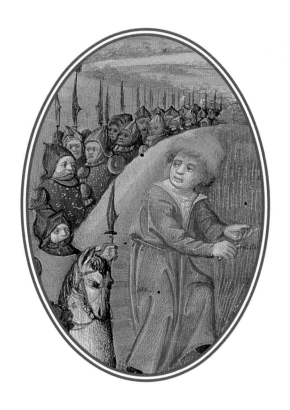

Flight into Egypt

Unknown artist, c. 1470–80.
Illumination from Salting Manuscript:
Hours of Margaret de Foix.
Victoria & Albert Museum, London.

Mary and Joseph make haste to flee the soldiers, who are massacring all the newborn male infants by Herod's decree. The artist has made the biblical passage come to life, showing a medieval peasant interrupted in his labor (harvesting corn) by the mounted expedition.

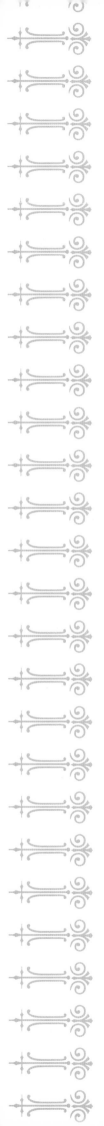

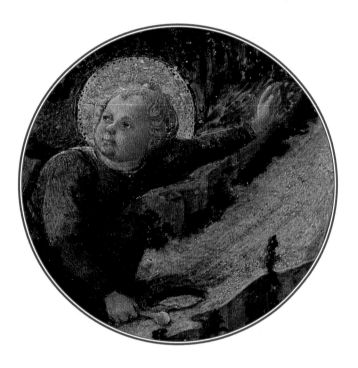

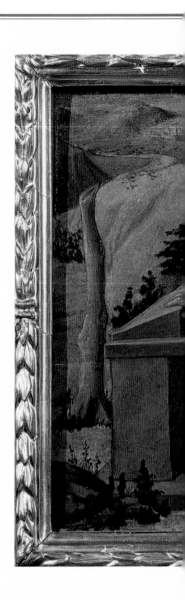

The Vision of St. Augustine

Fra Filippo Lippi, mid-fifteenth century; oil on panel. Hermitage, St. Petersburg.

St. Augustine is among the most important writers and thinkers of the Christian church. There is a legend that while he was walking along the seashore one day he met a boy who was trying to empty the ocean by pouring it into a hole in the sand. When the Saint told the child that he was attempting the impossible, the boy replied, 'No more so than for thee to explain the mysteries on which thou art meditating.' By giving the boy a circular halo, Filippo Lippi may be suggesting that the boy Augustine encountered was the infant Christ.

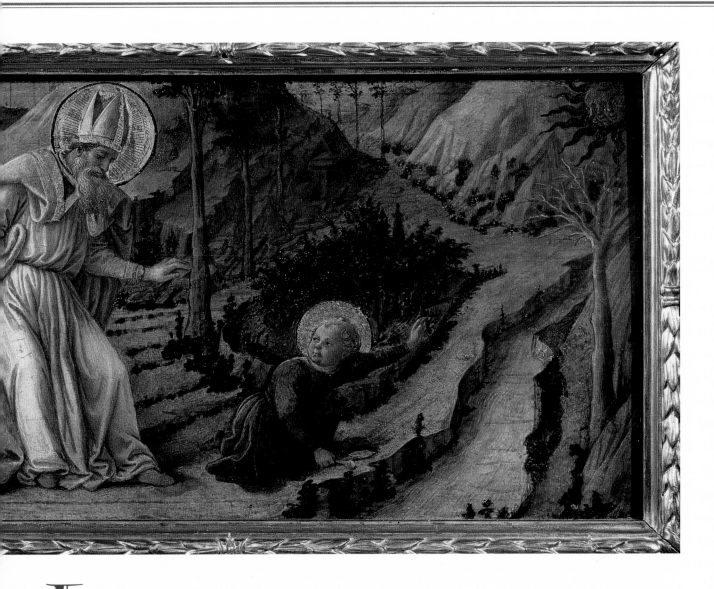

Late have I loved Thee, O Beauty so ancient and so new; late have I loved Thee: for behold Thou wert within me, and I outside; and I sought Thee outside and in my unloveliness fell upon those lovely things that Thou hast made. Thou wert with me, and I was not with Thee. I was kept from Thee by those things, yet had they not been in Thee, they would not have been at all. Thou didst call and cry to me to break open my deafness: and Thou didst send forth Thy beams and shine upon me and chase away my blindness: Thou didst breathe fragrance upon me, and I drew in my breath and do now pant for Thee: I tasted Thee, and now hunger and thirst for Thee: Thou didst touch me, and I have burned for Thy peace.

—*St. Augustine.*

Index

D1299058

JOURNEYS

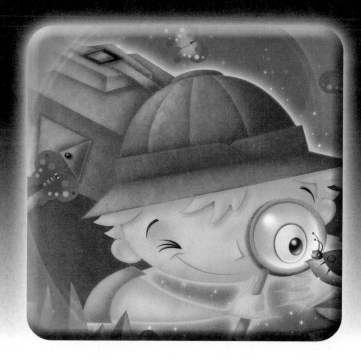

Program Consultants

Shervaughnna Anderson · Marty Hougen
Carol Jago · Erik Palmer · Shane Templeton
Sheila Valencia · MaryEllen Vogt

Consulting Author · Irene Fountas

Cover illustration by Jimmy Pickering.

Copyright © 2017 by Houghton Mifflin Harcourt Publishing Company

All rights reserved. No part of this work may be reproduced or transmitted in any form or by any means, electronic or mechanical, including photocopying or recording, or by any information storage and retrieval system, without the prior written permission of the copyright owner unless such copying is expressly permitted by federal copyright law. Requests for permission to make copies of any part of the work should be addressed to Houghton Mifflin Harcourt Publishing Company, Attn: Contracts, Copyrights, and Licensing, 9400 Southpark Center Loop, Orlando, Florida 32819-8647.

Common Core State Standards © Copyright 2010. National Governors Association Center for Best Practices and Council of Chief State School Officers. All rights reserved.

This product is not sponsored or endorsed by the Common Core State Standards Initiative of the National Governors Association Center for Best Practices and the Council of Chief State School Officers.

Printed in the U.S.A.

ISBN 978-0-54-454330-0

13 14 0690 23 22 21 20 19
4500752808   B C D E F G

If you have received these materials as examination copies free of charge, Houghton Mifflin Harcourt Publishing Company retains title to the materials and they may not be resold. Resale of examination copies is strictly prohibited.

Possession of this publication in print format does not entitle users to convert this publication, or any portion of it, into electronic format.

Unit 3

Nature Near and Far 9

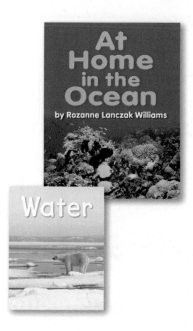

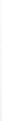

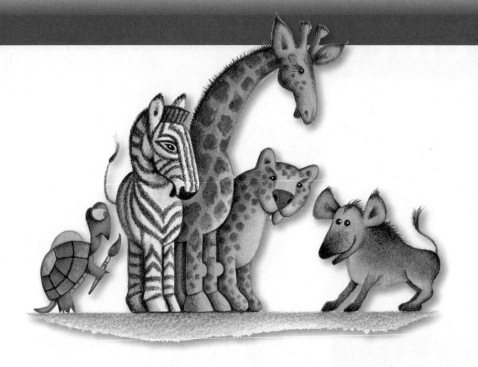

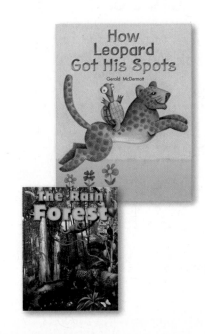

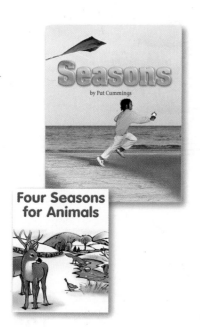

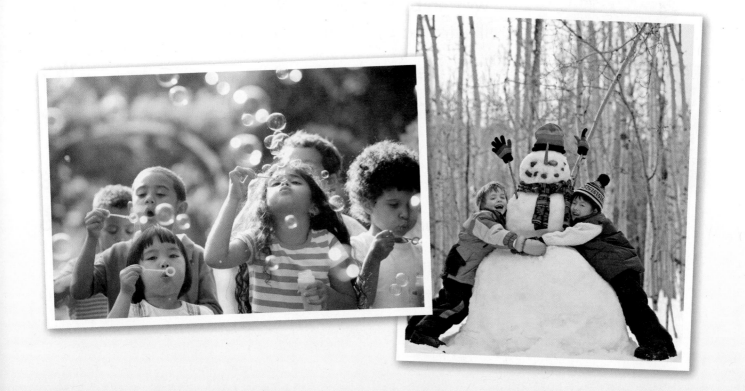

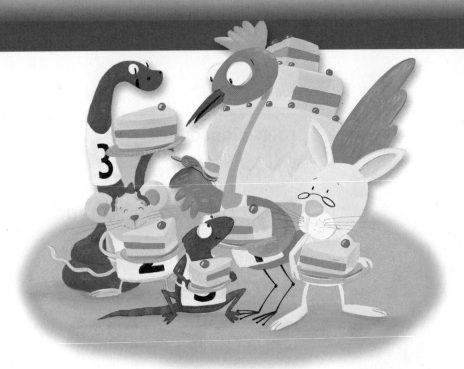

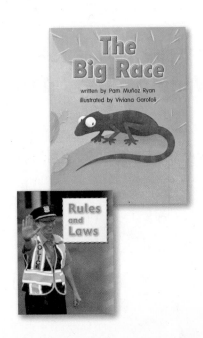

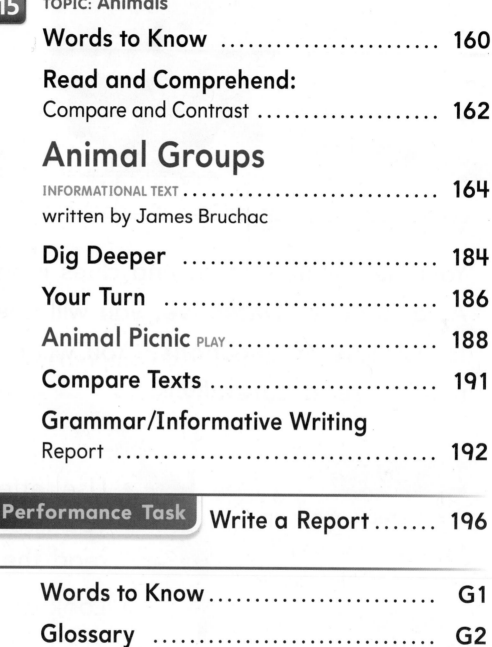
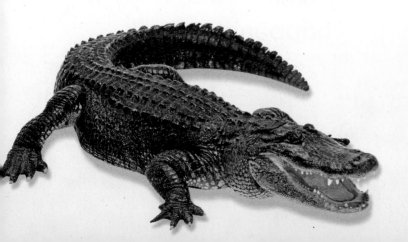

Be a
Reading
Detective!

Welcome, Reader!

Your help is needed to find clues in texts. As a **Reading Detective**, you will need to **ask lots of questions.** You will also need to **read carefully.**

📓 myNotebook

As you read, mark up the text. Save your work to **myNotebook**.

- Highlight details.
- Add notes and questions.
- Add new words to **myWordList**.

- Use letters and sounds you know to help you read the words.

- Look at the pictures.

- Think about what is happening.

Let's go!

Nature Near and Far

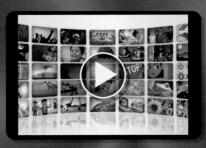

Stream to Start

> ❝In all things of nature there is something of the marvelous.❞
>
> — Aristotle

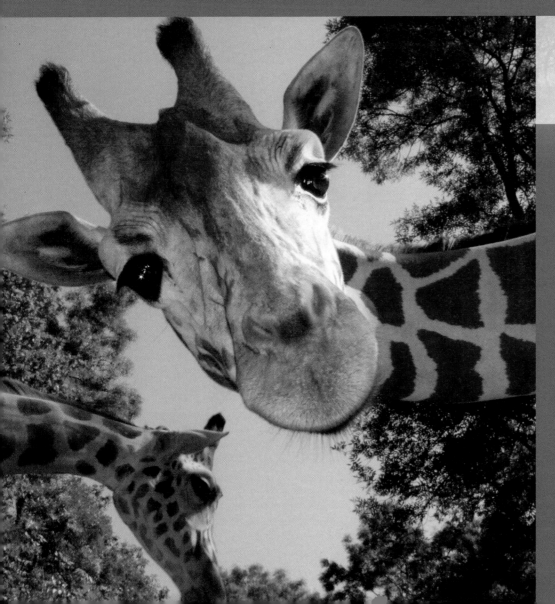

Performance Task Preview

At the end of this unit, you will write a report. It will be about reptiles! You will use facts from two texts you read to tell what reptiles are like.

hmhfyi.com

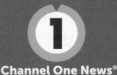

Channel One News®

9

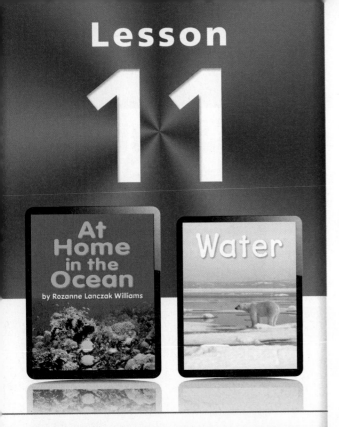

At
Home
in the
Ocean
by Rozanne Lanczak Williams

Water

🔍 **LANGUAGE DETECTIVE**

Talk About Words
Work with a partner. Choose a **Context Card**. Take out the yellow word. Put in a word that means the same or almost the same thing. Tell how the sentences are the same and different.

📓 myNotebook

Add new words to **myWordList**. Use them in your speaking and writing.

Words to Know

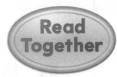
Read Together

▶ Read each **Context Card**.

▶ Make up a new sentence that uses a blue word.

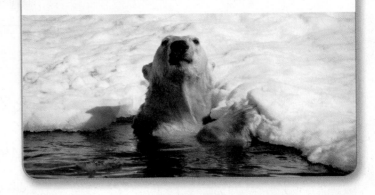

① **cold**
This ocean water is very cold.

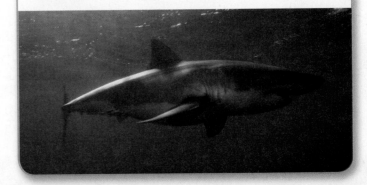

② **where**
Sharks live where the ocean is deep.

3 **blue**

Today the ocean water looks blue.

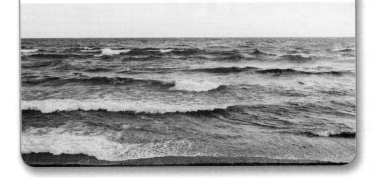

4 **live**

Whales live in all the oceans of the world.

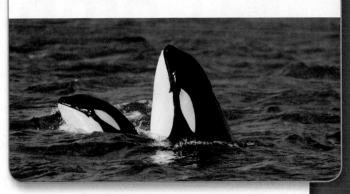

5 **far**

Squid swim far below the ocean's surface.

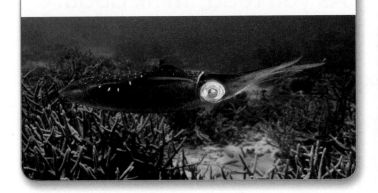

6 **their**

Their home is by the ocean.

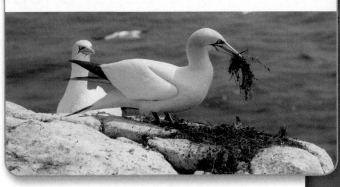

7 **little**

Many little fish live in the ocean.

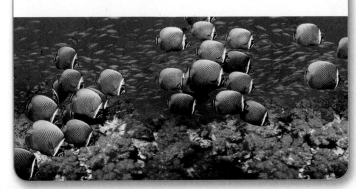

8 **water**

Some people take photos in the water.

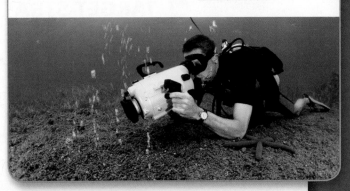

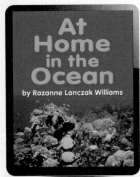

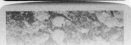
by Rozanne Lanczak Williams

Read and Comprehend

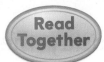
Read Together

☑ **TARGET SKILL**

Author's Purpose Authors may write to make you laugh or to give information. The reason an author writes is called the **author's purpose**. In informational texts, the author's purpose is to give information about a topic. As you read, think about what the author wants you to learn. List details that explain the author's purpose.

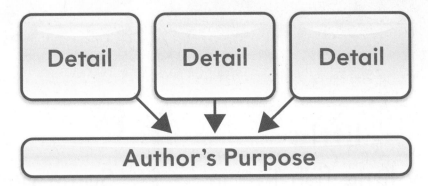

☑ **TARGET STRATEGY**

Analyze/Evaluate Tell what you think and how you feel about the selection. Tell why.

ELA RI.1.8, SL.1.4, SL.1.6, L.1.1j

Marine Habitats

Oceans are very big. They are filled with many kinds of plants and animals. Some animals live on the bottom of the ocean. Other animals swim far in the water. They come to the top to breathe. Some fish live deep down under the water where it is cold and dark. Some of them can even light up!

You will read more about life in the ocean in **At Home in the Ocean**.

💬 Talk About It

What can you see in the ocean? Write sentences to answer the question. Share your ideas with classmates.

ANCHOR TEXT

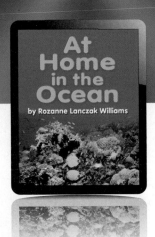

At Home
in the
Ocean
by Rozanne Lanczak Williams

✅ **GENRE**

Informational text
gives facts about a
topic. Look for:

▶ information and
   facts in the words
▶ photos that show
   the real world
▶ labels for photos

Meet the Author

Rozanne Lanczak Williams

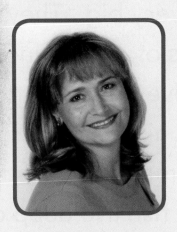

When Rozanne Lanczak Williams first became a teacher, she lived far from the ocean. She and her students learned a lot about sea life, though, from their research and by making beautiful underwater murals. Now Ms. Williams lives only seven miles from the ocean! To write this story, she hunted for fun fishy facts. She visited a big aquarium, the library, a bookstore, a friend's classroom library—and the ocean!

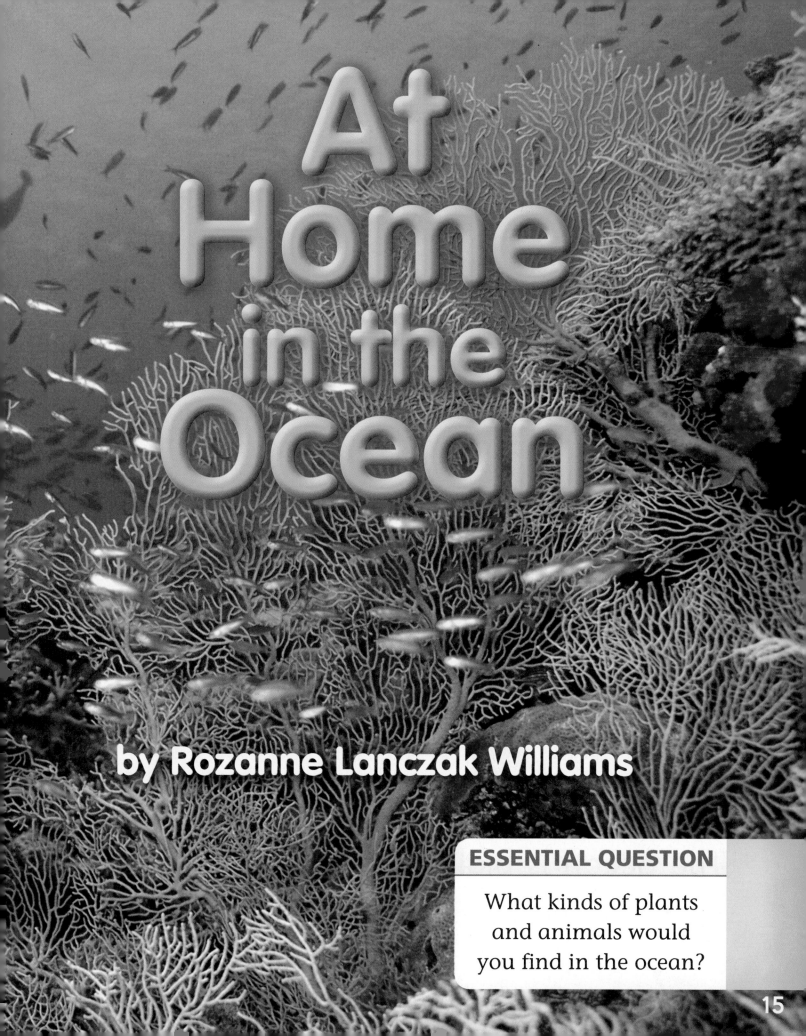

At Home in the Ocean

by Rozanne Lanczak Williams

ESSENTIAL QUESTION

What kinds of plants and animals would you find in the ocean?

15

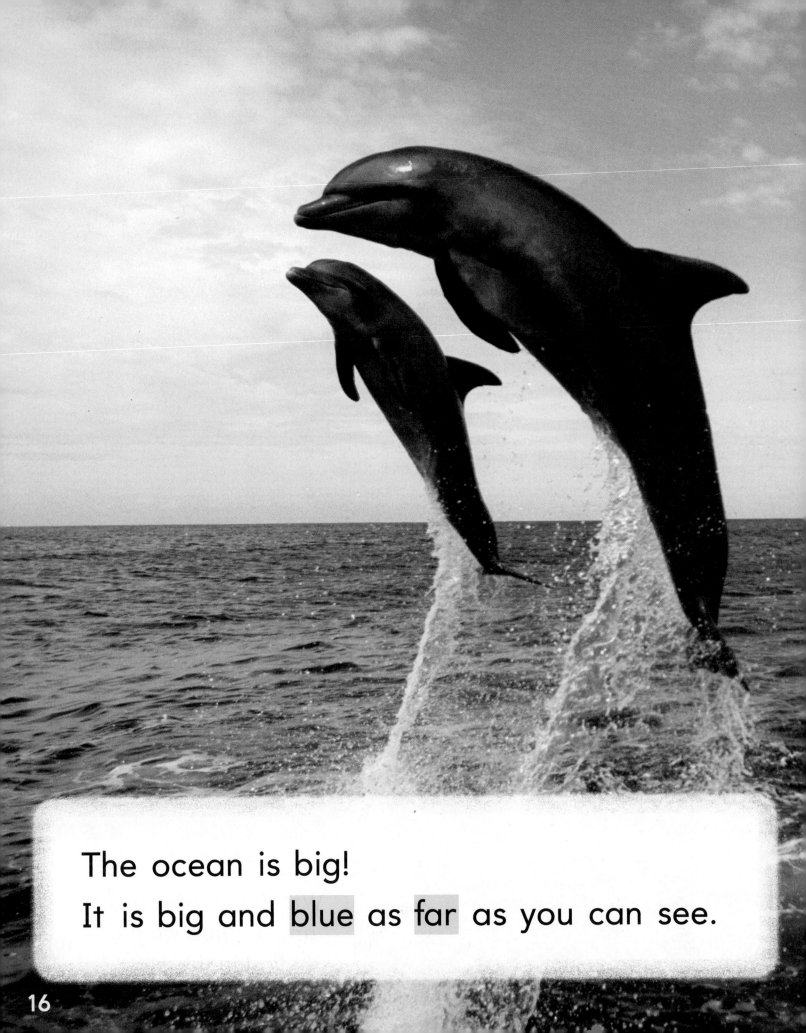

The ocean is big!
It is big and blue as far as you can see.

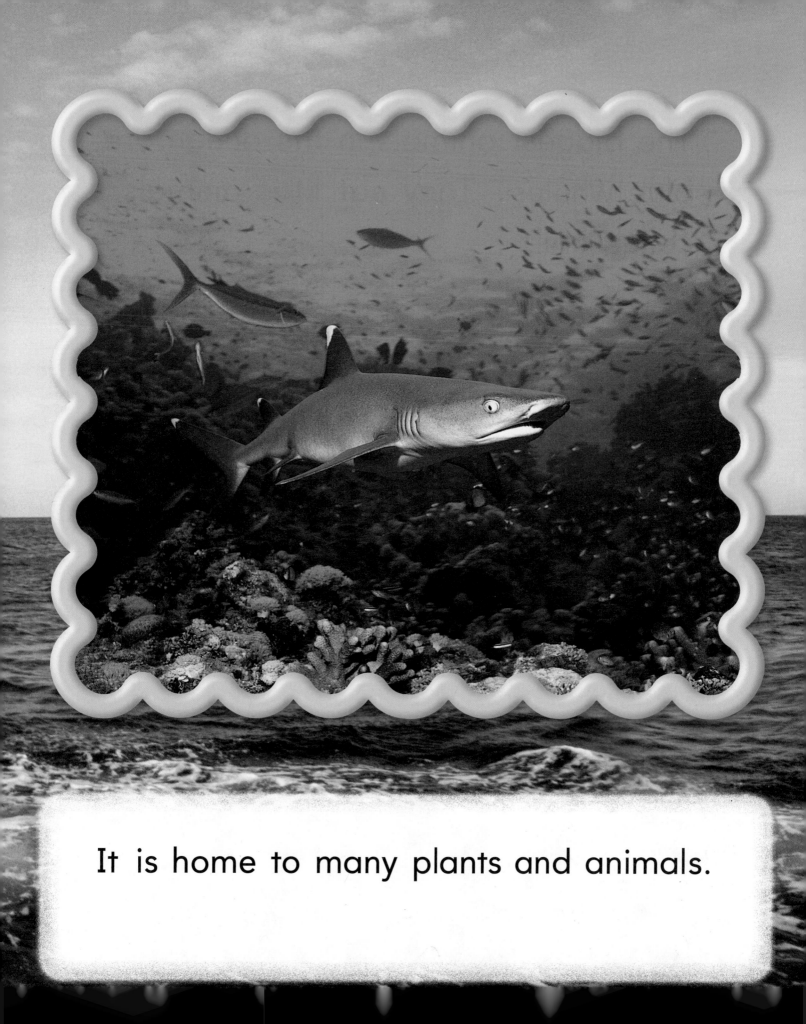

It is home to many plants and animals.

The biggest animals in the ocean are blue whales. They eat little animals called krill.

blue whale

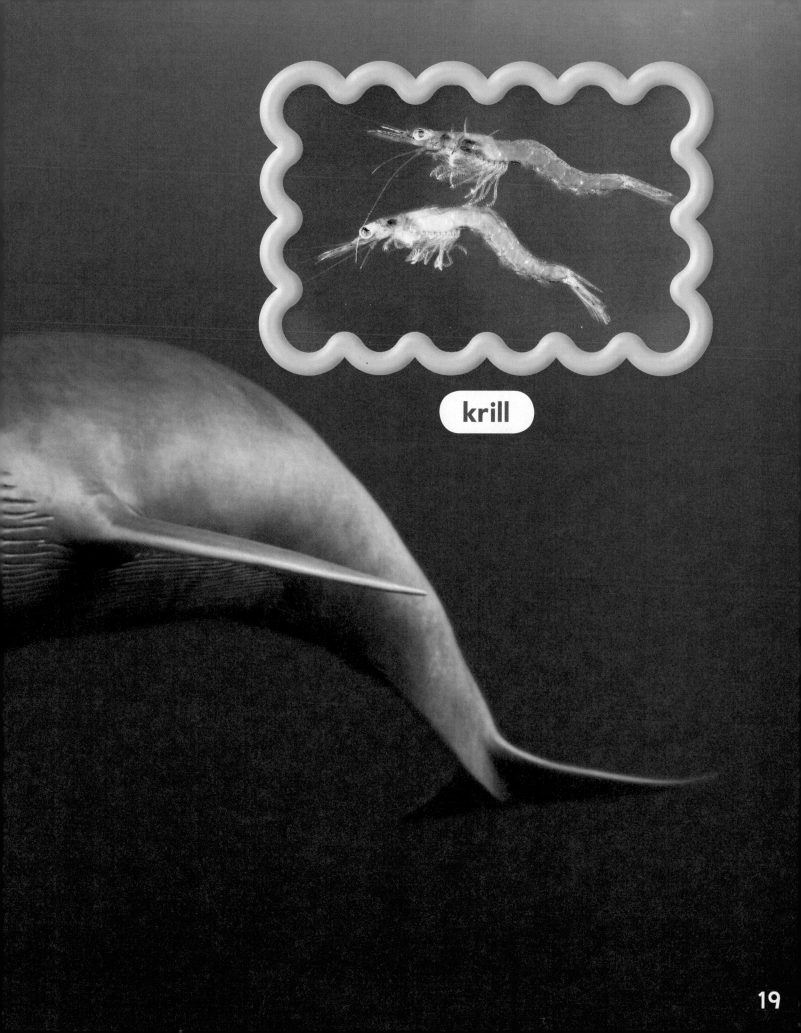

krill

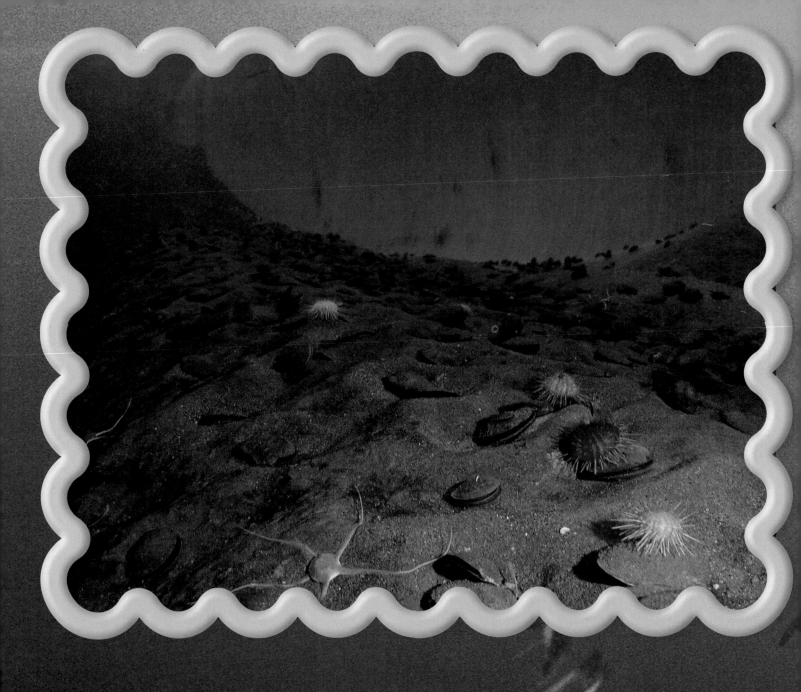

Many animals live in cold water.
Brrr!

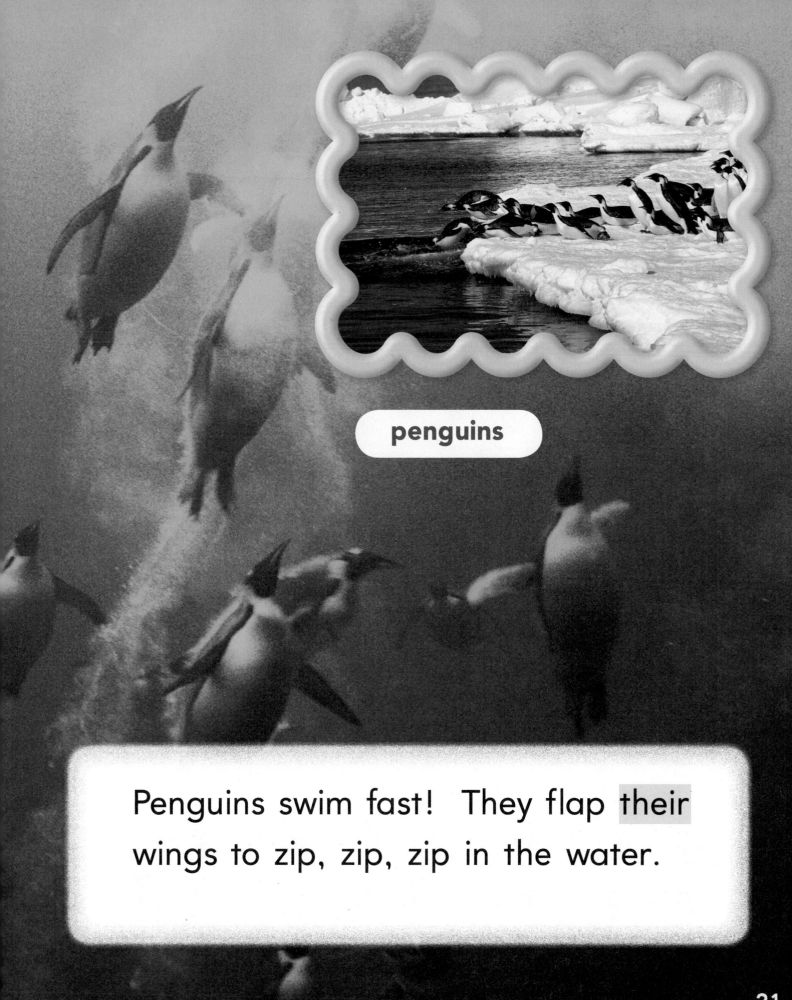

penguins

Penguins swim fast! They flap their wings to zip, zip, zip in the water.

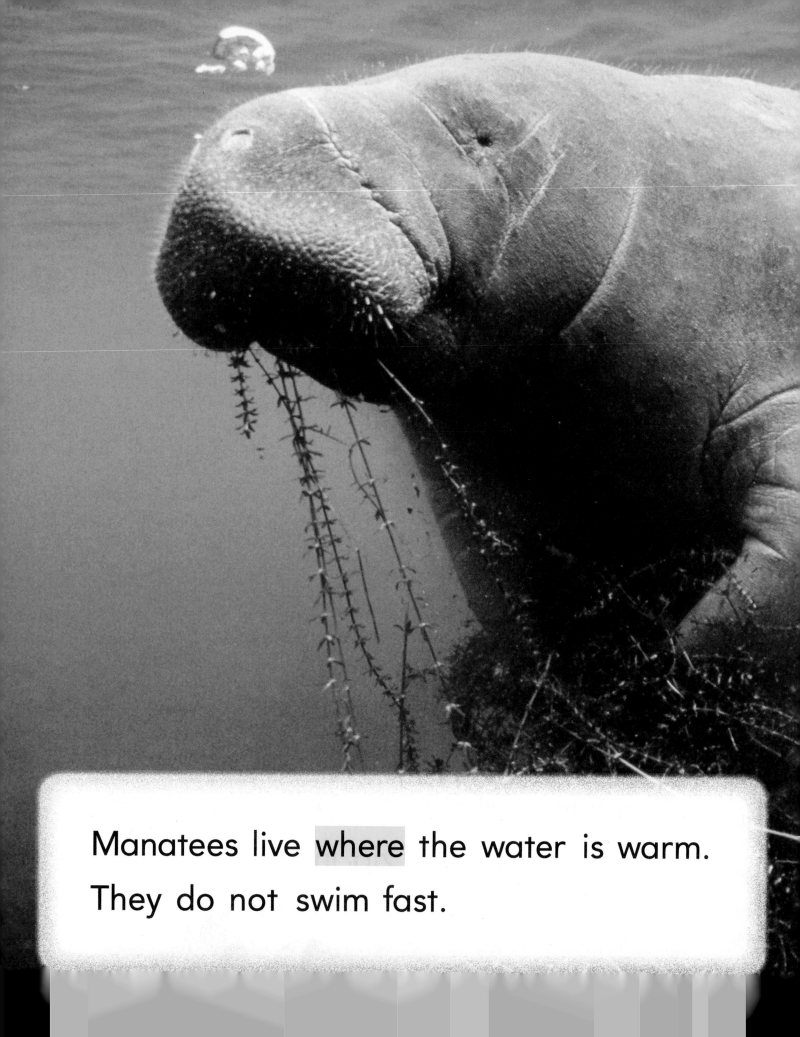

Manatees live where the water is warm.
They do not swim fast.

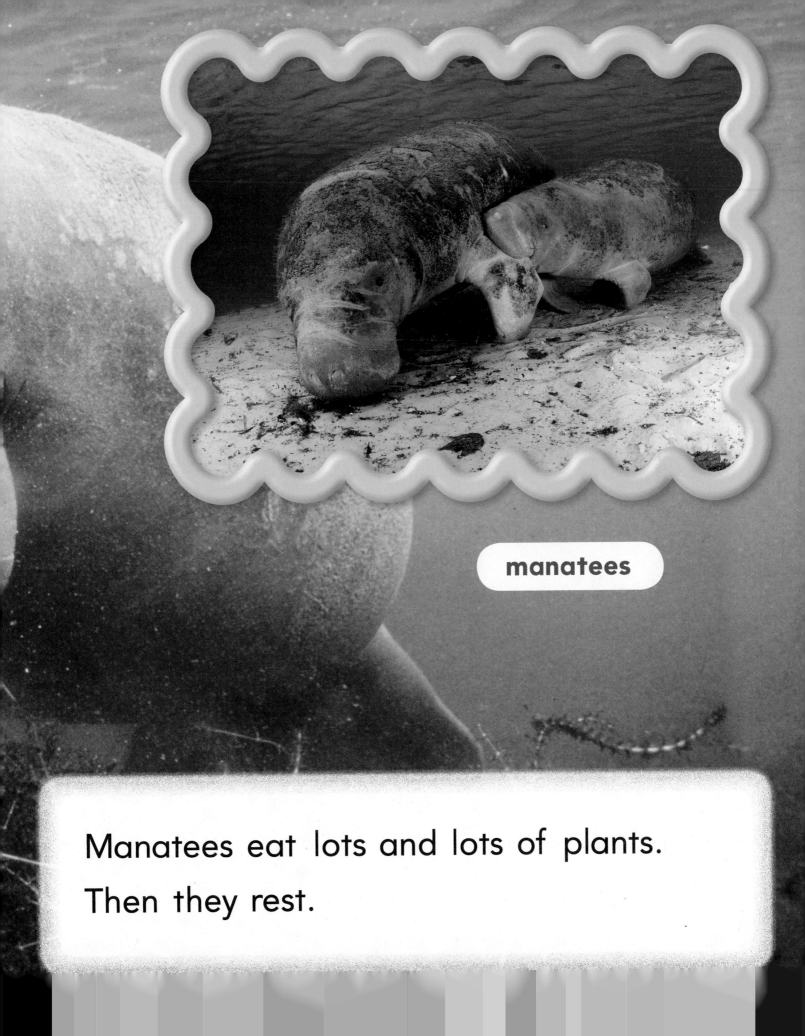

manatees

Manatees eat lots and lots of plants.
Then they rest.

This turtle swims far!

It digs in the sand and lays its eggs.

Then it swims back to its ocean home.

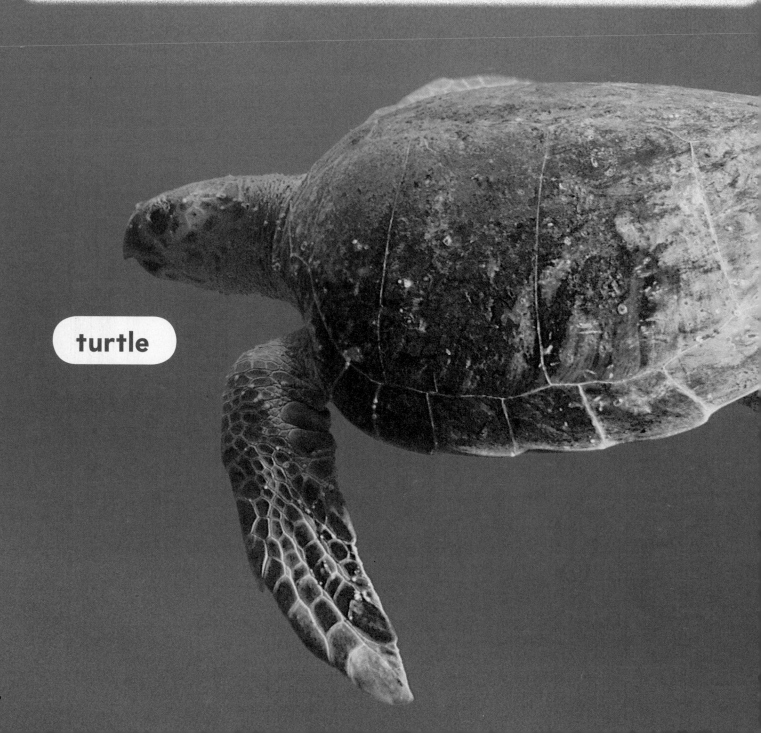

turtle

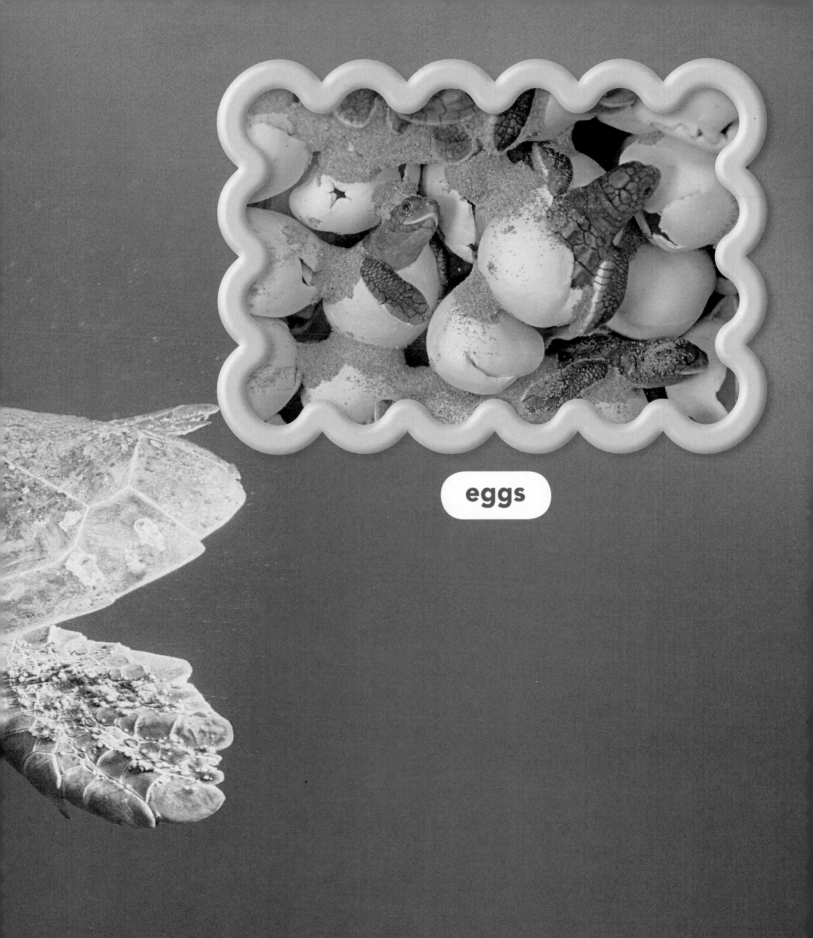

eggs

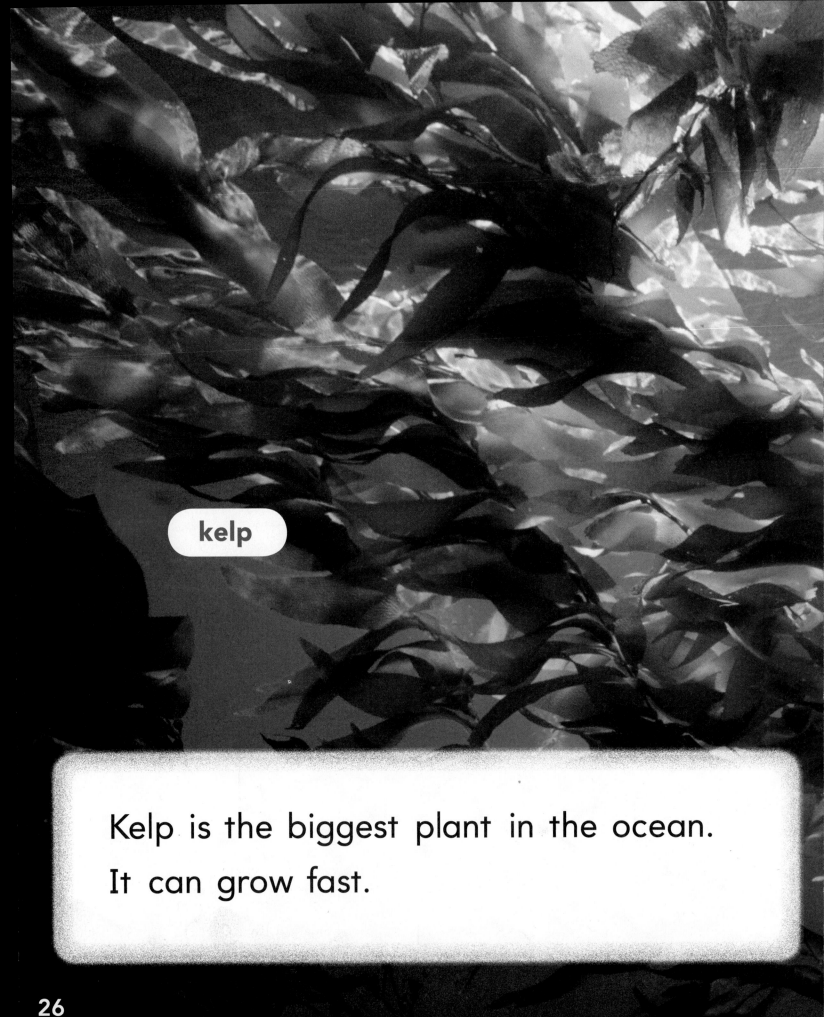

kelp

Kelp is the biggest plant in the ocean.
It can grow fast.

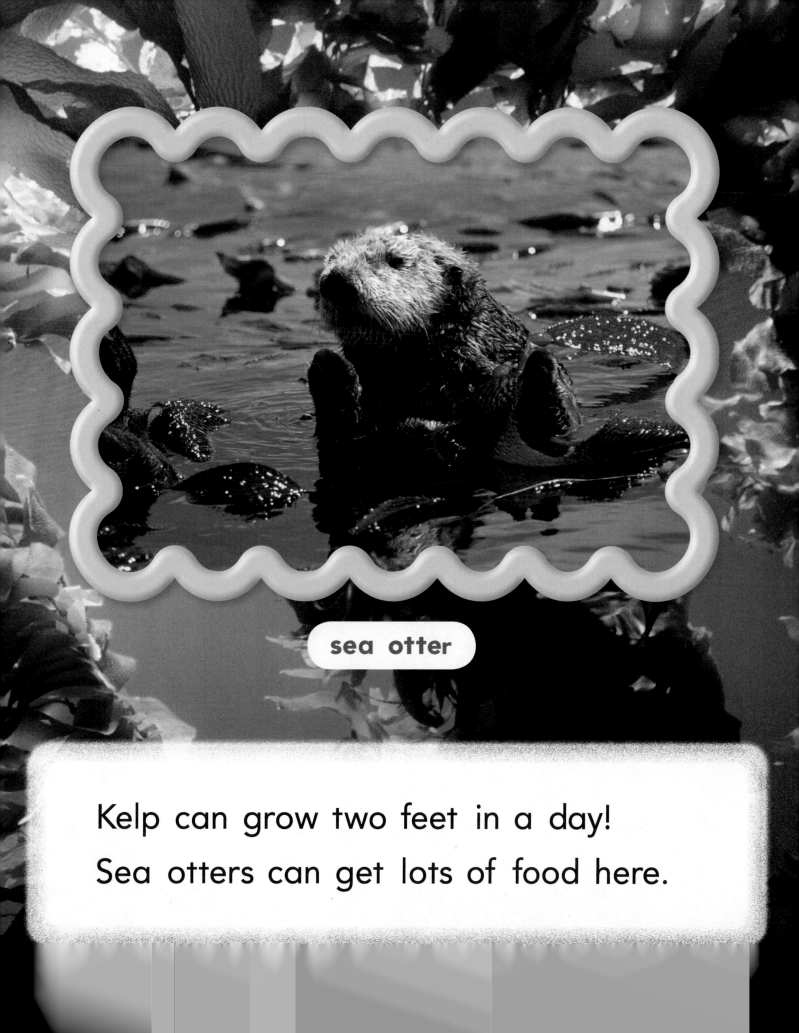

sea otter

Kelp can grow two feet in a day!
Sea otters can get lots of food here.

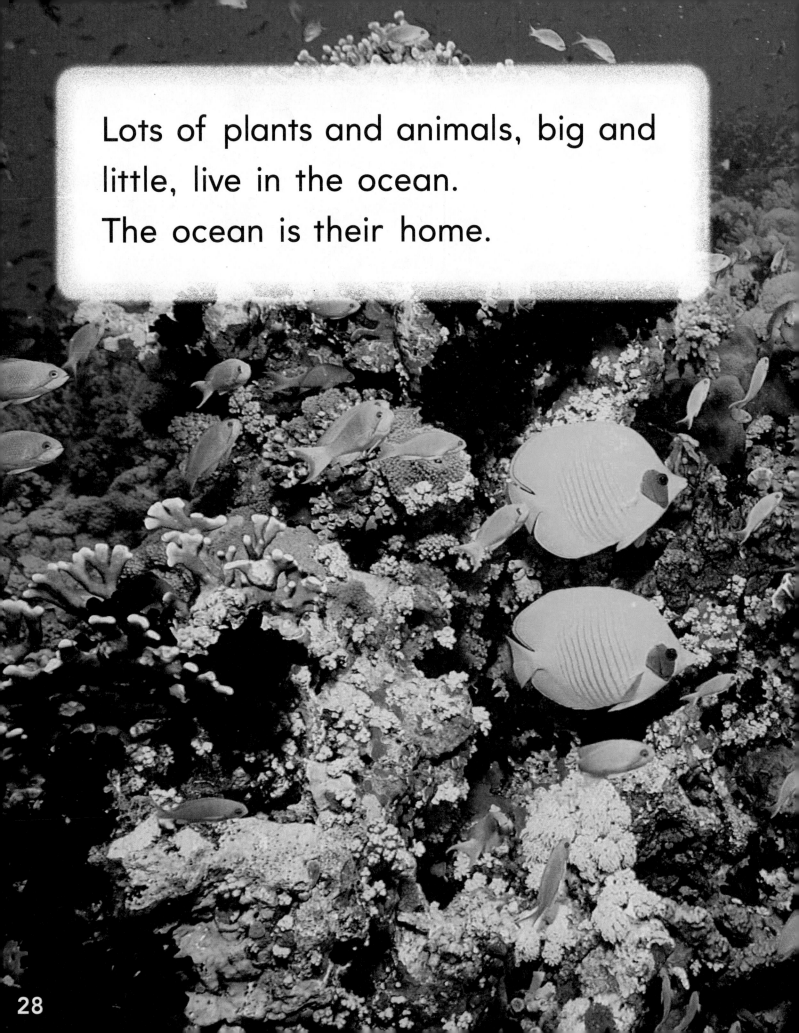

Lots of plants and animals, big and
little, live in the ocean.
The ocean is their home.

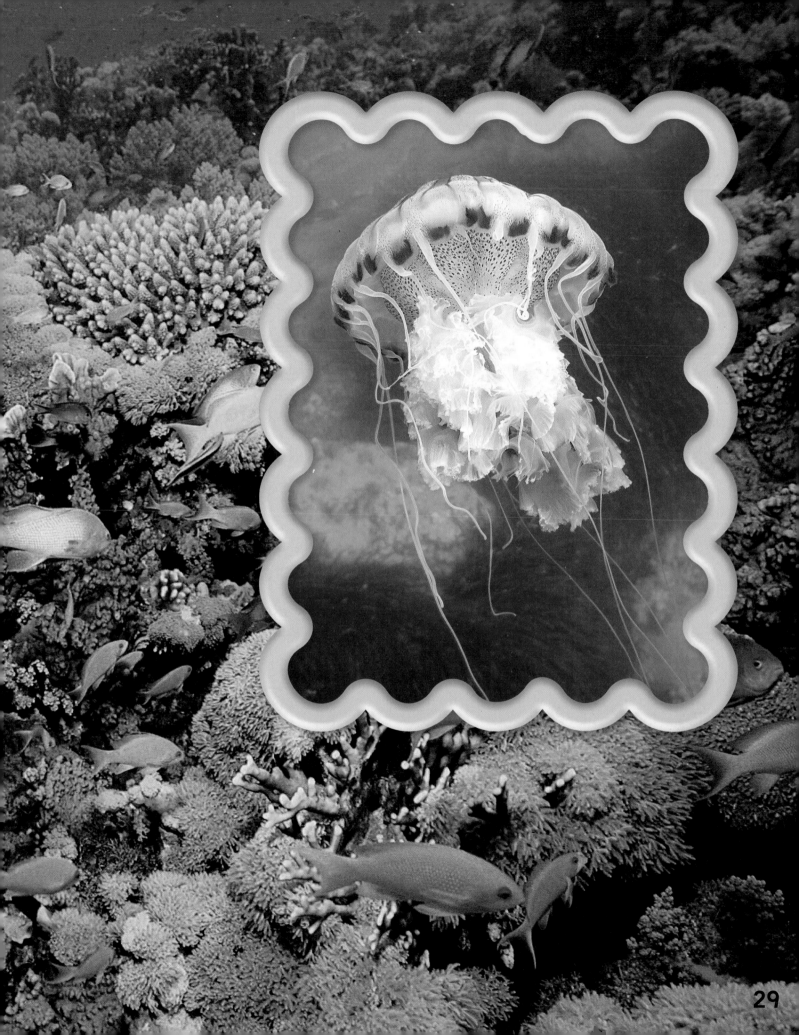

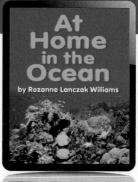
At Home in the Ocean
by Rozanne Lanczak Williams

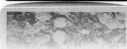

Dig Deeper

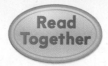
Read Together

Use Clues to Analyze the Text

Use these pages to learn about Author's Purpose and Details. Then read **At Home in the Ocean** again.

Author's Purpose

Authors write for many different reasons. Why do you think the author wrote **At Home in the Ocean**? What topic does she want you to learn about? You can find important details in the selection that help explain the author's topic. Use a chart to list the details and the author's purpose.

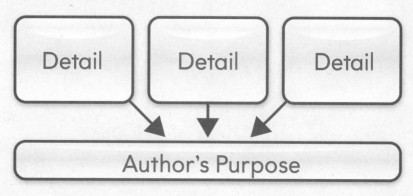

Detail   Detail   Detail

Author's Purpose

Details

Details are facts and other bits of information. They tell more about a topic. A detail you learned in **At Home in the Ocean** is that manatees eat lots of plants.

What other details from this selection teach you about life in the ocean? You can find important details in the words and pictures.

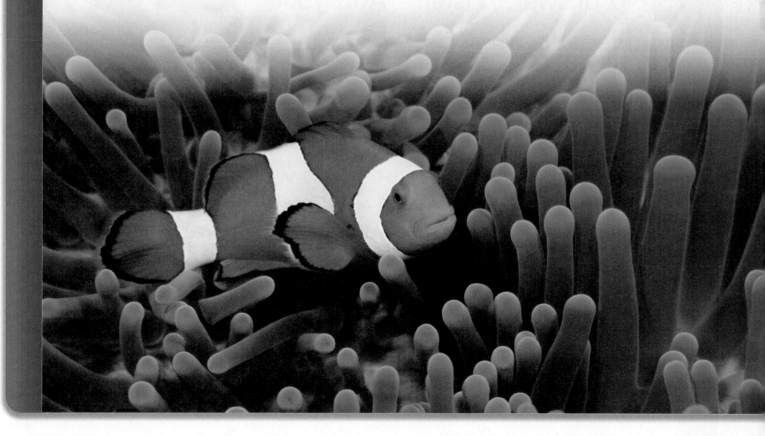

Your Turn

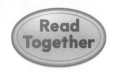

RETURN TO THE ESSENTIAL QUESTION

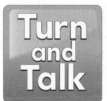 **Turn and Talk**

What kinds of plants and animals would you find in the ocean? Talk with a small group about what you learned. Use details from **At Home in the Ocean** to answer. Listen. Add your ideas to what others say.

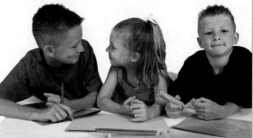

💬 Classroom Conversation

Talk about these questions with your class.

1. Describe an animal or plant you learned about. Use details to tell more.

2. How are all the animals the same?

3. Which animal or plant would you like to learn more about? Why?

WRITE ABOUT READING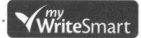

Response Write two facts that you learned from **At Home in the Ocean**. Find text evidence in the words and photos to get ideas. Use your own words when you write your facts.

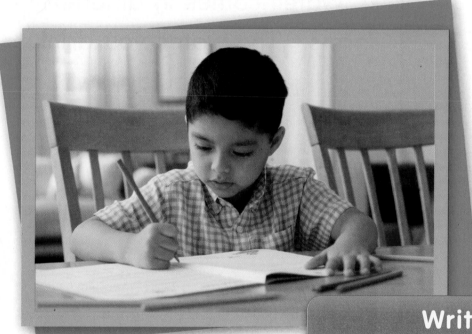

Writing Tip

Add details that give more information about your topic.

INFORMATIONAL TEXT

Read Together

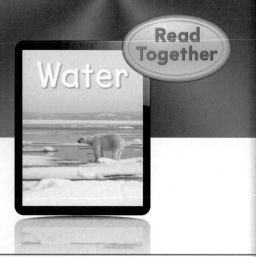

Water

✓ GENRE

Informational text gives facts about a topic. This is from a science textbook.

✓ TEXT FOCUS

A **diagram** is a drawing that can show how something works or the parts that make up something. What does the diagram on page 35 show?

Water

What is one thing that all living things, whether they are big or little, have in common? They need water to live.

Water comes in different forms. The water you drink is a liquid. A liquid flows and takes the shape of the container it is in.

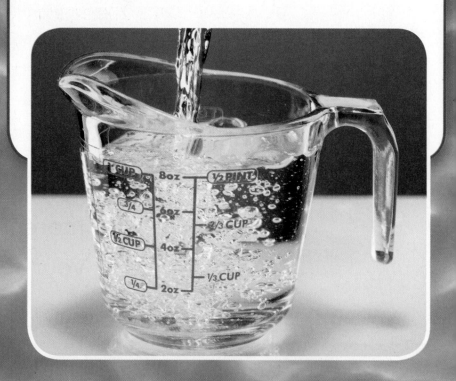

ELA RI.1.5, RI.1.10

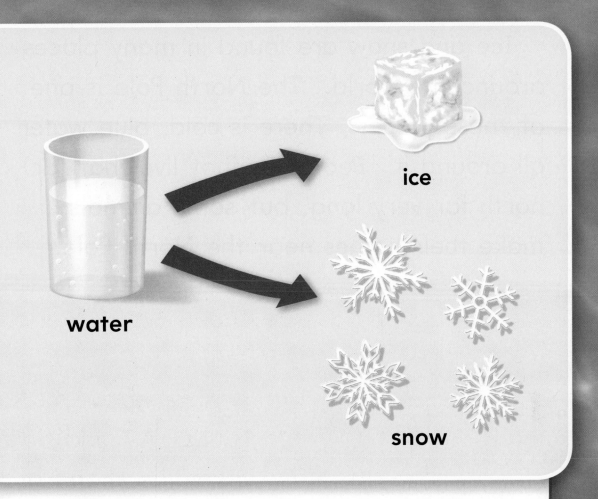

ice

water

snow

Water can freeze into ice or snow.
Frozen water is a solid. A solid has
its own shape.

What is ice? Ice is water that has
frozen. It is hard and cold.

Where does snow come from?
Snow is tiny pieces of frozen water
that fall from the clouds.

Ice and snow are found in many places around the world. The North Pole is one of these places. There is cold, blue water all around it. People cannot live that far north for very long, but some animals make their homes near the North Pole.

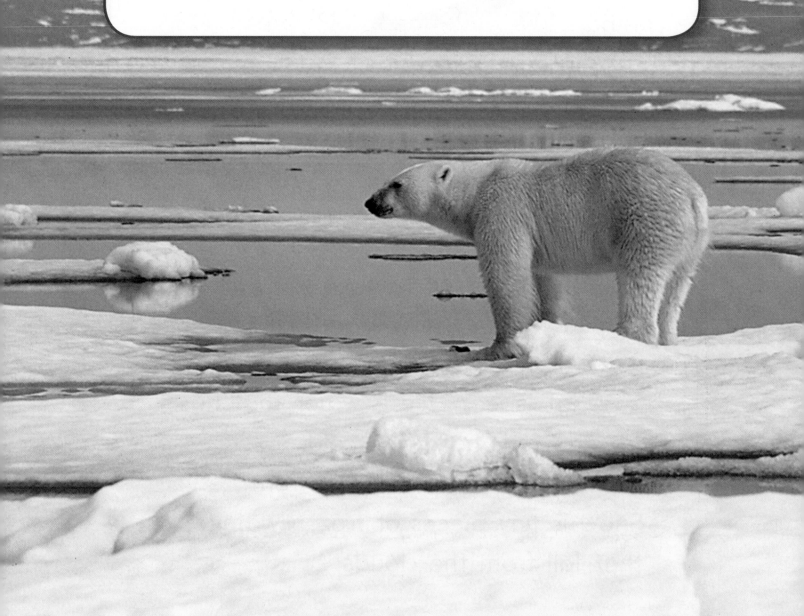

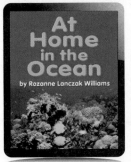 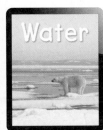

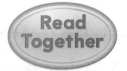

Compare Texts

Read Together

TEXT TO TEXT

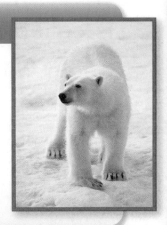

Compare Animals Use text evidence to compare the polar bear with an animal from **At Home in the Ocean**. How are they alike and different?

TEXT TO SELF

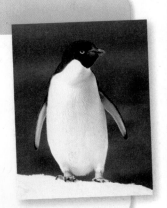

Describe It Find the photo of your favorite animal from either selection. How does it look? What does it do? Use the photo to help describe it.

TEXT TO WORLD

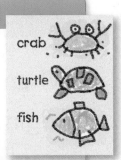

Use a Globe Use a globe to find two different oceans. Draw and label animals that you think might live in each ocean.

ELA RI.1.3, RI.1.7, RI.1.9, SL.1.4, SL.1.5

Grammar

Digital Resources

► **Multimedia Grammar Glossary**

Proper Nouns A noun that names a special person, animal, place, or thing is called a **proper noun**. Proper nouns begin with capital letters.

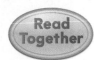

Read Together

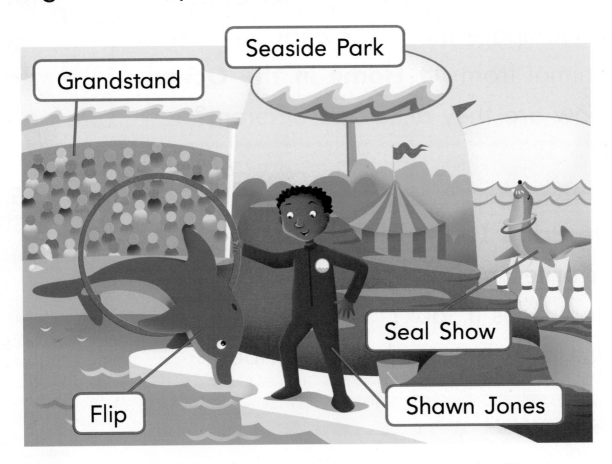

Seaside Park

Grandstand

Flip

Seal Show

Shawn Jones

When a **title** is used before a name, it begins with a capital letter, too. A title usually ends with a period.

Mr. Diaz   **Mrs. Sims**   **Miss Reed**

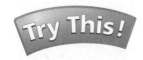

Write each sentence on another sheet of paper. Find the proper nouns. Use capital letters and periods where they belong.

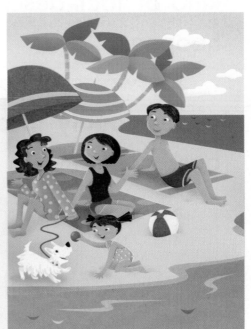

1. My family went to florida.

2. We drove on beach street.

3. We met mrs bell.

4. Her dog is named skippy.

5. I went on the super sun slide.

6. We all ate at snack shack.

Connect Grammar to Writing

When you proofread your writing, be sure you have used capital letters to write proper nouns.

Informative Writing

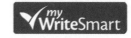

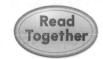

☑ **Evidence** Sometimes you will write **sentences** that give readers facts. One kind of fact describes how something happens.

Joy wrote about sea lions. Then she added **loudly** to describe how sea lions bark.

Revised Draft

loudly
A sea lion can bark.
                   ∧

Writing Checklist

☑ **Evidence** Do my sentences have words that tell **how**?

☑ Does my writing tell facts?

☑ Did I use capital letters correctly?

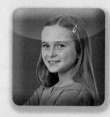

Final Copy

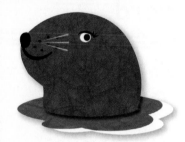

Sea Lions

Sea lions do amazing things. A sea lion can bark loudly. It uses its flippers to move quickly on land or in water.

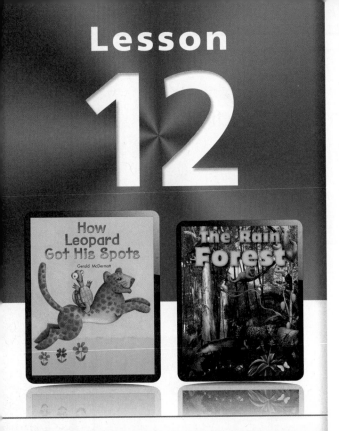

Talk About Words
Work with a partner. Choose your favorite photo. Tell why it's your favorite. Use as many of the blue words as possible. Be sure to use complete sentences.

Words to Know

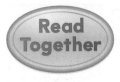
Read Together

▶ Read each **Context Card**.

▶ Describe a picture, using the blue word.

---

1   **brown**

Some hyenas have brown fur.

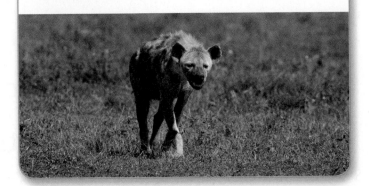

---

2   **own**

Zebras know their own mother by her stripes.

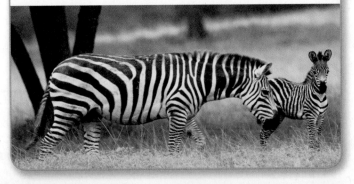

3. very

The snake in that tree is **very** long.

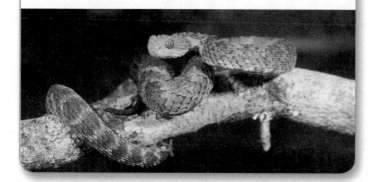

4. off

The bird flew **off** the rock and into the air.

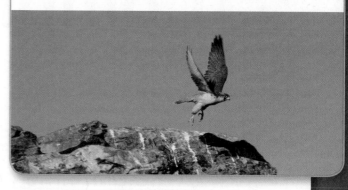

5. never

Rhinos eat plants. They **never** eat meat.

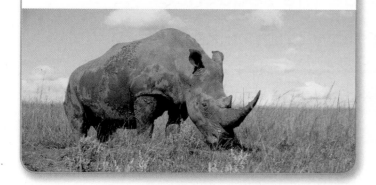

6. know

Leopards **know** how to climb trees.

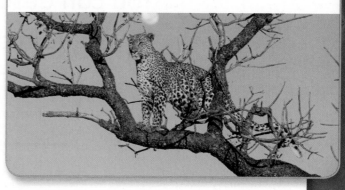

7. out

I called **out** to Mom, "Look at that turtle!"

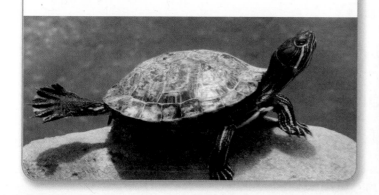

8. been

The giraffes have **been** moving fast.

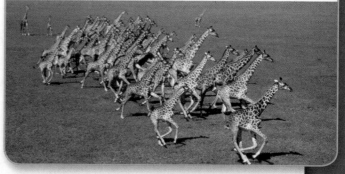

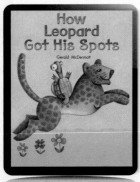

Read and Comprehend

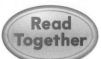

☑ **TARGET SKILL**

Sequence of Events Most story events are told in time order. This order is called the **sequence of events.** Good readers think about what happens **first, next,** and **last** so that a story makes sense. You can describe the sequence of events in a flow chart like this.

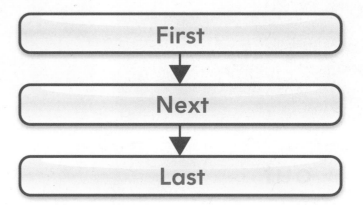

☑ **TARGET STRATEGY**

Question Ask yourself questions as you read. Look for text evidence to answer.

Jungle Animals

Many animals live in the jungle. Monkeys swing on vines. Frogs and snakes hide in the bushes. Birds fly through the trees. Which jungle animal is your favorite? You will read about jungle animals in **How Leopard Got His Spots.**

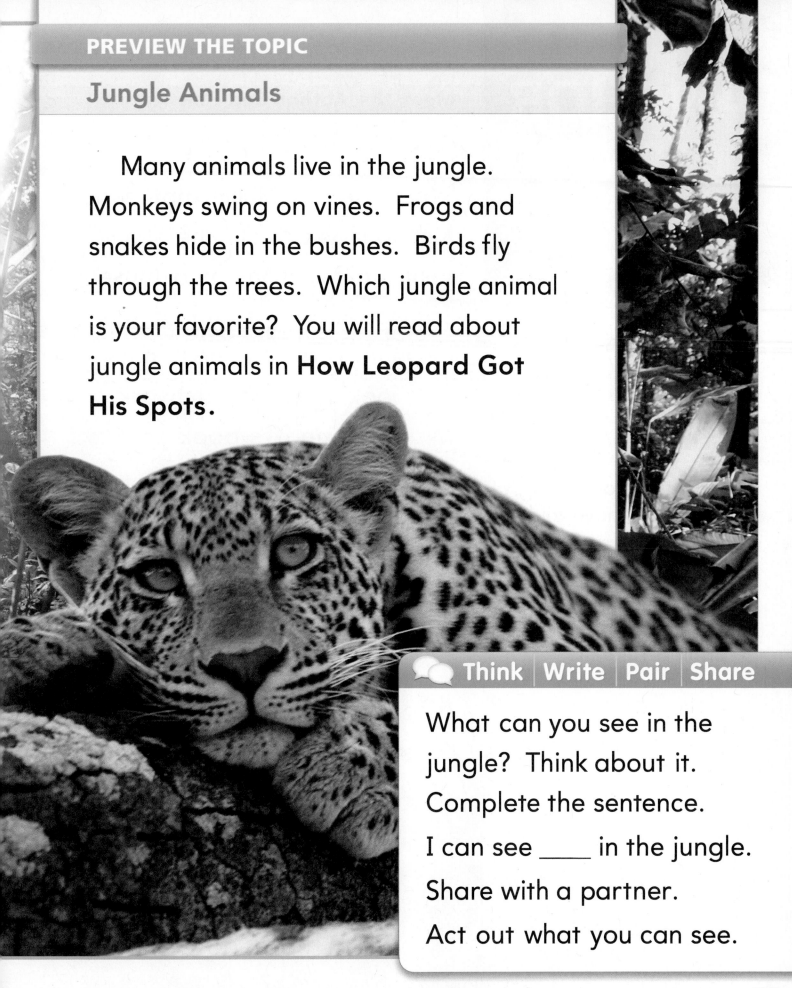

💬 **Think | Write | Pair | Share**

What can you see in the jungle? Think about it. Complete the sentence.

I can see ____ in the jungle.

Share with a partner.

Act out what you can see.

ANCHOR TEXT

How Leopard Got His Spots
Gerald McDermott

✅ GENRE

A **folktale** is an old story people have told for many years. As you read, look for:

- a lesson about life
- the words **once upon a time**

Meet the Author and Illustrator

Gerald McDermott

When Gerald McDermott was just four years old, he started taking art lessons at a museum. Saturdays were spent at the museum drawing, painting, and looking at the artwork. Mr. McDermott's book **Arrow to the Sun** won the Caldecott Medal for best illustrations.

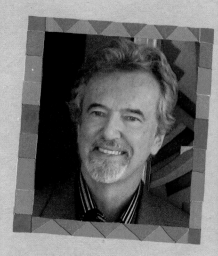

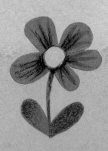

How Leopard Got His Spots

written and illustrated by Gerald McDermott

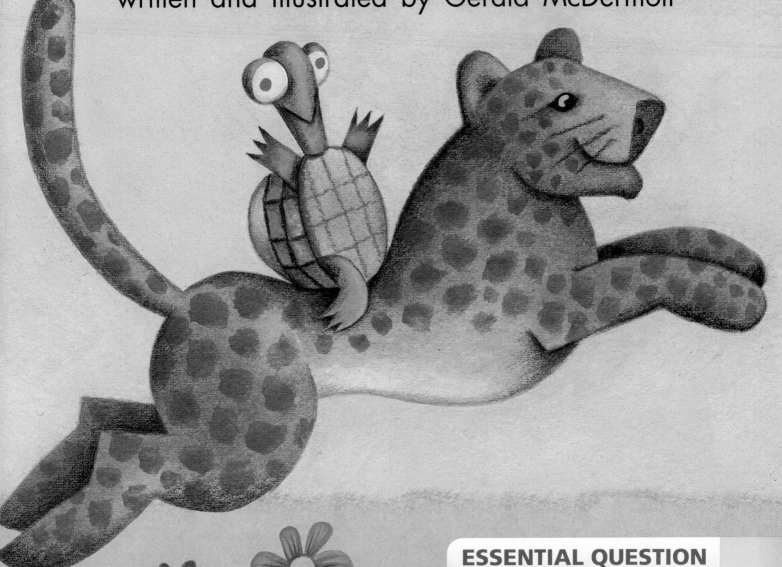

ESSENTIAL QUESTION

How are jungle animals different from animals on a farm?

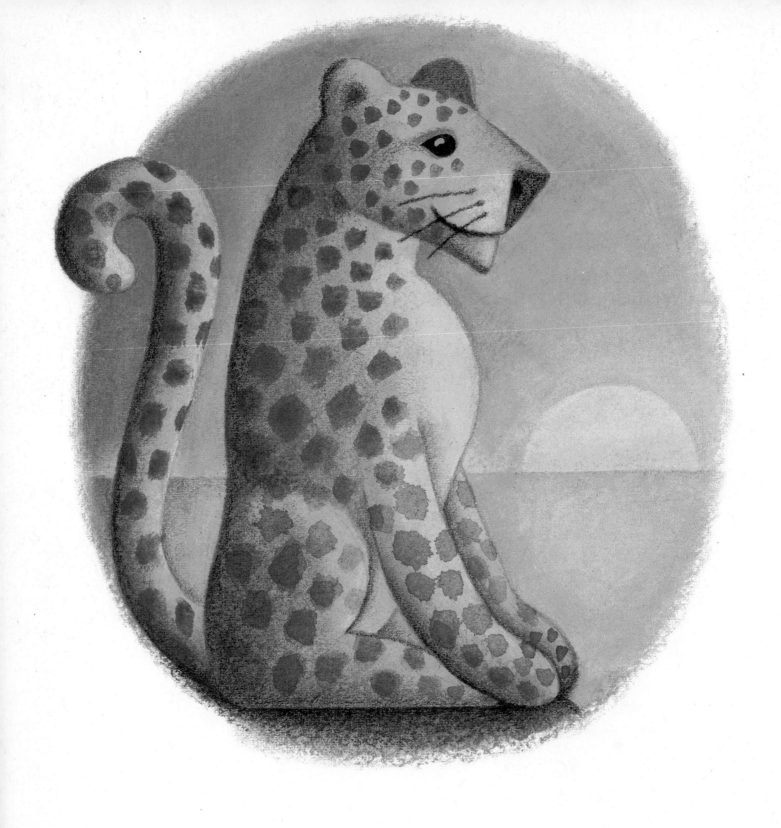

Do you know how
Leopard got his spots?

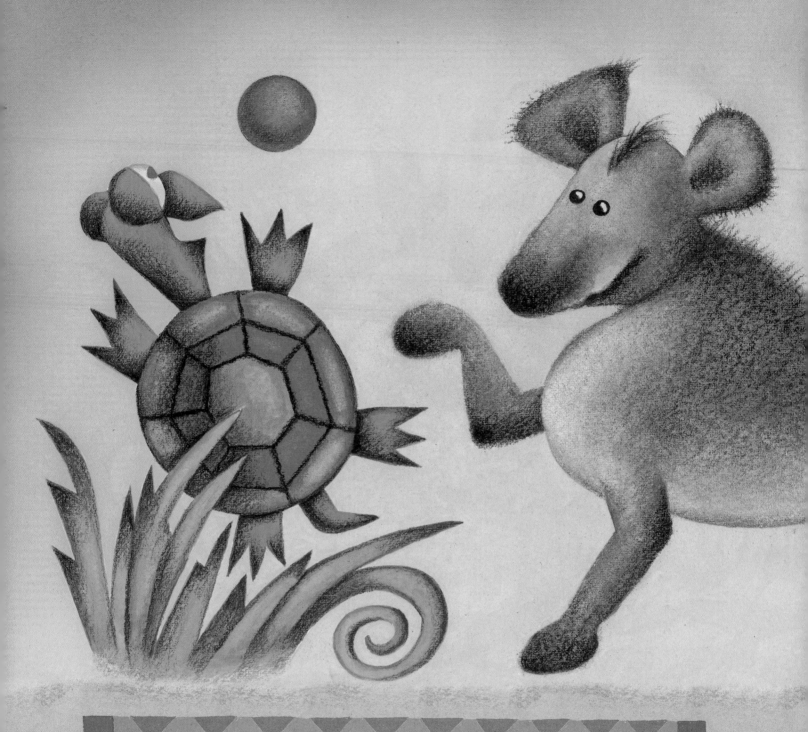

Once upon a time, Fred
Turtle was playing catch with
Hal Hyena. Hal tricked Fred.
Then he ran away.

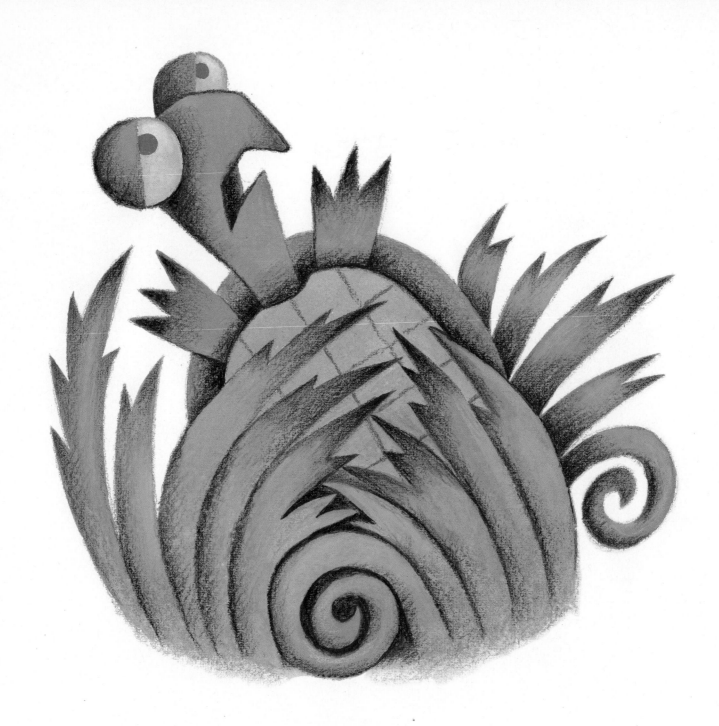

Fred felt very sad.
He called out for help.
"Help! I am stuck in
the plants," he yelled.

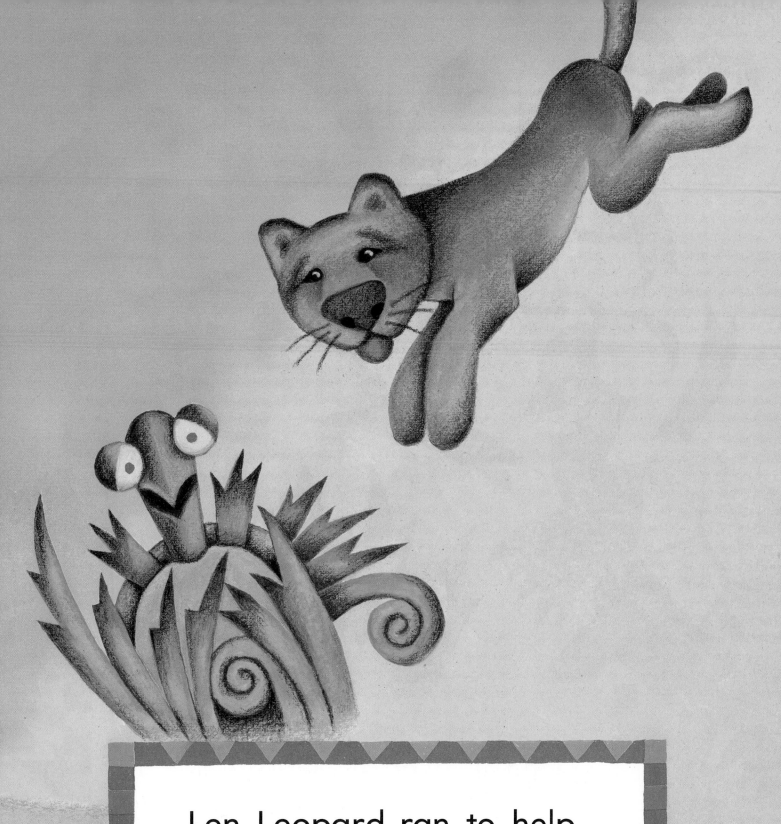

Len Leopard ran to help.

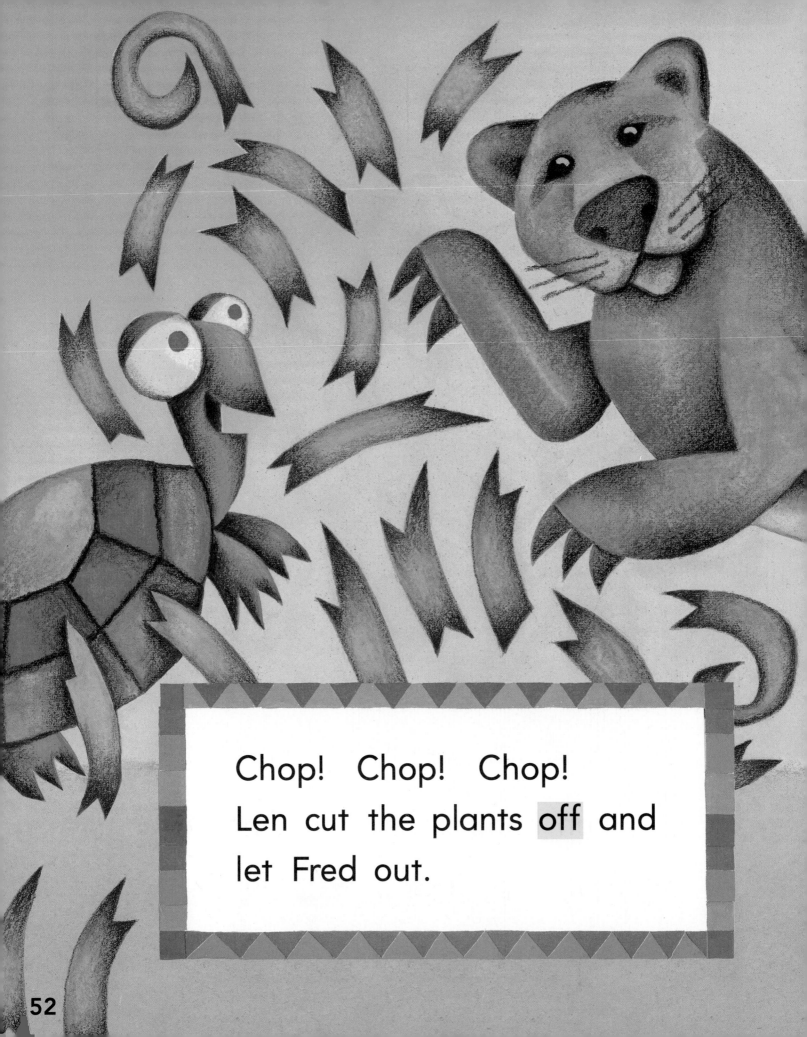

Chop! Chop! Chop!
Len cut the plants off and
let Fred out.

52

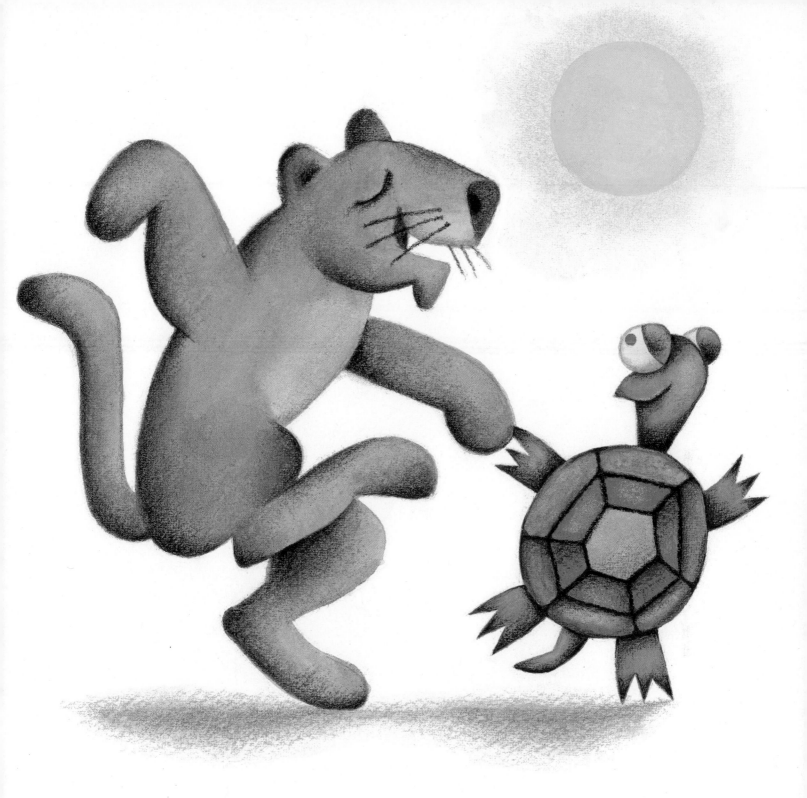

Fred and Len danced in the sun.
"This is such fun!" they said.

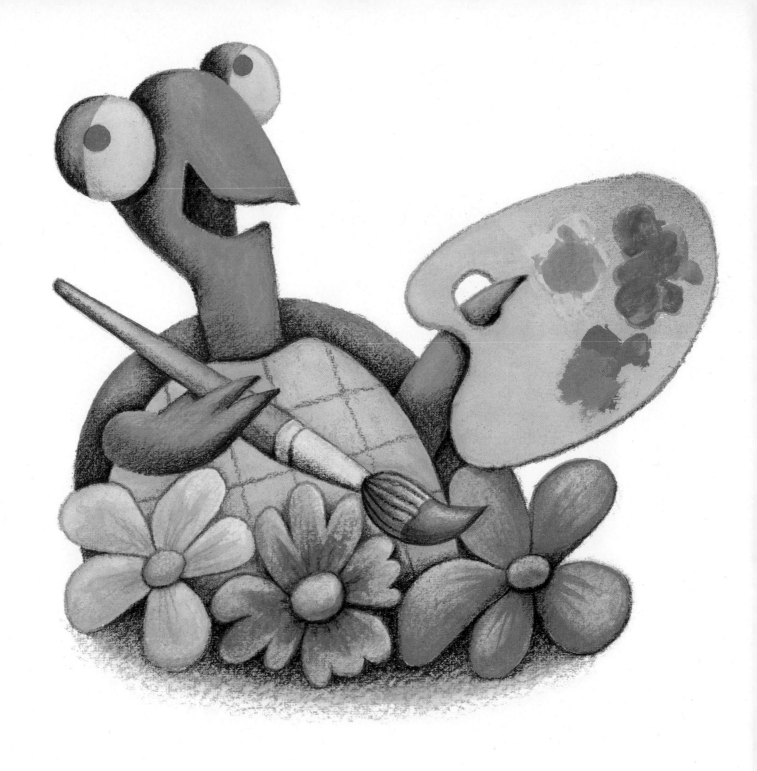

"I have never been this glad,"
said Fred. "I like to paint if I
am glad!"

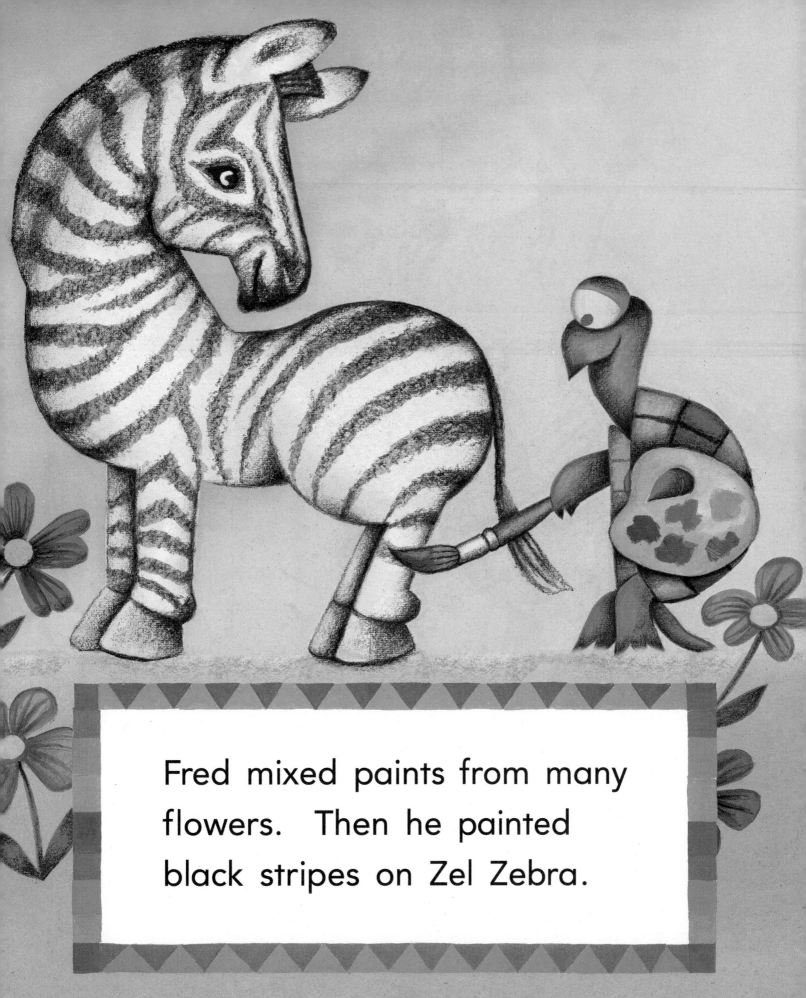

Fred mixed paints from many flowers. Then he painted black stripes on Zel Zebra.

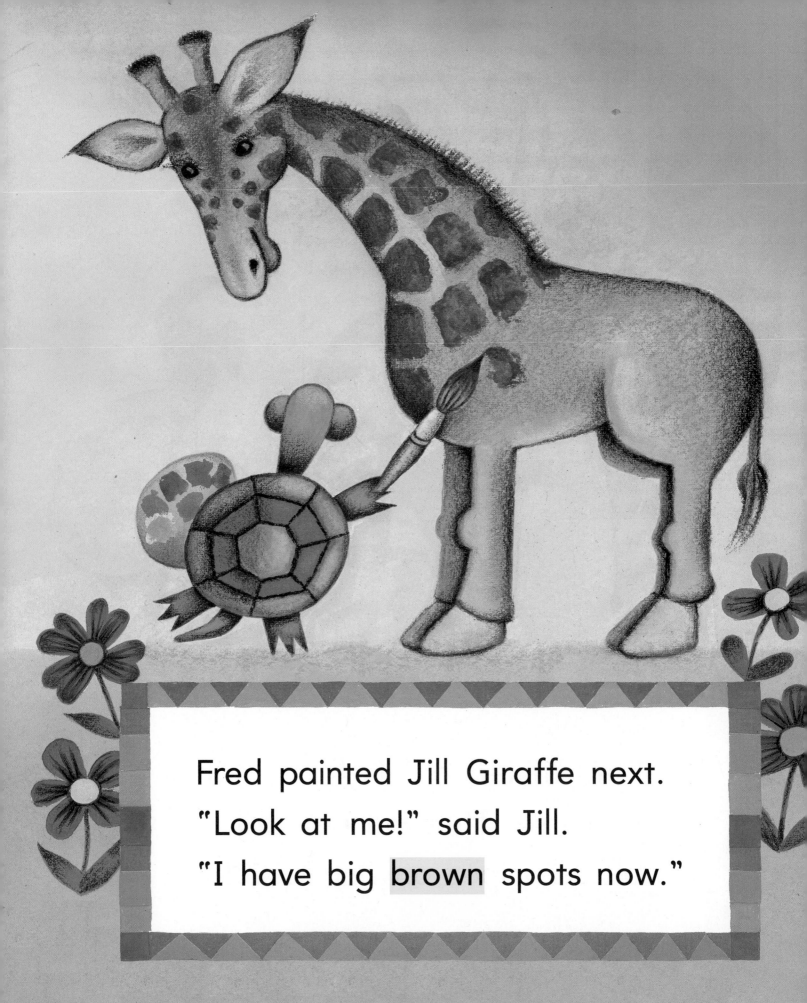

Fred painted Jill Giraffe next.
"Look at me!" said Jill.
"I have big brown spots now."

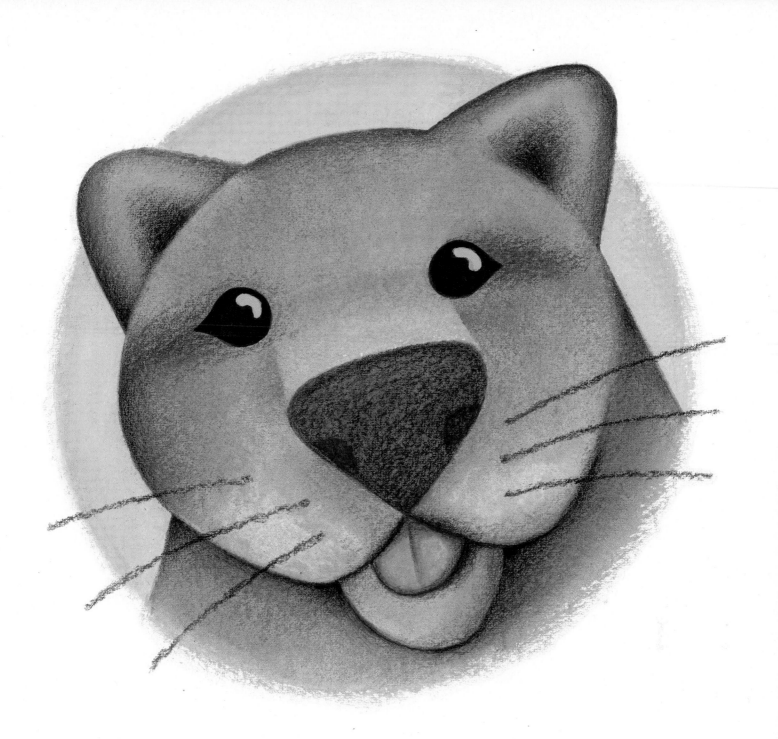

"I like spots very much.
Can I have spots, too?"
asked Len.

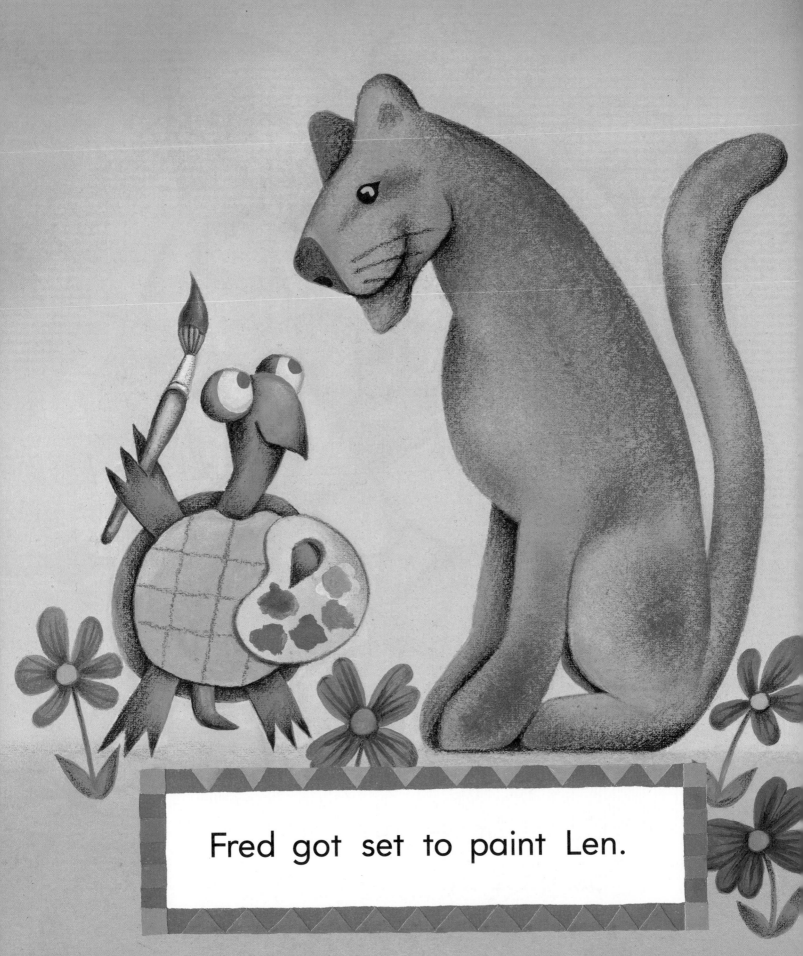

Fred got set to paint Len.

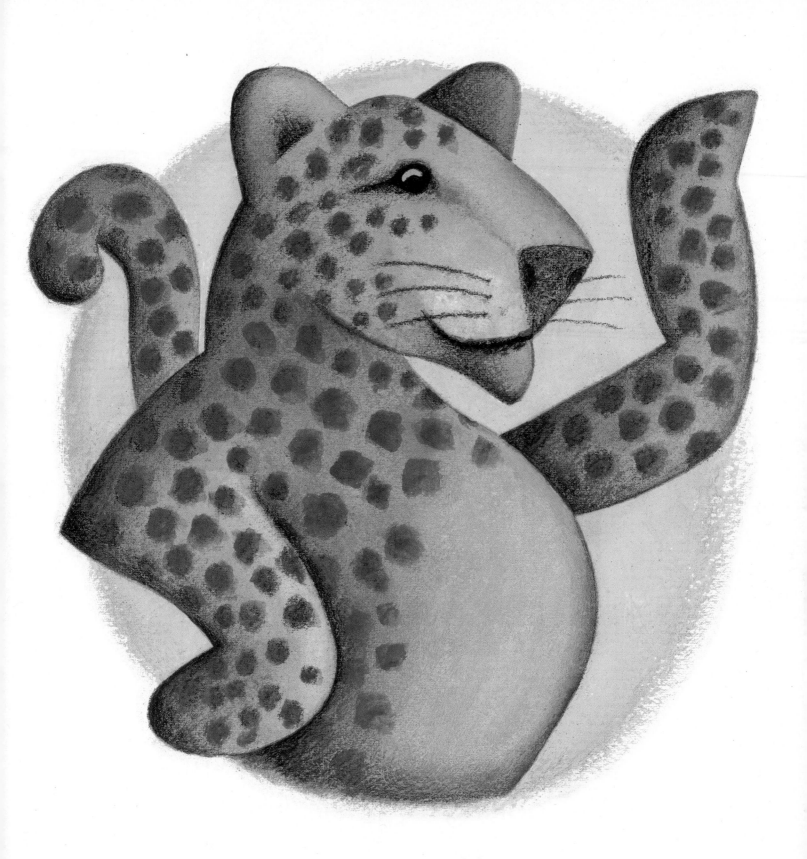

Now Len had spots
of his very own.

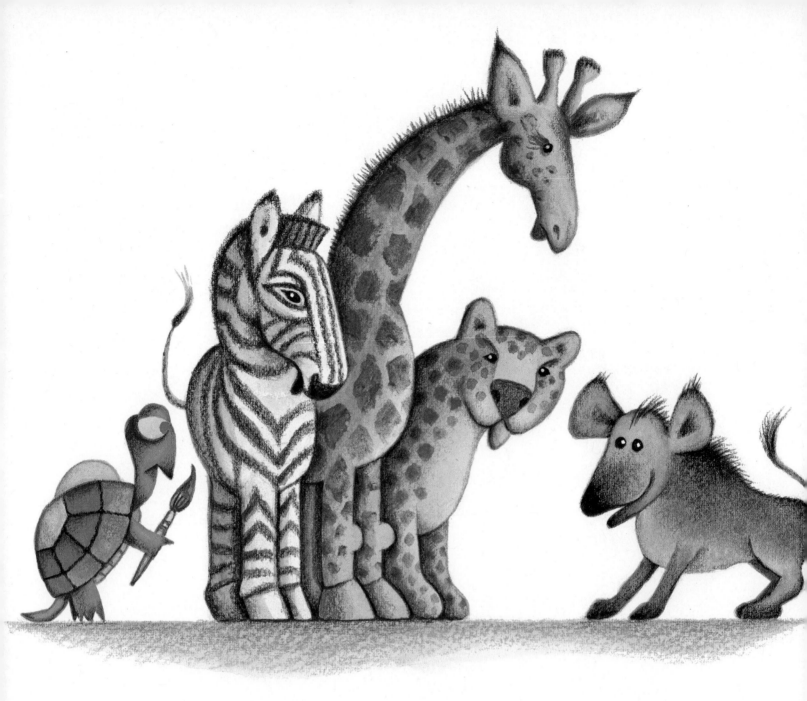

Zel, Jill, and Len had such
fun looking at their spots
and stripes.
Hal said, "Paint me, too!"

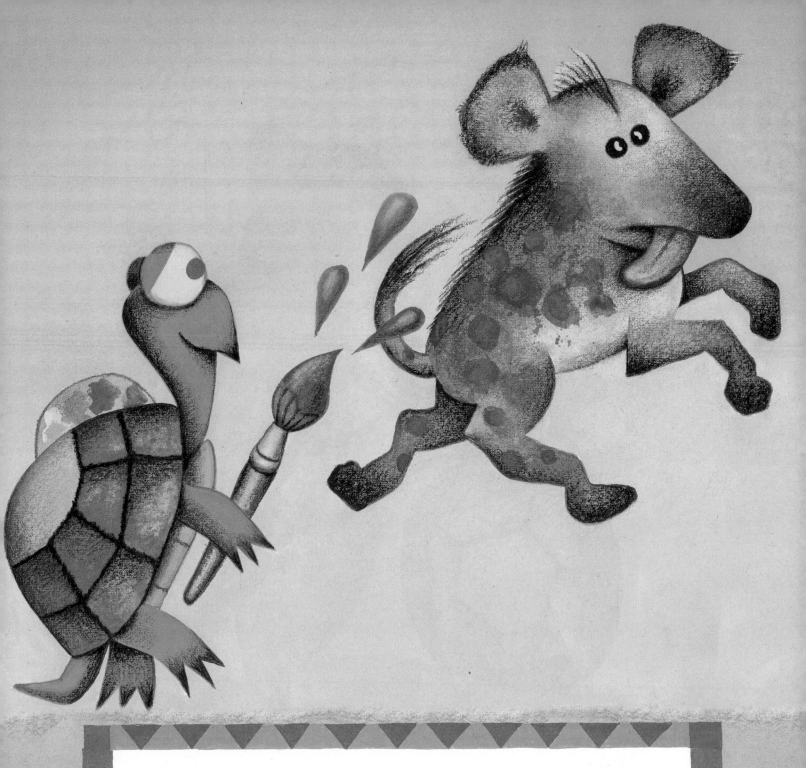

But Fred had a trick for Hal.
He splashed Hal with brown
paint. Hal yelled and ran off.

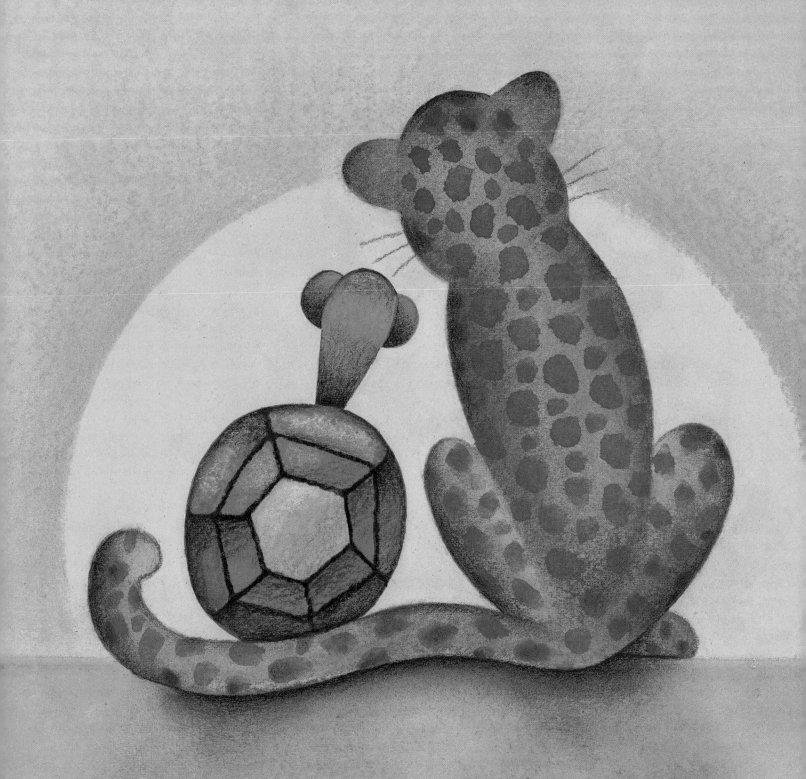

Now Fred and Len
are best friends.

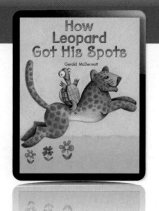

Dig Deeper

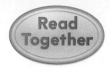
Read Together

Use Clues to Analyze the Text

Use these pages to learn more about Sequence of Events and Story Lesson. Then read **How Leopard Got His Spots** again.

Sequence of Events

In **How Leopard Got His Spots**, Fred Turtle helps Len Leopard get his spots. Think about the important events in the story. What happens **first**, **next**, and **last?** This order is called the **sequence of events**. Use a flow chart like this to describe the order of events in the story.

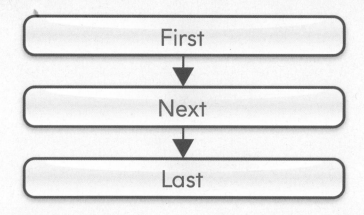

First

↓

Next

↓

Last

Story Lesson

How Leopard Got His Spots is a folktale. People told this story for many years before it was written down. Folktales often teach a lesson. What lesson do you learn from Hal Hyena?

Folktales can also tell why something is the way it is. Think about Len Leopard's spots. What does this folktale try to explain?

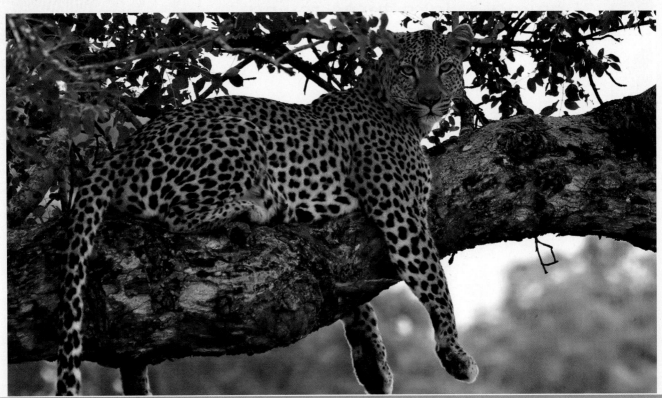

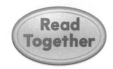

Your Turn

RETURN TO THE ESSENTIAL QUESTION

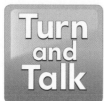 **Turn and Talk**

How are jungle animals different from animals on a farm? Use the words and pictures in the story to describe the jungle animals. Then draw a jungle animal and a farm animal. Take turns telling how the animals are different.

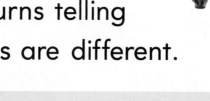

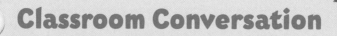 **Classroom Conversation**

Now talk about these questions with your class.

1. How does Len Leopard help Fred Turtle?

2. Why does Fred splash paint on Hal?

3. What do you think will happen the next time Hal Hyena sees the other animals?

ELA RL.1.1, RL.1.2, RL.1.7, W.1.3, SL.1.1a

WRITE ABOUT READING ··································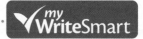

Response Write the story the way Hal Hyena would tell it. Write sentences to tell what happens in the beginning, middle, and end of the story.

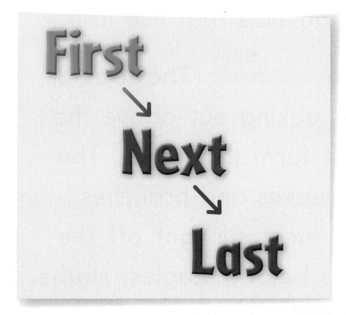

Writing Tip

Add words like **first**, **next**, and **last** to tell the events in order.

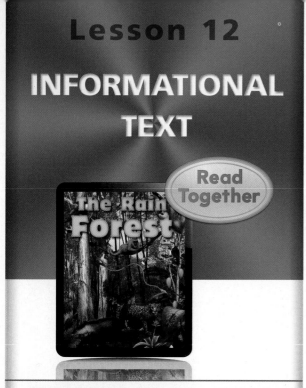

Read Together

GENRE

Informational text gives facts about a topic. This is from a science textbook. What facts do the words give? What do the pictures show?

TEXT FOCUS

A **map** is a drawing of a town, state, country, or the world. A map **key** tells more about what the map shows. What do you learn from the map on page 70?

The Rain Forest

A rain forest is a very wet and warm place. Rain forests have layers. Each layer has its own animals that live in it.

Canopy Layer The tops of trees poking out above the forest form this layer. The tree leaves and branches keep most sunlight off the layers below. Eagles, sloths, and monkeys live here.

Understory Layer This layer is above the ground. It is shady. Young trees and bushes grow here. Frogs, birds, and snakes live here.

ELA RI.1.5, RI.1.10

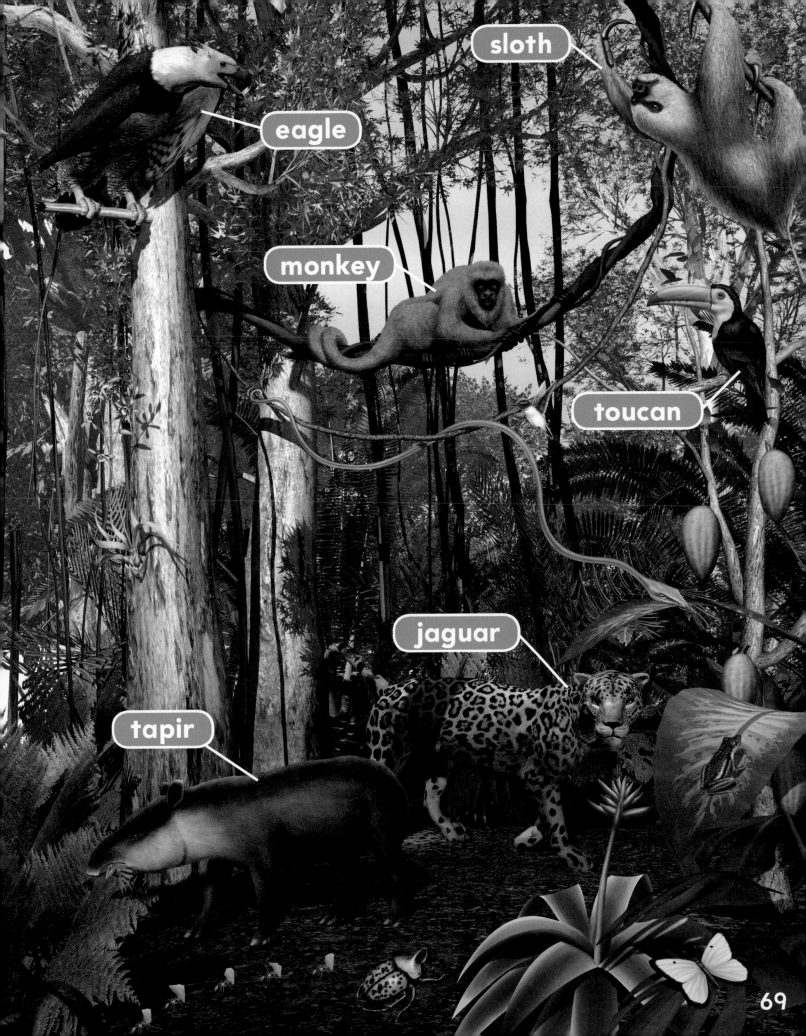

sloth

eagle

monkey

toucan

jaguar

tapir

69

Forest Floor Not much sunlight reaches this layer. Tapirs, jaguars, and beetles live on the brown forest floor. Ants and giant anteaters also live there. Anteaters have been known to eat thirty thousand insects in a single day!

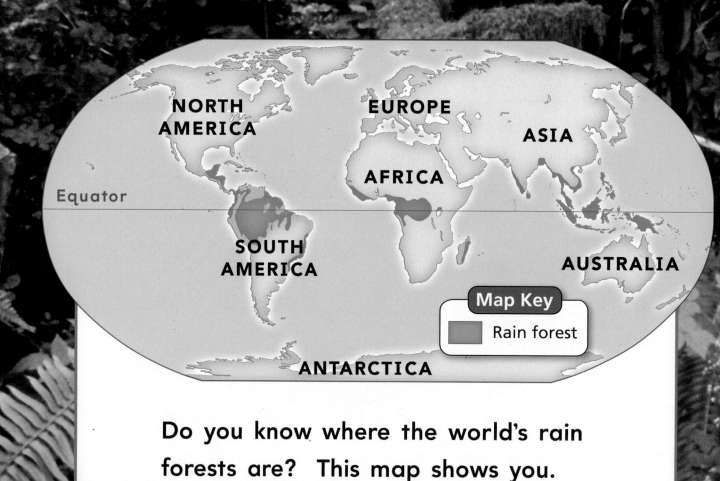

Do you know where the world's rain forests are? This map shows you.

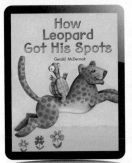
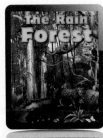

Compare Texts

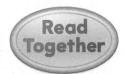

TEXT TO TEXT

Compare Settings Look at both selections. Tell how the settings are alike and different. Make a chart.

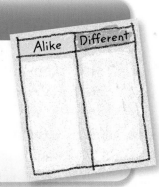

TEXT TO SELF

Write a Story What does **once upon a time** mean? Write a story about an animal you might see near your home. Begin your story with **once upon a time**.

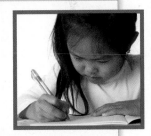

TEXT TO WORLD

Make a Map Pretend that you are going to visit a rain forest. Draw a map showing where you will go. Explain any symbols or words you use on your map.

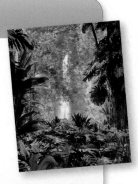

ELA RL.1.3, RI.1.3, RI.1.5, W.1.3, L.1.6

Grammar

Commands A sentence that tells someone to do something is a **command**. A command can end with a period. A command can end with an exclamation point when it is said with strong feeling.

Commands
Pick up that pencil.
Draw stripes on the zebra.
Help the turtle right now!
Save the rain forest!

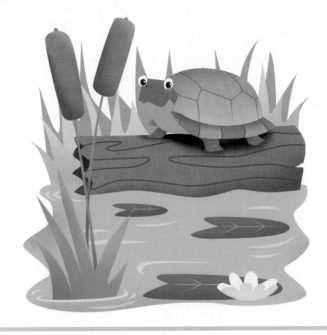

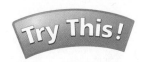

Read the sentences. Decide which ones are commands. Write each command on another sheet of paper. Then read the commands to a partner to check them.

1. Paint more spots on the giraffe.

2. Does the leopard like his spots?

3. Stand still while you paint.

4. Those paints are new.

5. Stay away from that wet paint!

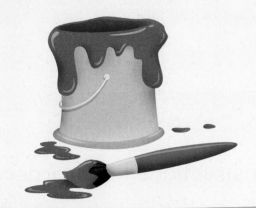

Connect Grammar to Writing

When you proofread your writing, be sure you have written commands correctly.

Informative Writing

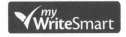

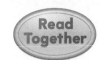

✓ Organization   In good **instructions**, the sentences tell the steps in order.   Order words help make the steps easy to follow.

Akil drafted his instructions in a letter to his friend Pam.   Later, he added the order word **Last**.

Revised Draft

Last,
4. ~~C~~olor brown spots.

Writing Checklist

✓ Organization   Do my instructions have order words?

✓ Did I tell the steps in order?

✓ Did I include a greeting and a closing in my letter?

ELA W.1.2, L.1.1j

Revise your writing using the Checklist. You can follow the instructions in Akil's final copy to make a puppet!

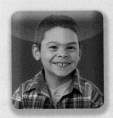

Final Copy

Dear Pam,

I made a leopard puppet. Here is how you can make one, too.

1. First, get a small paper bag.
2. Next, fold the sides of the flap.
3. Then, glue on ears, eyes, a nose, and whiskers.
4. Last, color brown spots.

I hope you have fun making your puppet.

Your friend,
Akil

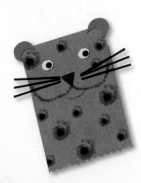

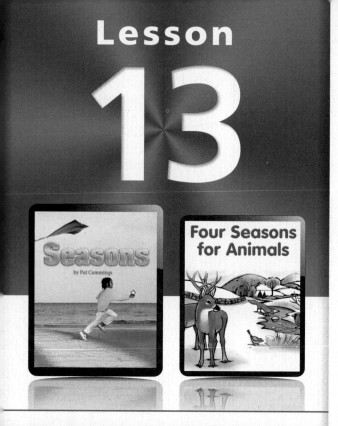

Seasons
by Pat Cummings

Four Seasons
for Animals

🔍 LANGUAGE DETECTIVE

Talk About Words
Adjectives describe
people, animals,
places, or things by
telling their size,
shape, color, and
number. Work with
a partner. Find the
blue words that are
adjectives. Use them
in complete sentences.

ELA RF.1.3g, SL.1.6, L.1.1f, L.1.1j, L.1.6

Words to Know

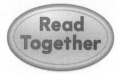
Read Together

▶ Read each **Context Card**.

▶ **Choose two blue words.**
Use them in sentences.

1 **green**
The green buds come
out in the spring sun.

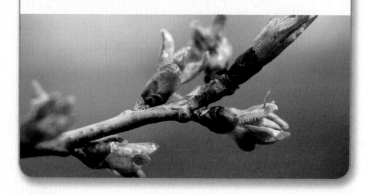

2 **yellow**
He put on yellow boots
on a rainy day.

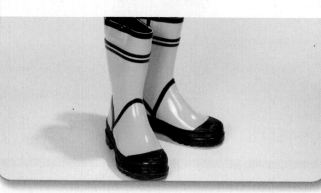

3 **grow**

Many flowers grow in the summer.

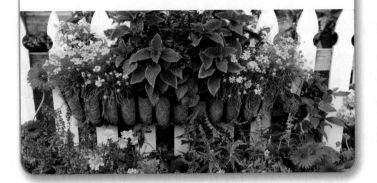

4 **open**

The windows can be open on a hot day.

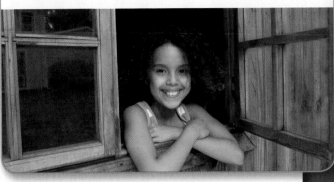

5 **fall**

The leaves change color in fall.

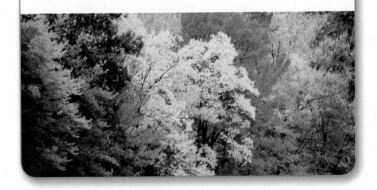

6 **new**

She has a brand new backpack for school.

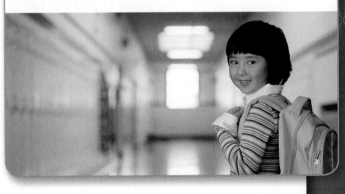

7 **down**

Snow comes down on a cold day.

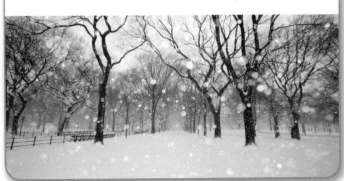

8 **goes**

She goes to the park to skate with her mom.

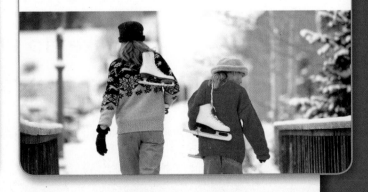

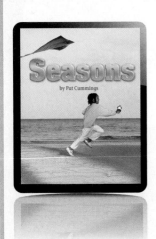

Read and Comprehend

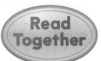

✓ **TARGET SKILL**

Cause and Effect Sometimes one event can **cause** another event to happen. The **cause** happens first. It makes something else happen. The **effect** is what happens next. As you read, think about what happens and why. You can use a chart like this to show how events are connected.

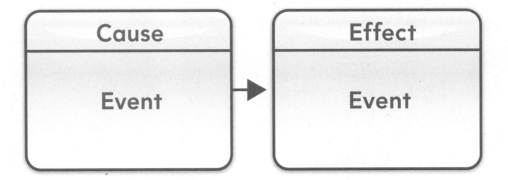

Cause	Effect
Event	Event

✓ **TARGET STRATEGY**

Visualize To understand a selection, picture events in your mind as you read.

78

ELA RI.1.3, SL.1.4, SL.1.6, L.1.1j

Seasons

There are four seasons. In winter it is cold. It snows in some places. Then it gets warmer, and the snow melts. It becomes spring. In spring, plants begin to grow. Summer comes next. It gets hot. Then in fall, the leaves turn colors. It is cool. After fall, it's winter again!

You will read about changes that happen each year in **Seasons**.

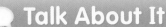

Talk About It

What do you know about the seasons?

What would you like to know?

Share your ideas with your classmates.

What did you learn from others?

ANCHOR TEXT

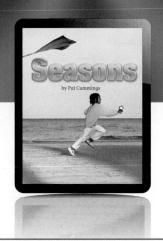

☑ **GENRE**

Informational text gives facts about a topic. As you read, look for:

▸ information and facts in the words

▸ photos that show the real world

Meet the Author

Pat Cummings

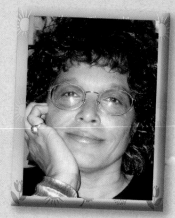

Pat Cummings loves getting letters from kids who have read her books. Sometimes they send her other things too, such as T-shirts, mugs, drawings, and even science projects. **Clean Your Room, Harvey Moon!** is just one of her many books.

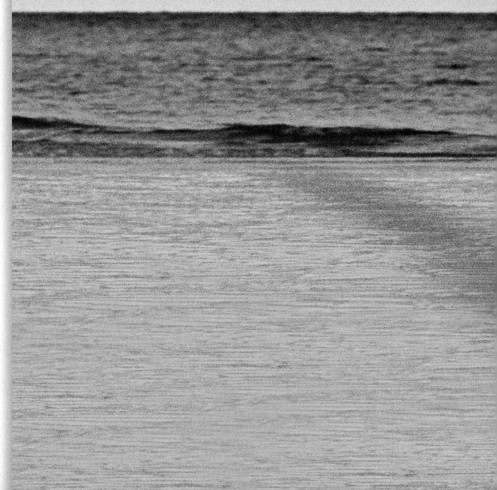

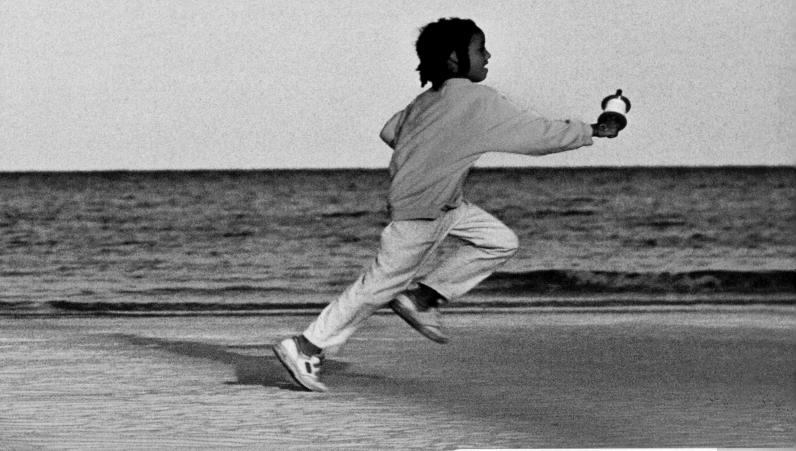

Seasons

written by Pat Cummings

ESSENTIAL QUESTION

What changes do the different seasons cause?

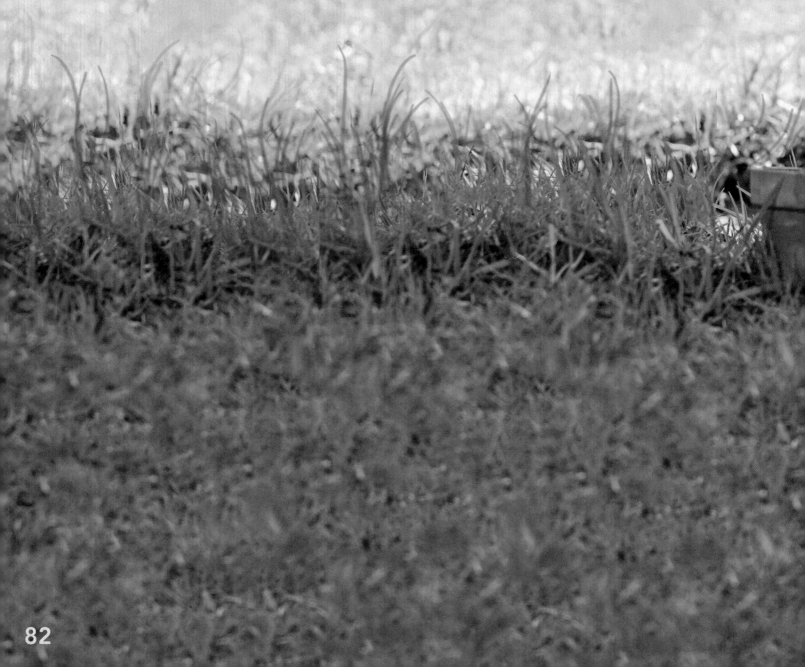

Spring

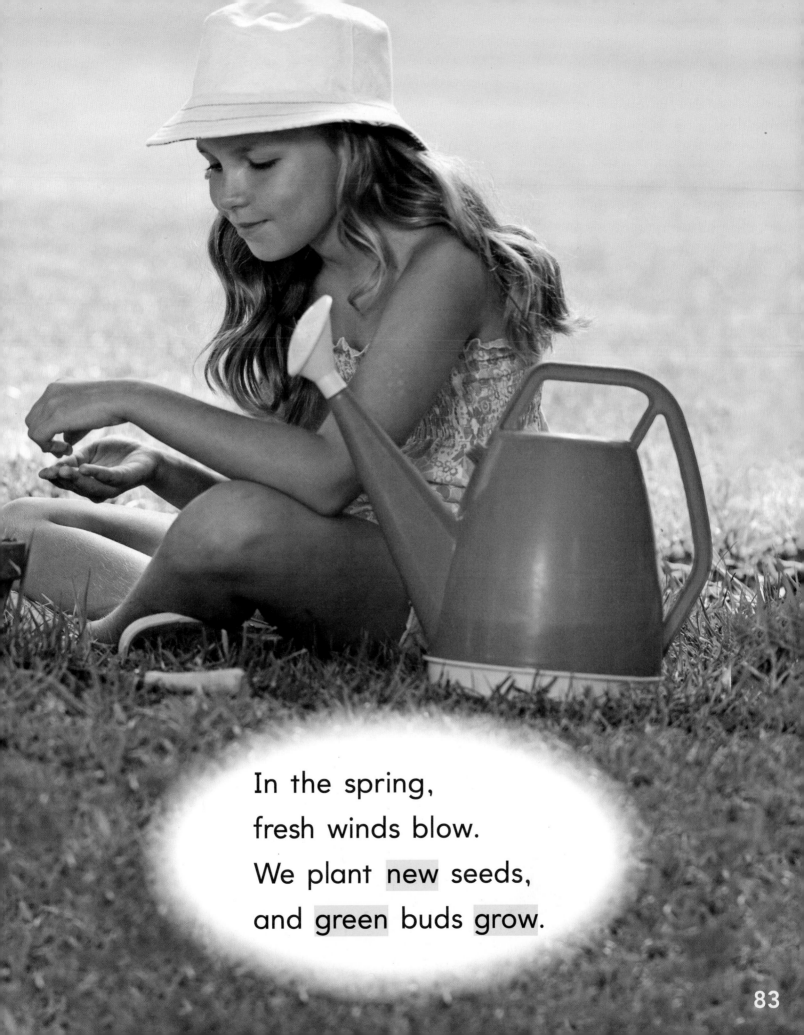

In the spring,
fresh winds blow.
We plant new seeds,
and green buds grow.

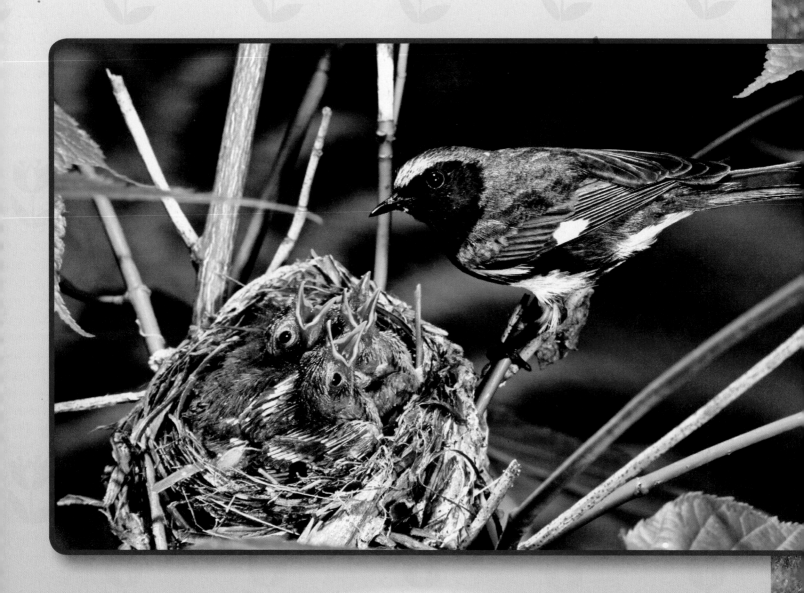

Eggs hatch open.
Little chicks sing.
The sun is out.
It must be spring!

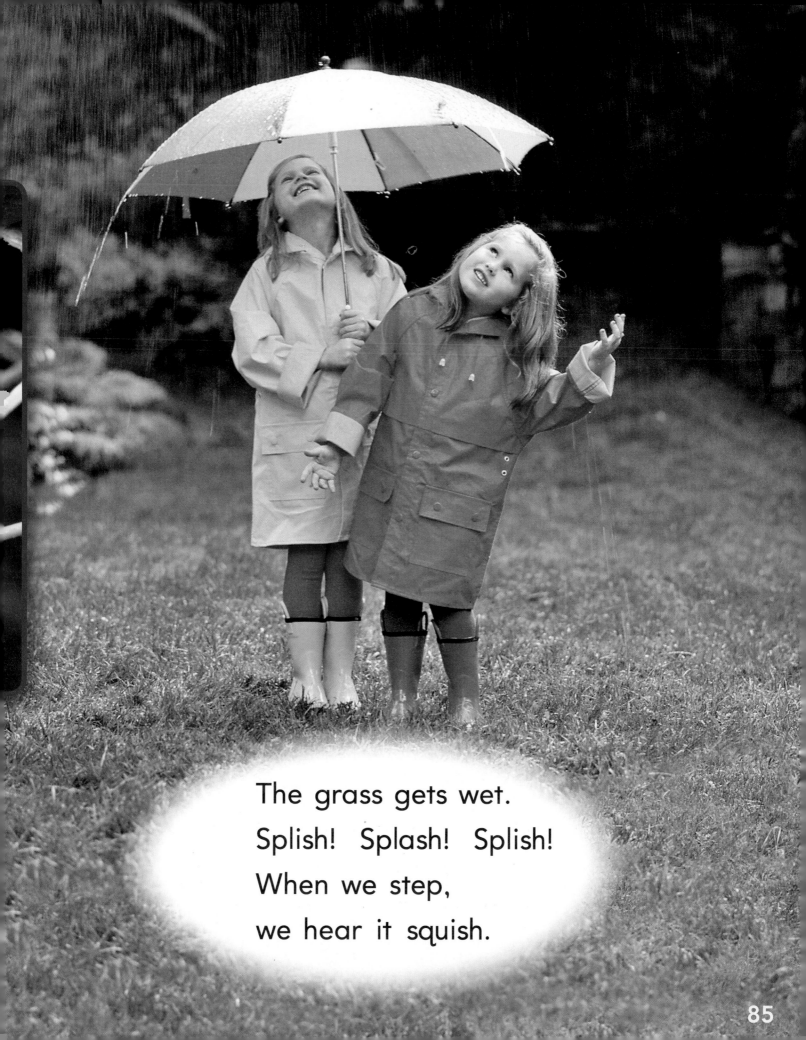

The grass gets wet.
Splish! Splash! Splish!
When we step,
we hear it squish.

Summer

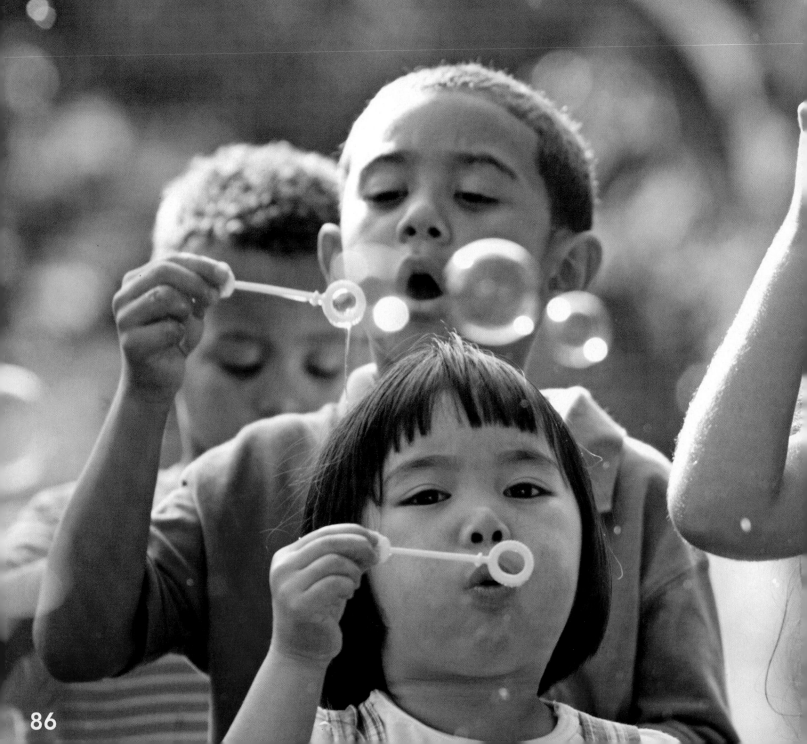

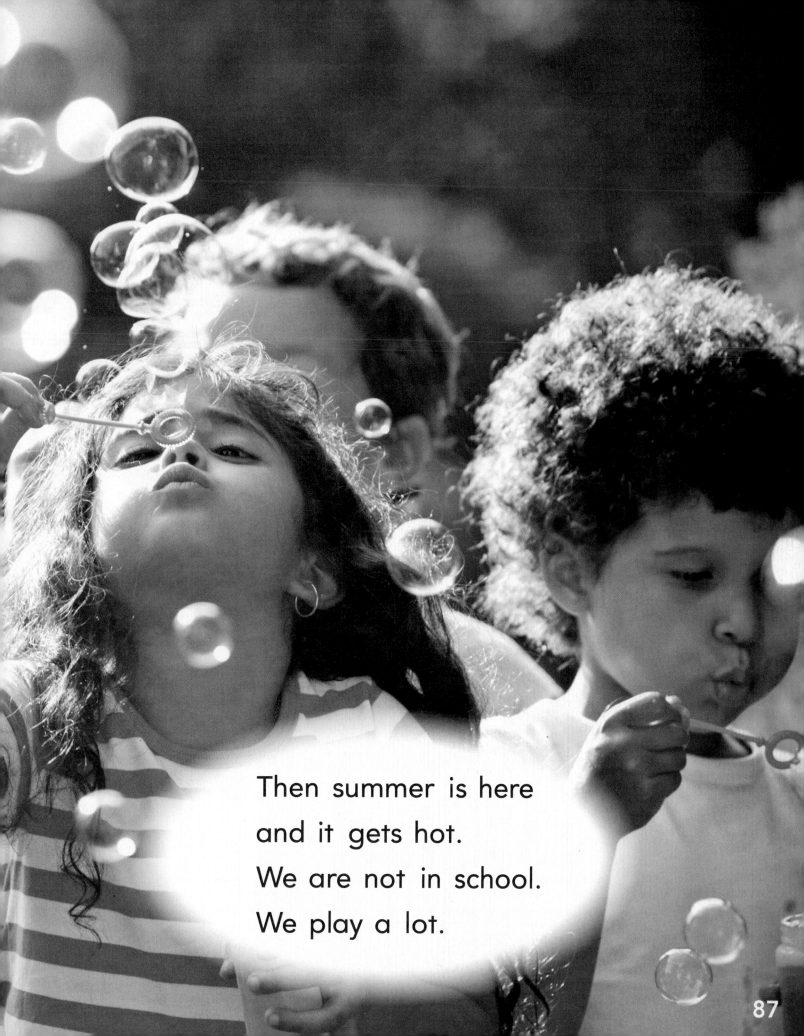

Then summer is here
and it gets hot.
We are not in school.
We play a lot.

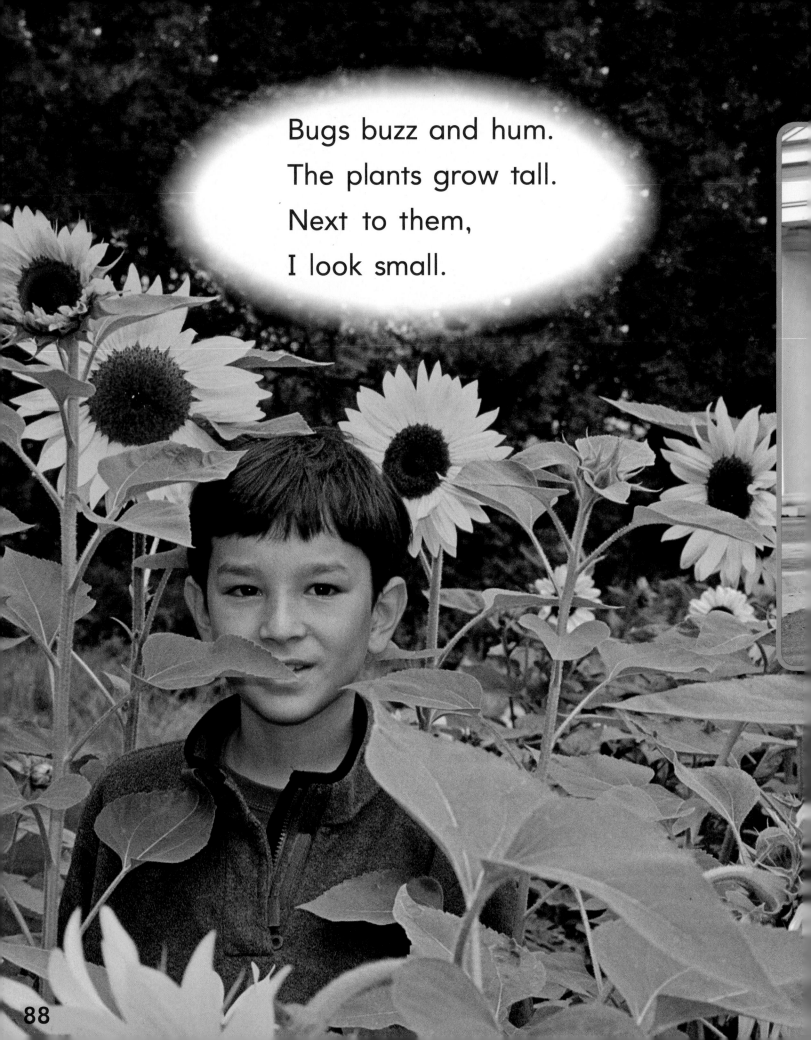

Bugs buzz and hum.
The plants grow tall.
Next to them,
I look small.

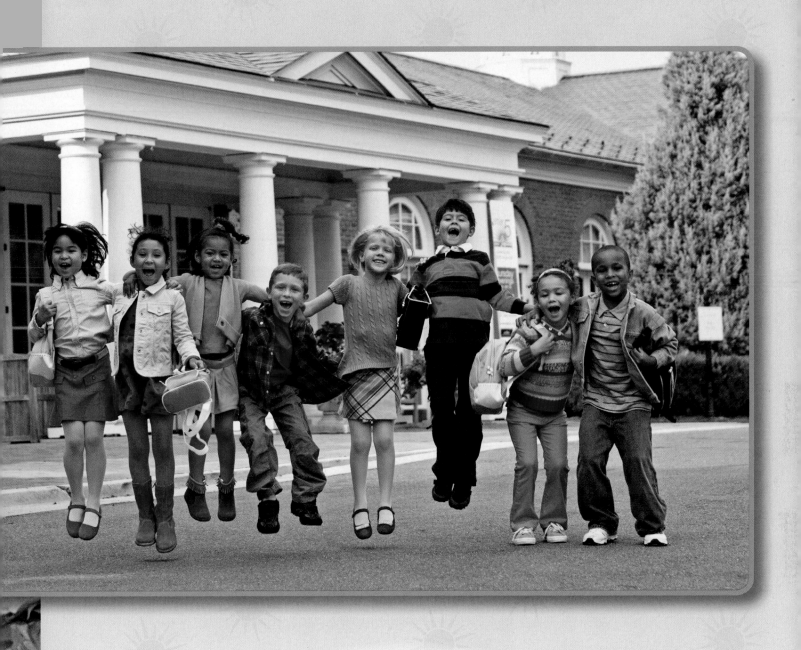

Summer goes fast,
and when it ends,
we will go back to school
with all our friends.

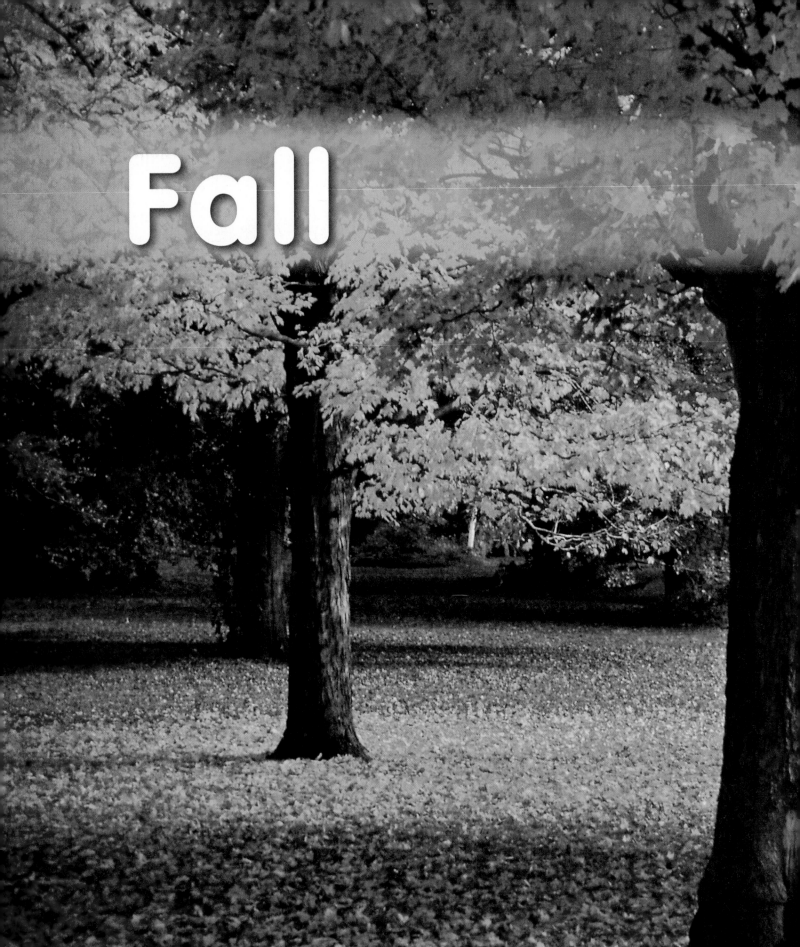

Fall

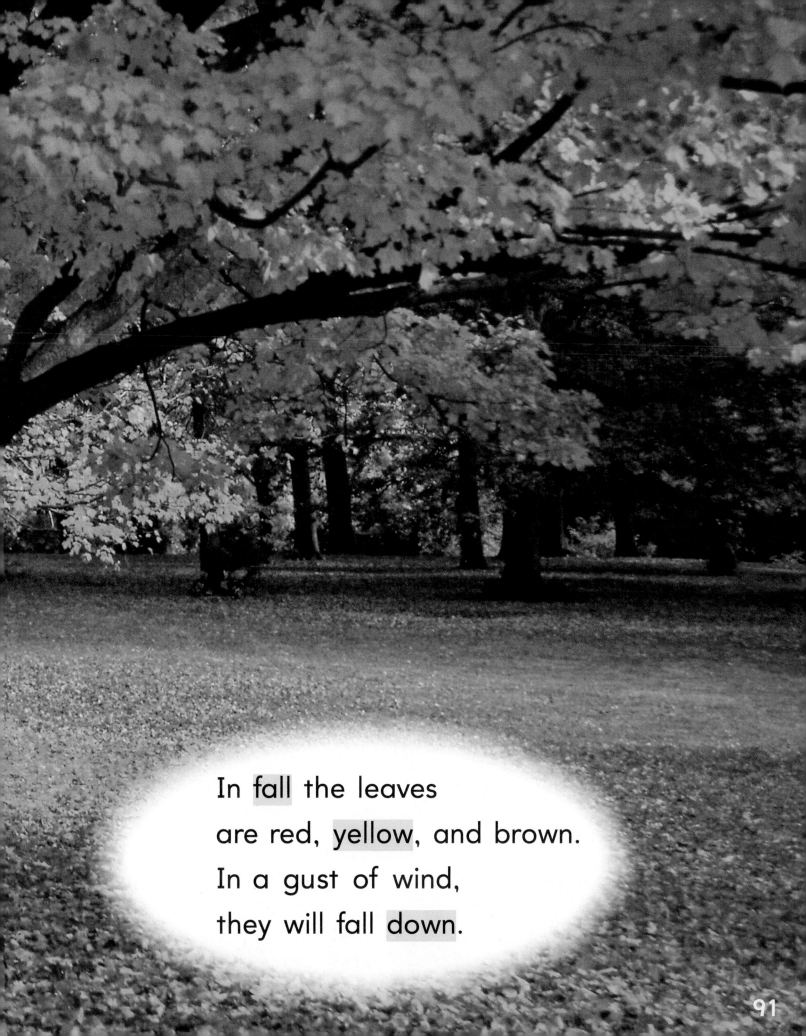

In fall the leaves
are red, yellow, and brown.
In a gust of wind,
they will fall down.

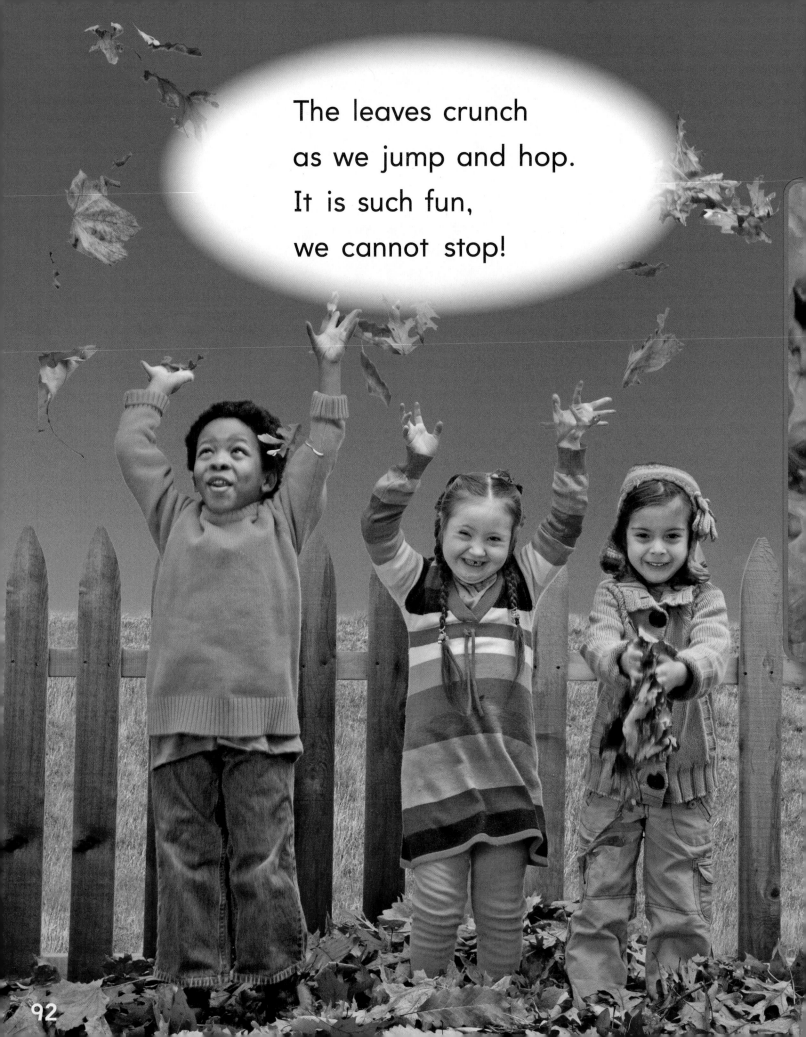

The leaves crunch
as we jump and hop.
It is such fun,
we cannot stop!

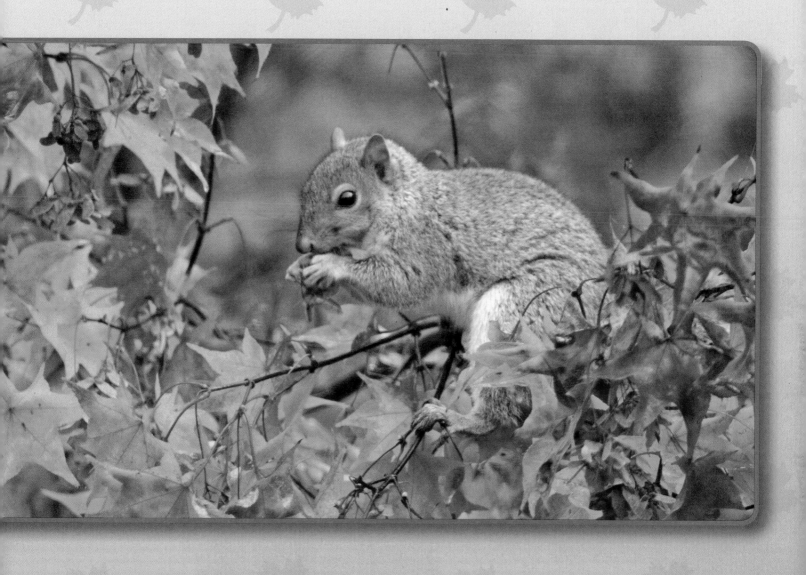

Animals get nuts
and pack them away.
They will have lots to eat
on a cold day.

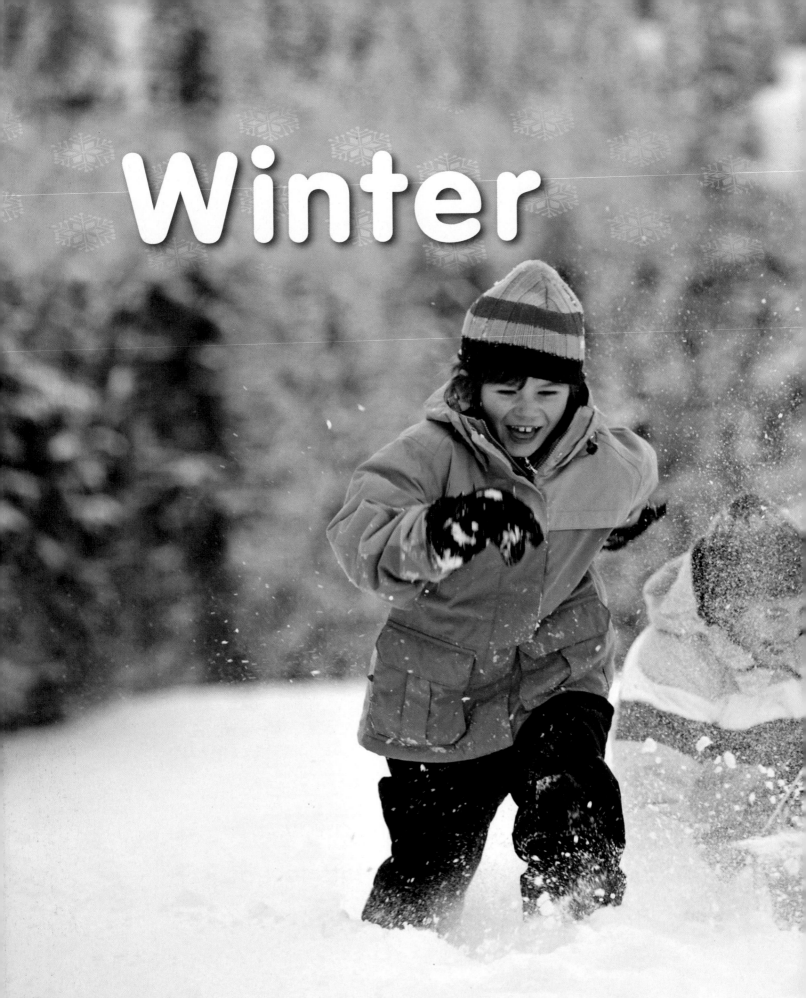

Winter

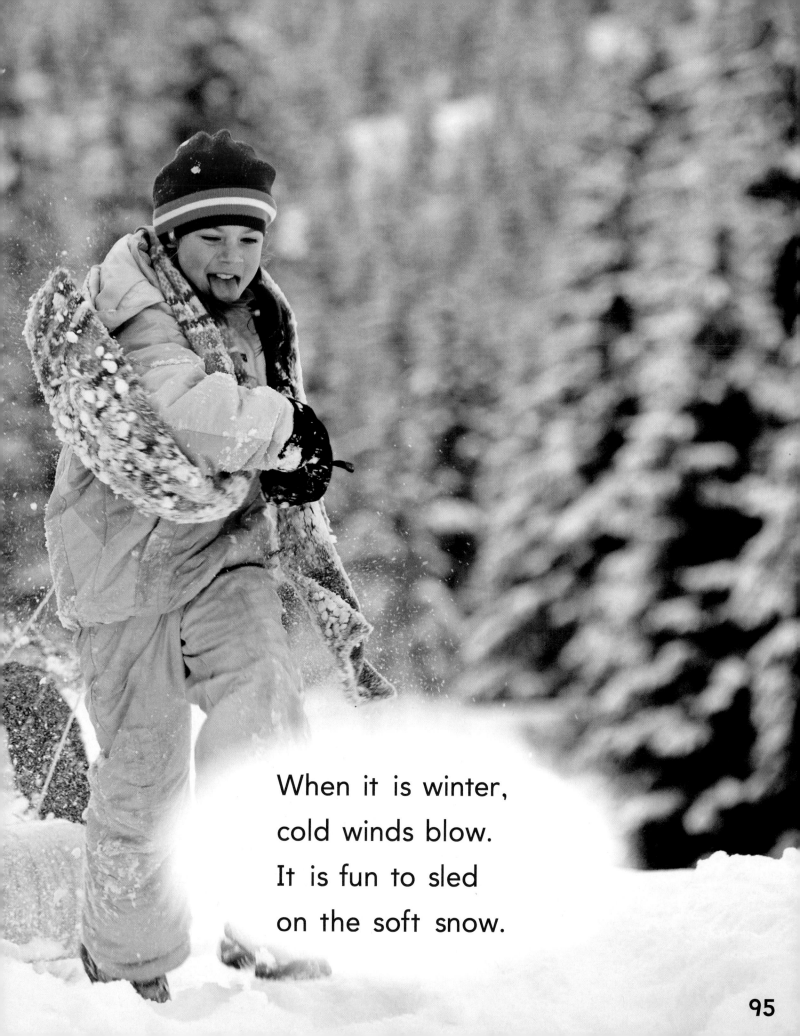

When it is winter,
cold winds blow.
It is fun to sled
on the soft snow.

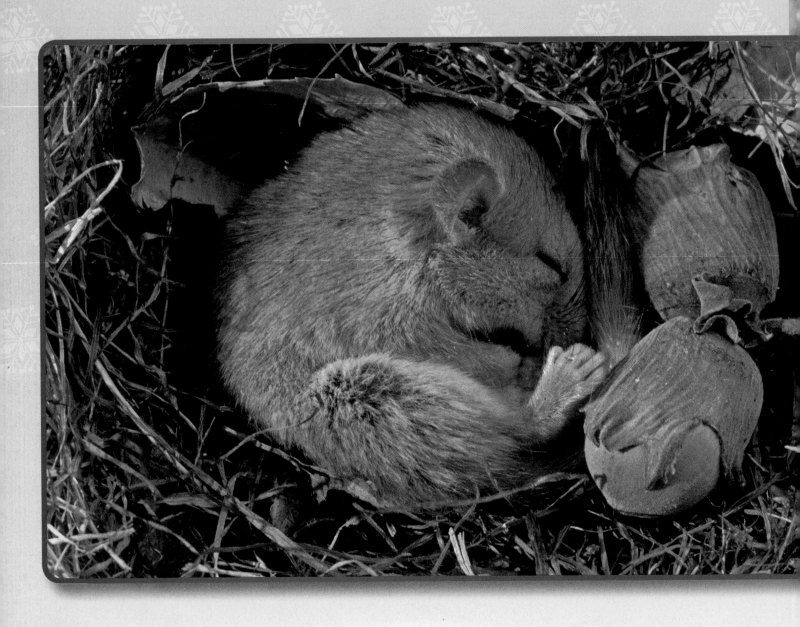

When it is cold,
some animals rest.
This animal has
a nap in a nest.

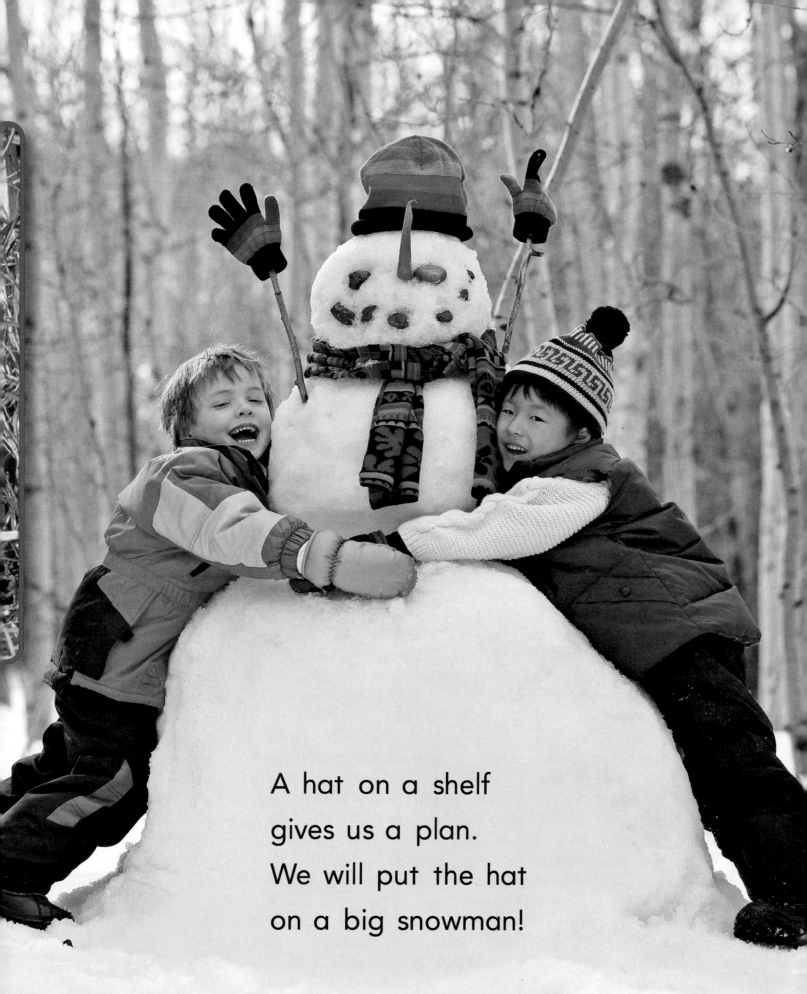

A hat on a shelf
gives us a plan.
We will put the hat
on a big snowman!

Winter

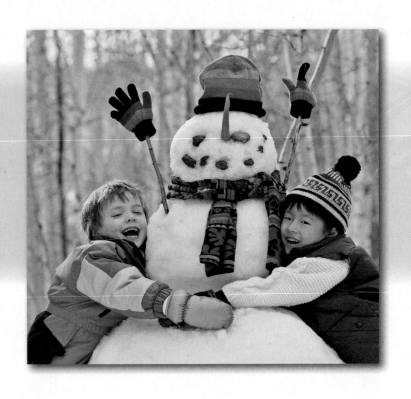

Spring

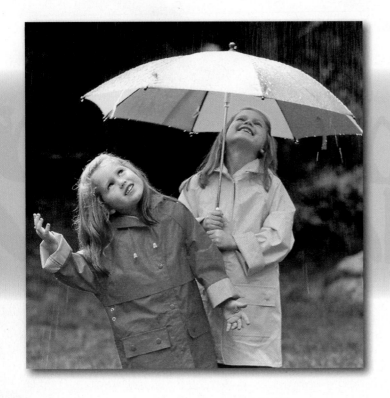

Summer

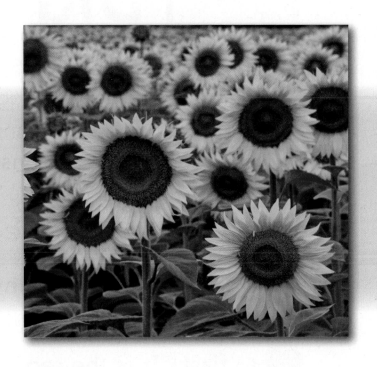

Winter, Spring,
Summer, Fall.
Which is best?
We like them all!

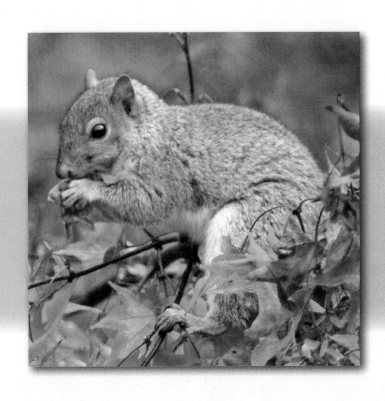

Fall

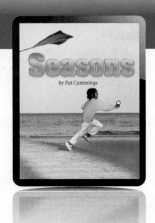

Dig Deeper

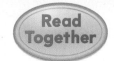

Use Clues to Analyze the Text

Use these pages to learn about Cause and Effect and Sound Words. Then read **Seasons** again.

Cause and Effect

In **Seasons**, many events cause other events to happen. The **cause** happens first. It is the reason why something else happens. The **effect** is what happens next. In **Seasons**, you read that it is cold in winter. What does the cold cause some animals to do? Use a chart to show what happens and why.

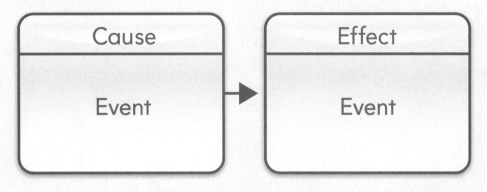

Cause		Effect
Event	→	Event

Sound Words

An author can use words that sound like real noises. In the part about spring, the author uses the words **Splish! Splash! Splish!** These words describe the sounds of rain and wet grass.

Find other words that tell about sounds in **Seasons.** Ask yourself what the words mean and what they describe. Use the other words and sentences to help you. Do sound words help you know what real things are like?

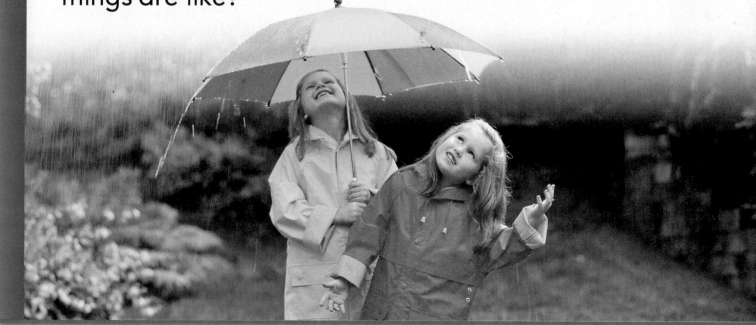

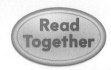

Your Turn

RETURN TO THE ESSENTIAL QUESTION

Turn and Talk

What changes do the different seasons cause? Talk with a partner about why changes happen in each season. Then look for text evidence to explain your answer. Take turns.

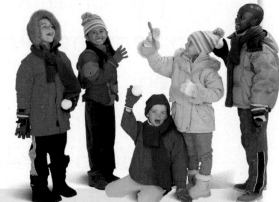

Classroom Conversation

Talk about these questions with your class.

1. What do animals do in different seasons?

2. How do plants change from spring to summer to fall?

3. Tell what the seasons are like where you live.

 ELA RI.1.1, RI.1.3, W.1.1, SL.1.1a

WRITE ABOUT READING

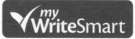

Response Write about your favorite season. First, tell what your topic is. Then give reasons why you like the season. Use text evidence from **Seasons** for ideas. Write an ending sentence.

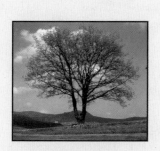

Spring

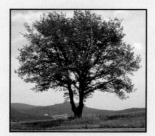

Summer

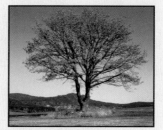

Fall

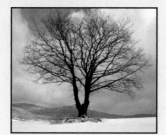

Winter

Writing Tip

An ending sentence can tell your opinion again in different words.

INFORMATIONAL TEXT

Read Together

Four Seasons for Animals

✓ GENRE

Informational text gives facts about a topic. Look for facts about what happens to plants and animals during the seasons.

✓ TEXT FOCUS

Headings are titles for different parts of an informational text. They tell you what each section will be about. What do the headings in this selection tell you?

Four Seasons for Animals

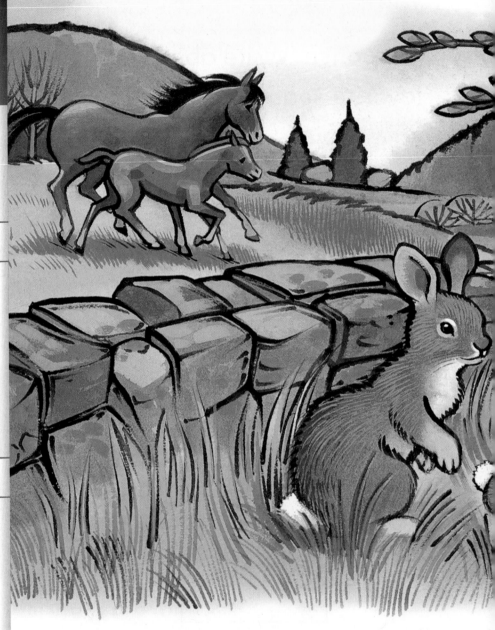

written and illustrated
by Ashley Wolff

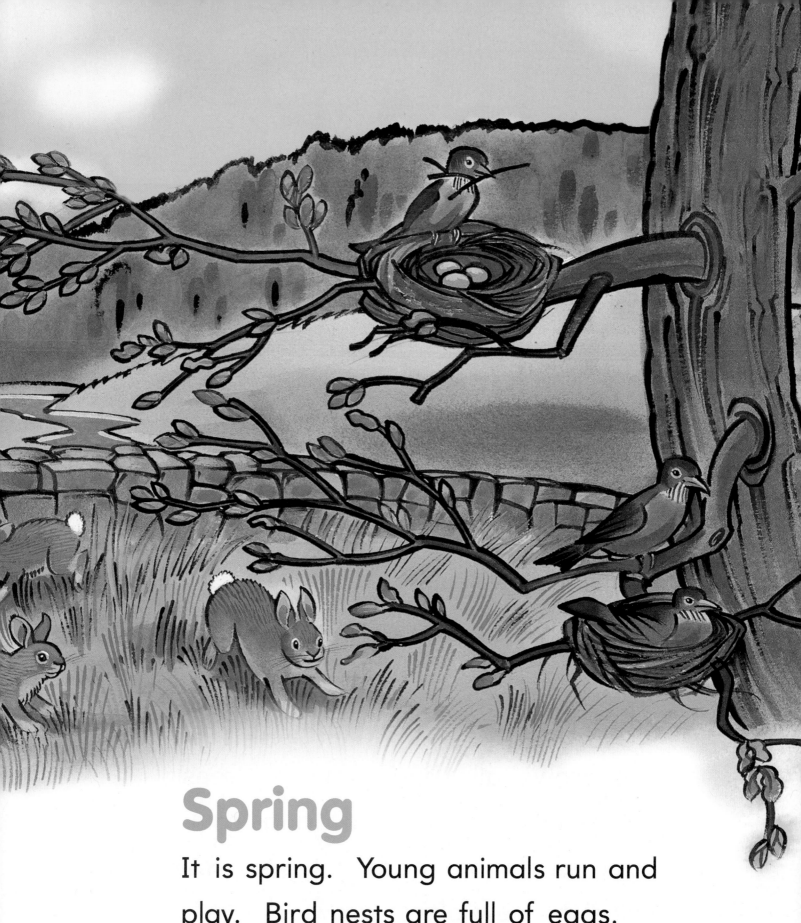

Spring

It is spring. Young animals run and
play. Bird nests are full of eggs.
Soon the eggs will hatch.

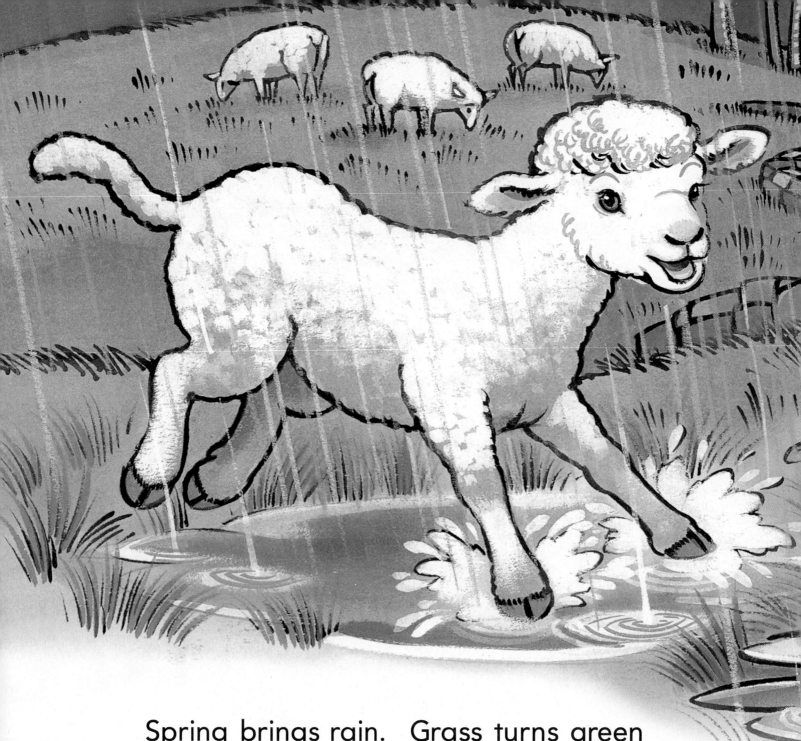

Spring brings rain. Grass turns green and grows tall. Buds grow on trees and plants. Spring also brings rain puddles! Flower buds get wet. Rain helps the new plants grow.

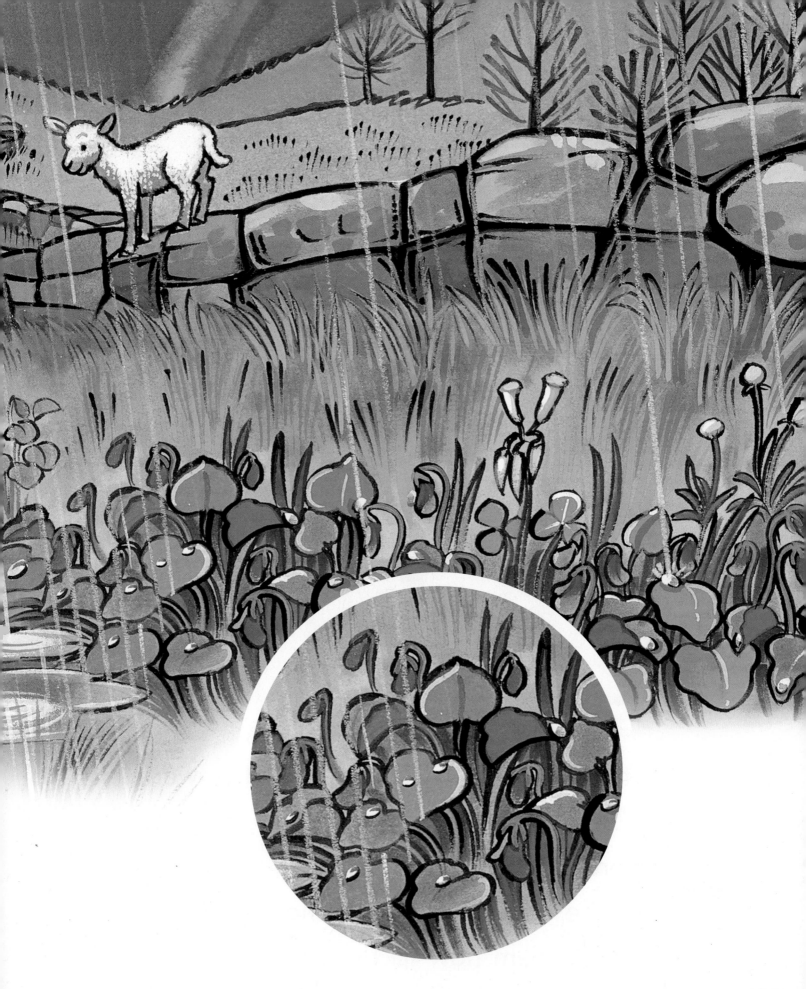

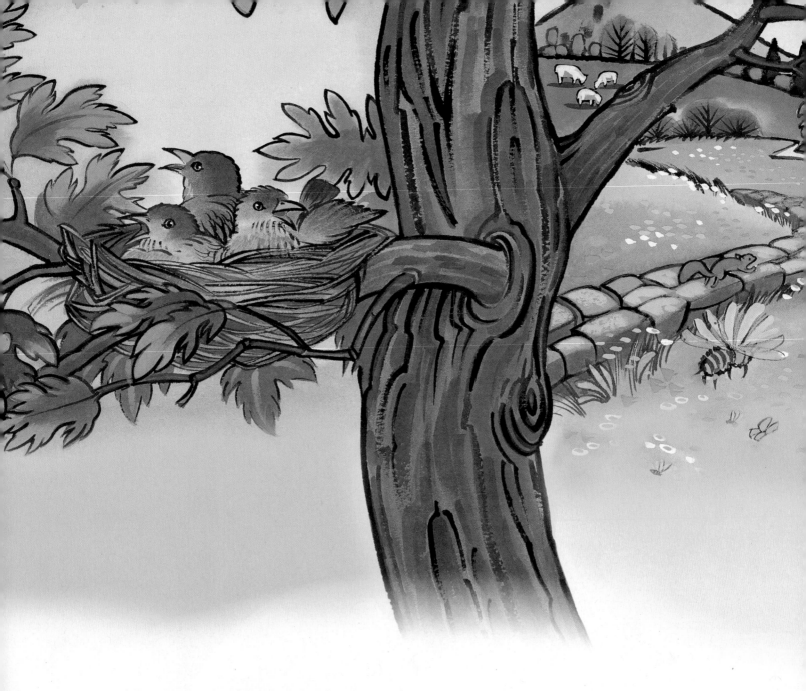

Summer

It is summer. Buds open and flowers bloom in the bright sun. Insects buzz here and there. Now there are chicks in the bird nest! Their mother will teach them how to fly.

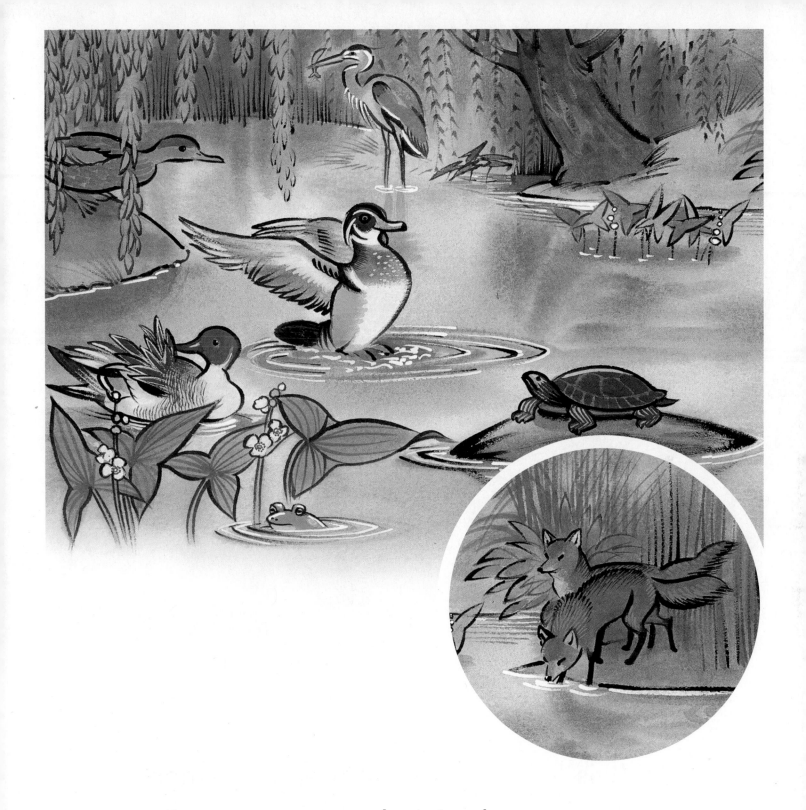

It can get very hot in the summer.
Many animals live near the pond.
Ducks swim in the pond. Fox pups
cool off in the shade.

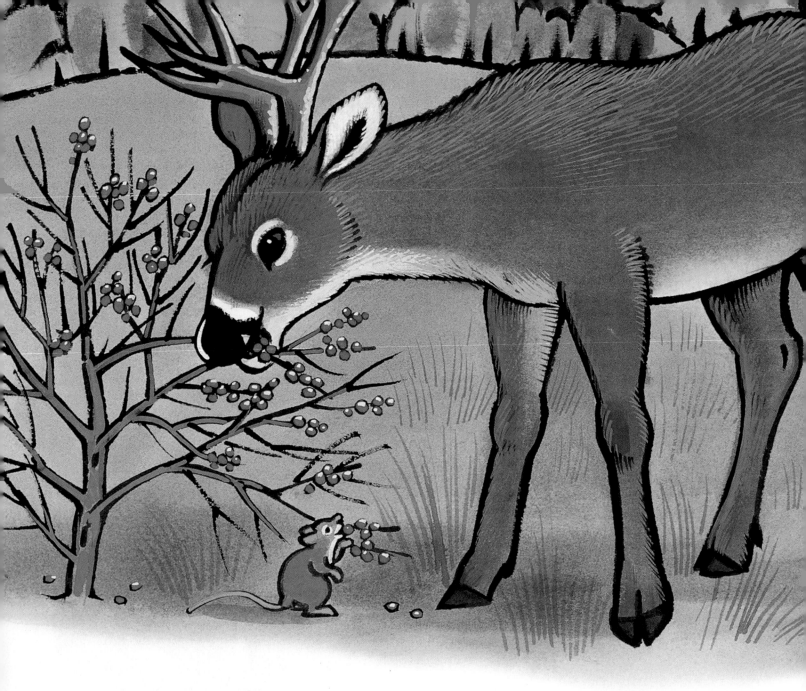

Fall

It is fall. Leaves fall down. Animals get ready for winter. Some animals eat as much as they can. They need to store fat because food is scarce in the winter.

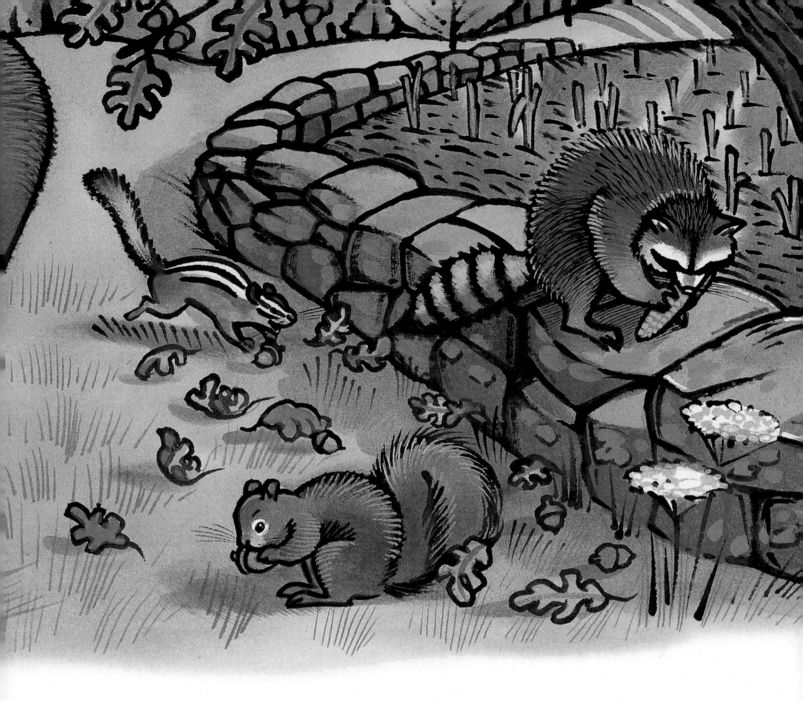

Squirrels and chipmunks gather nuts
so they will have enough food for
the winter.

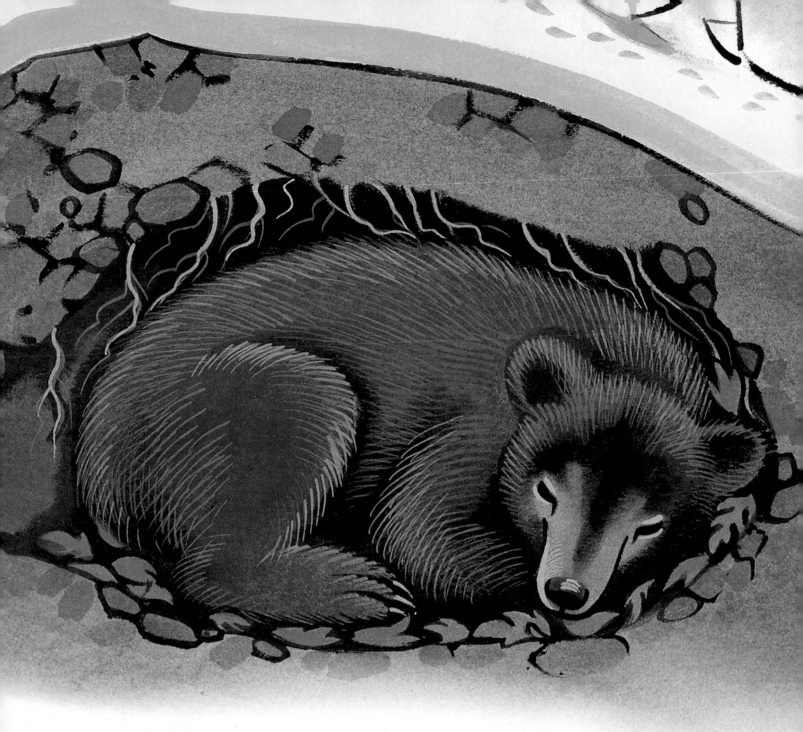

Winter

It is winter. Winter can be very cold and wet. Bears hibernate in the winter. That means they sleep.

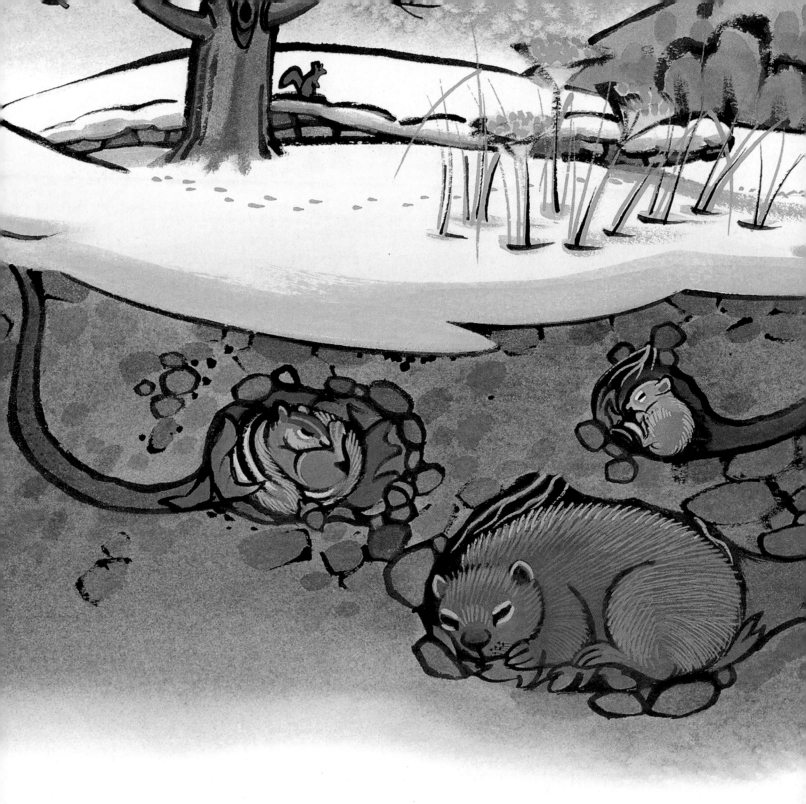

Many other animals hibernate in the winter. They curl up in dens to keep safe from the cold and wet.

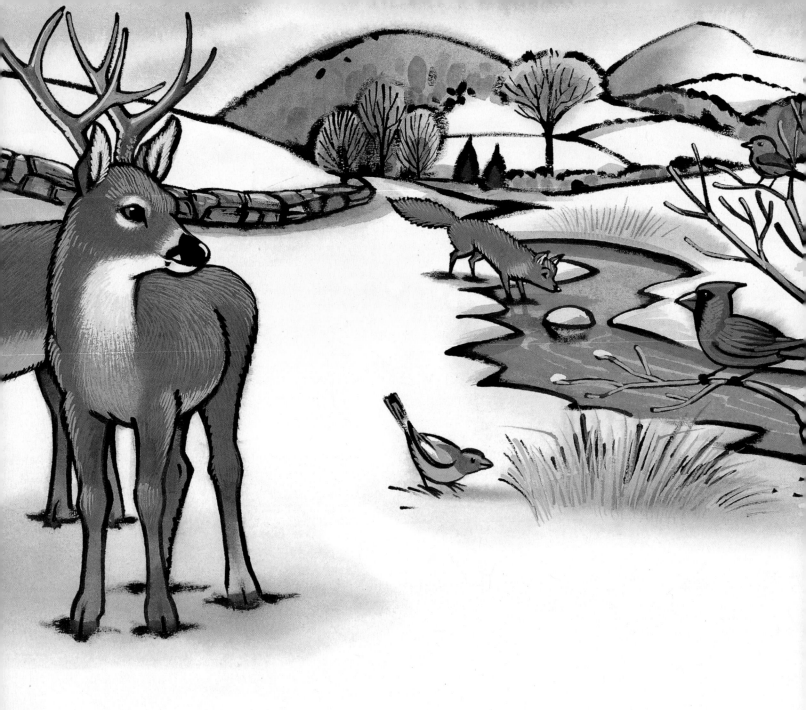

Like all the seasons, the winter will pass. The animals know that spring will come once again.

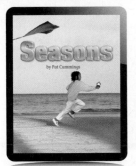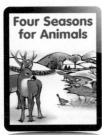

Compare Texts

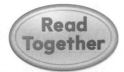

TEXT TO TEXT

Make a Chart How are the selections alike and different? Make a chart to show evidence.

Pictures	Facts	Descriptions

TEXT TO SELF

Describe a Season Describe your favorite season. Tell why you like it. Use details to make your ideas and feelings clear.

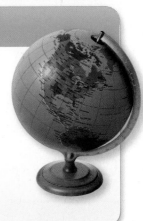

TEXT TO WORLD

Tell About Seasons Find your state on a globe. Then locate a country. Tell how you think the seasons in both places might be the same or different.

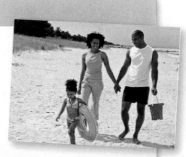

ELA RI.1.3, RI.1.9, SL.1.4

Grammar

Subjects and Verbs In a sentence, the subject and the verb have to agree. Both must tell about the same number of people or things. Add **s** to most **verbs** when they tell about a **noun** that names one.

Read Together

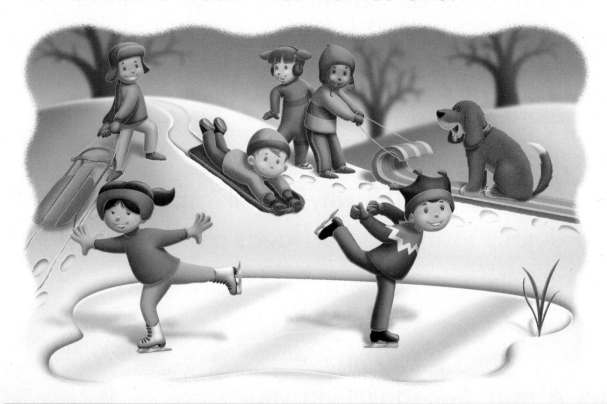

One	More Than One
One **boy** **pull<u>s</u>** his sled.	Two **girls** **pull** their dog.
Brett **slide<u>s</u>** down the hill.	**Children** **slide** across the pond.

116   ELA L.1.1c

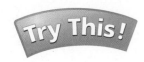

Choose the correct verb to finish each sentence. Take turns reading a sentence aloud with a partner. Then talk about how you chose the correct verb.

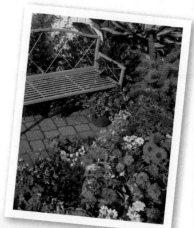

1. Raindrops ___?___ each spring.
          fall   falls

2. Flowers ___?___ in the garden.
       grow   grows

3. One bug ___?___ all night.
      hum   hums

4. Now the sun ___?___ brightly.
      shine   shines

5. The children ___?___ in the pool.
      swim   swims

Connect Grammar to Writing

When you proofread your writing, be sure you have written the correct verb to go with each noun.

Informative Writing

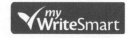

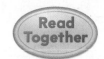

✓ Purpose When you write **sentences** that tell facts, be sure all your sentences are about one main idea.

Kyle wrote about winter. Then he took out a sentence that didn't belong.

Revised Draft

Winter is the coldest season.

Sometimes it snows here.

~~I have a dog.~~

Writing Checklist

✓ Purpose Are all my sentences about one main idea? Do the details tell facts?

✓ Did I write the correct verb to go with each noun?

✓ Did I write a good ending sentence?

Look for the main idea sentence in Kyle's final copy. Then revise your writing. Use the Checklist.

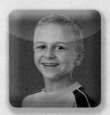

Final Copy

A Chilly Season

Winter is the coldest season.
Sometimes it snows here.
We go sledding.
The lake freezes.
People skate on it.
Winter is cold, but you can
still go out and play.

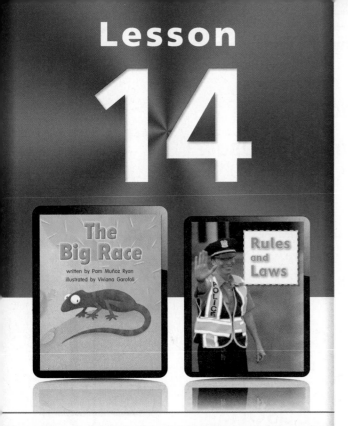

The Big Race
written by Pam Muñoz Ryan
illustrated by Viviana Garofoli

Rules and Laws

🔍 **LANGUAGE DETECTIVE**

Talk About Words
Work with a partner. Use two of the blue words in the same sentence. Be sure it is a complete sentence.

Words to Know

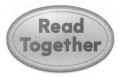
Read Together

▶ Read each **Context Card**.

▶ Use a blue word to tell about something you did.

1 **two**

Two desert lizards are sitting on the rock.

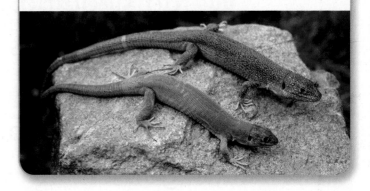

2 **into**

The bird flew into the big cactus.

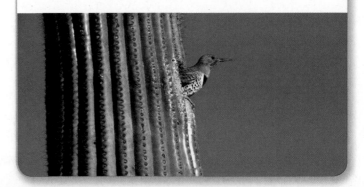

3 three

There are three birds resting in the sun.

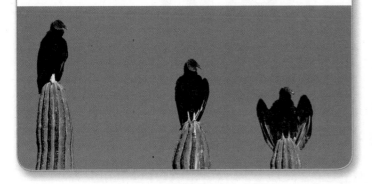

4 starts

The desert starts to cool down at sunset.

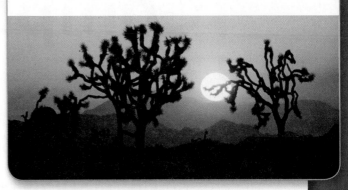

5 over

A hawk flew over the tall rocks.

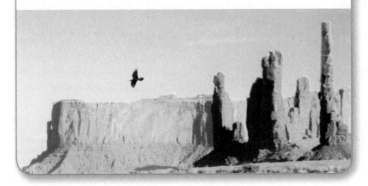

6 four

All four legs of this fox are strong.

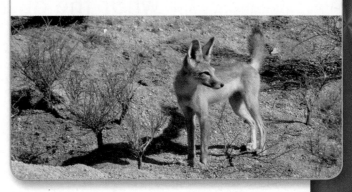

7 five

This desert flower has five red spots.

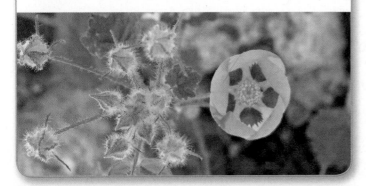

8 watch

The rabbits watch and listen for danger.

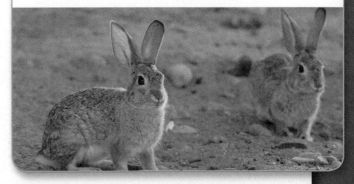

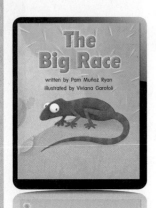

The Big Race
written by Pam Muñoz Ryan
illustrated by Viviana Garofoli

Read and Comprehend

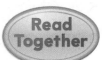

☑ **TARGET SKILL**

Conclusions Sometimes authors do not tell all the details in a story. Readers must use clues in the words and pictures and think about what they already know. This will help them make a smart guess about what the author does not tell. This smart guess is a **conclusion**. Use a chart to list the clues and your conclusions.

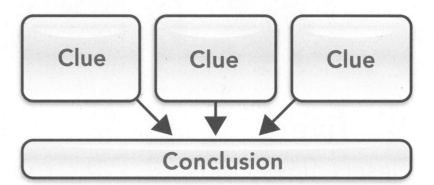

☑ **TARGET STRATEGY**

Infer/Predict Use text evidence to help you think of what might happen next.

ELA RL.1.3, RL.1.7, SL.1.4

Citizenship

Cross at the crosswalk. This rule keeps you safe. **Wash your hands.** This rule keeps you healthy. Following rules makes you a good classmate. It makes you a good neighbor, too.

When you read **The Big Race,** think about the rules and the different ways the animals race.

💬 Talk About It

What rules do you follow at school? What rules do you follow at home? Write your answers. Then share your ideas with your classmates.

ANCHOR TEXT

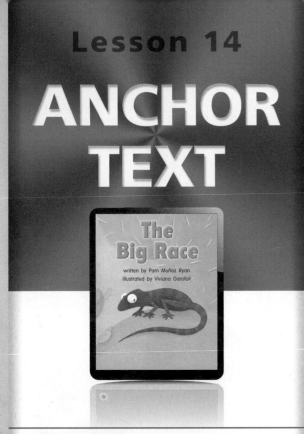

The Big Race

written by Pam Muñoz Ryan
illustrated by Viviana Garofoli

☑ GENRE

A **fantasy** could not happen in real life. As you read, look for:

▶ animals who talk and act like people
▶ events that could not really happen

Meet the Author

Pam Muñoz Ryan

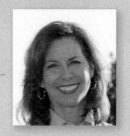

California summers can be very hot. When Pam Muñoz Ryan was growing up, she was often at the library on summer days. That's because the library was one of the few places nearby with air conditioning!

Meet the Illustrator

Viviana Garofoli

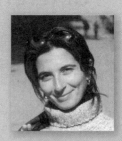

Viviana Garofoli and her family make their home in the country of Argentina. **Sophie's Trophy** and **My Big Rig** are two of the books she has illustrated.

The Big Race

written by Pam Muñoz Ryan

illustrated by Viviana Garofoli

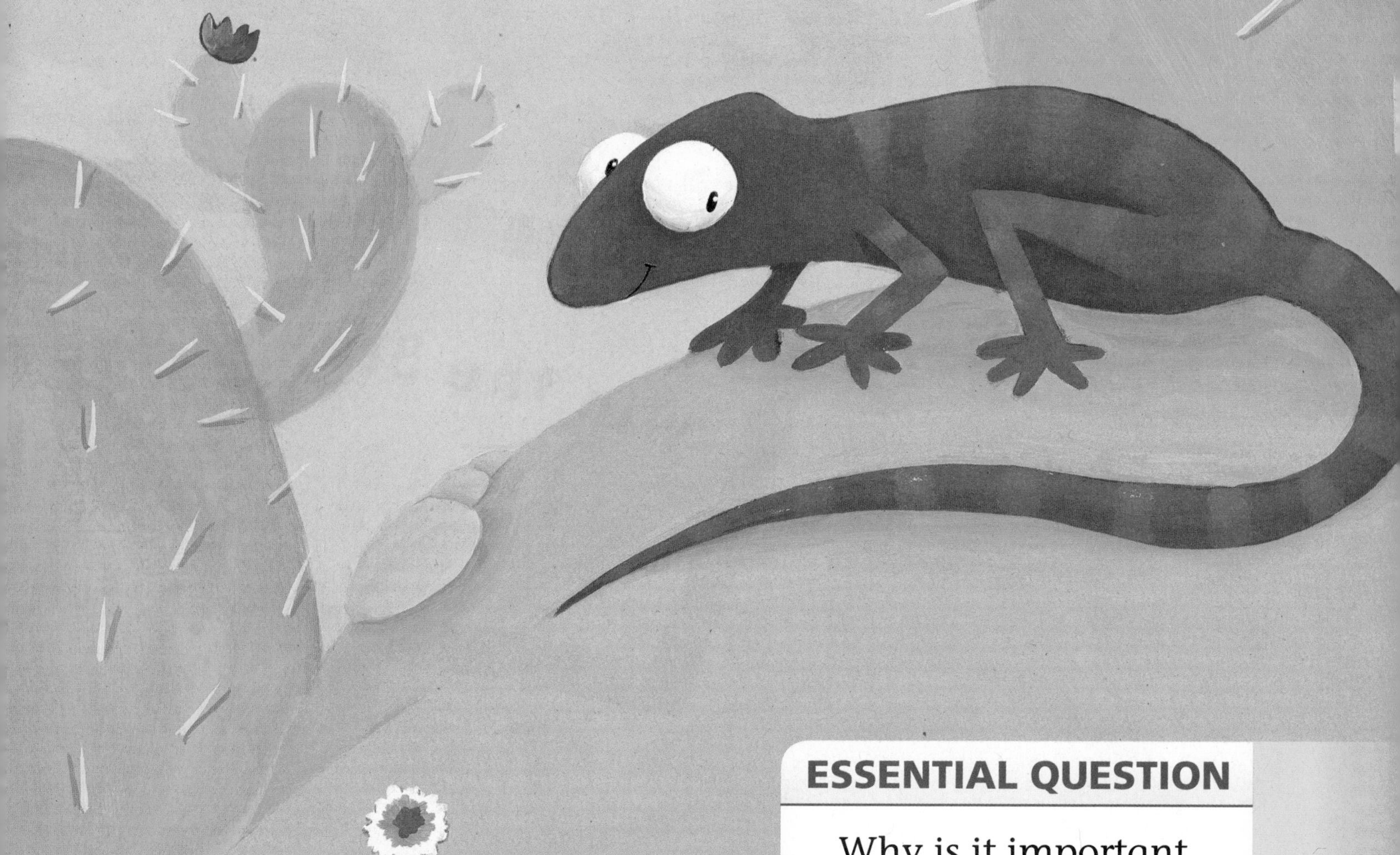

ESSENTIAL QUESTION

Why is it important
to have rules?

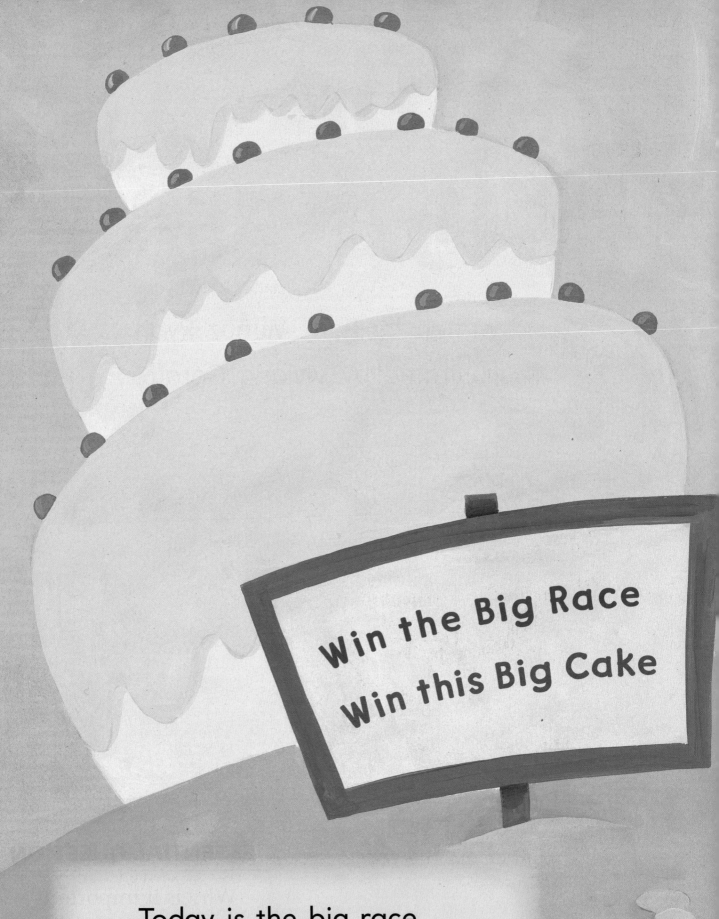

Win the Big Race
Win this Big Cake

Today is the big race.

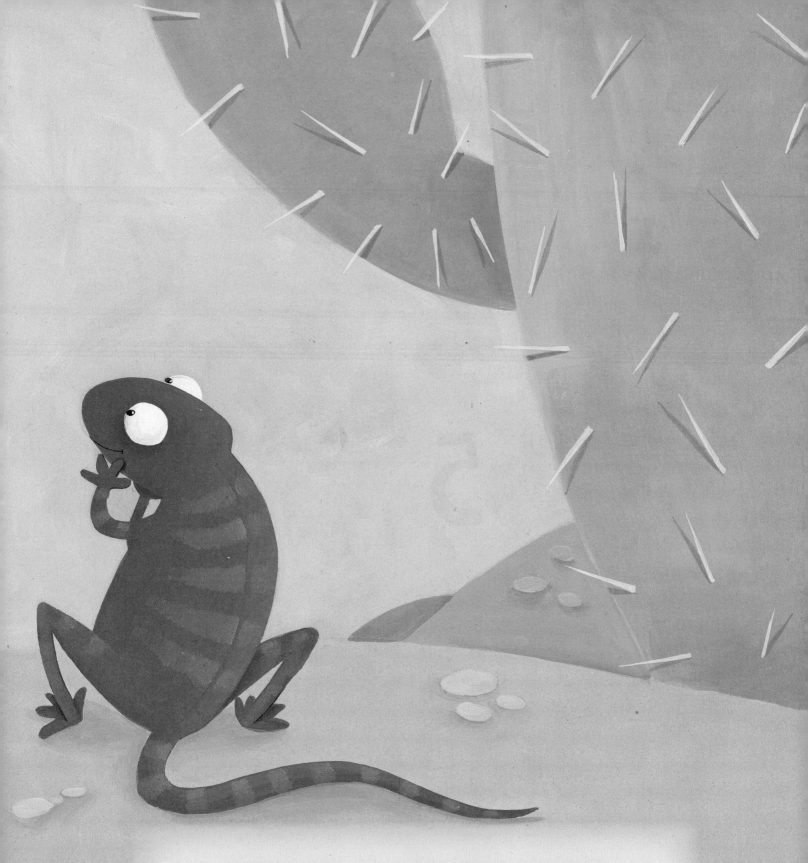

"I like cake!" said Red Lizard.
"I will run in that race."

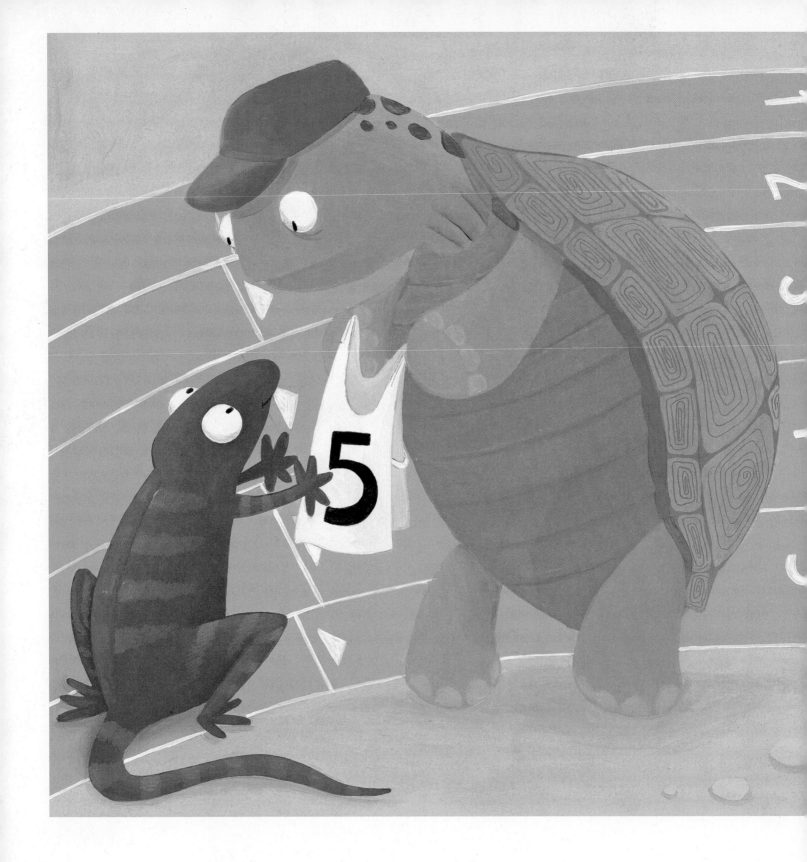

Red Lizard gets to the race.
Four animals will run with him.

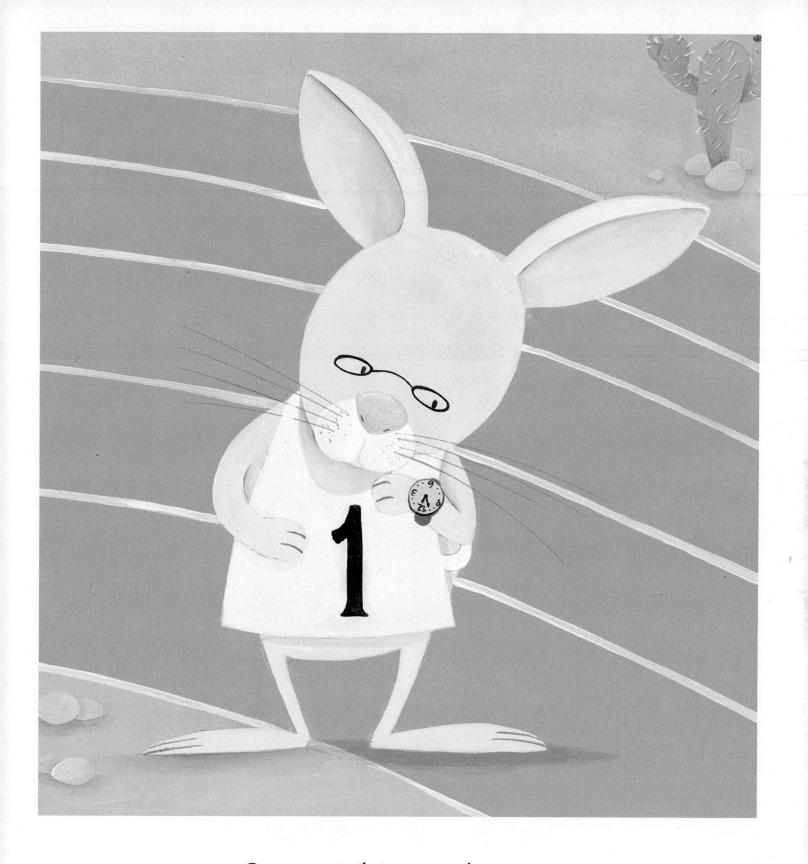

Cottontail is not late.
She will run in lane one.

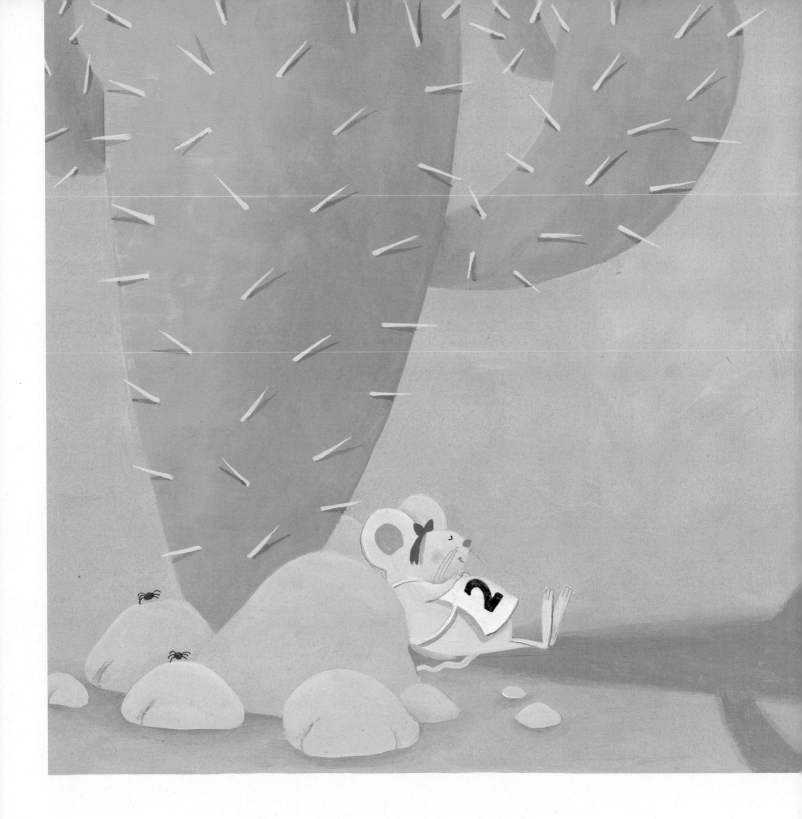

Rat naps in the shade.

She will run in lane two.

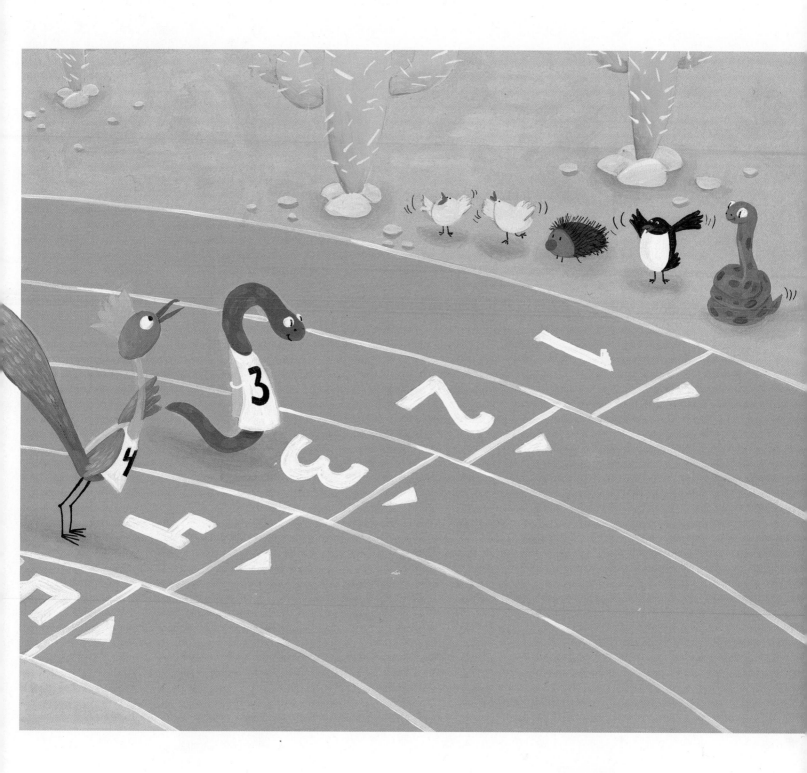

Snake takes his spot in lane three.

Roadrunner stands in lane four.

He waves to his pals.

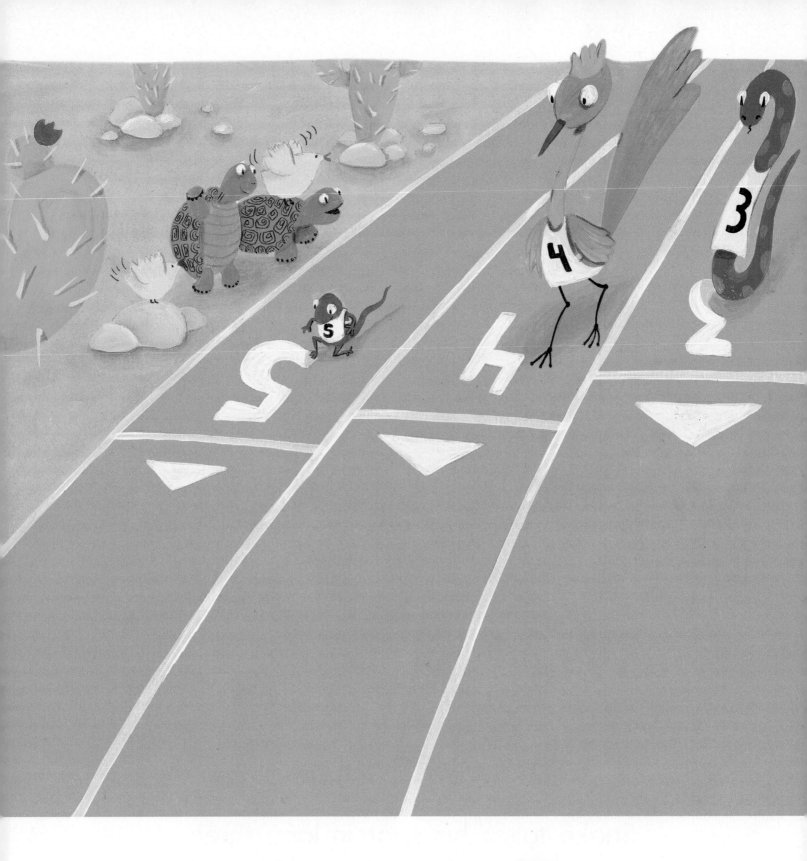

Red Lizard is in lane five.

The animals bend and hop.

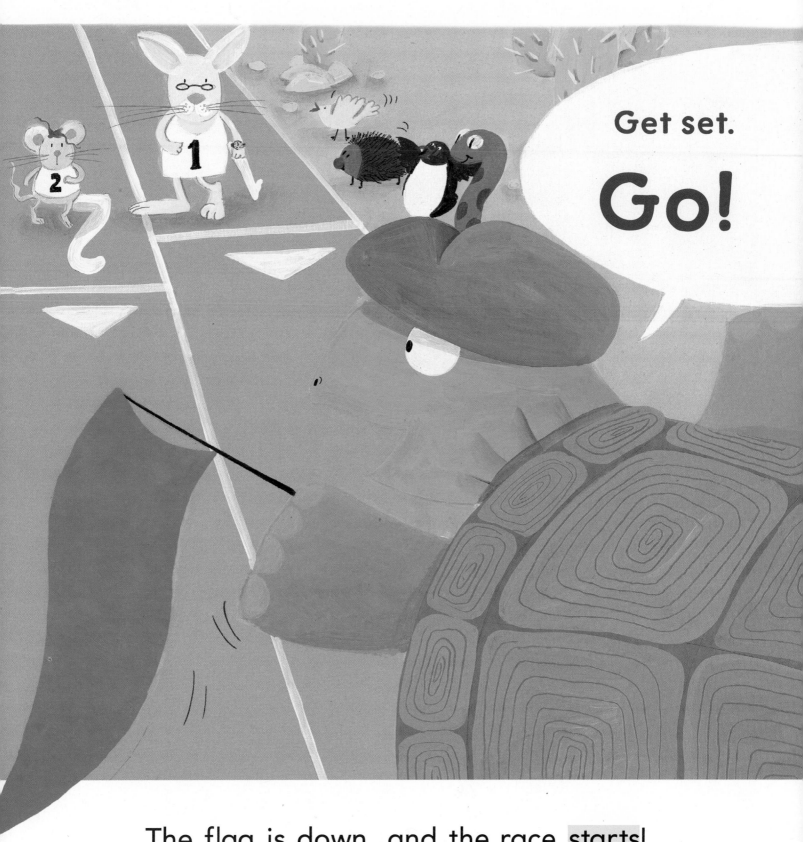

Get set.
Go!

The flag is down, and the race starts!
Many animals watch and clap.

133

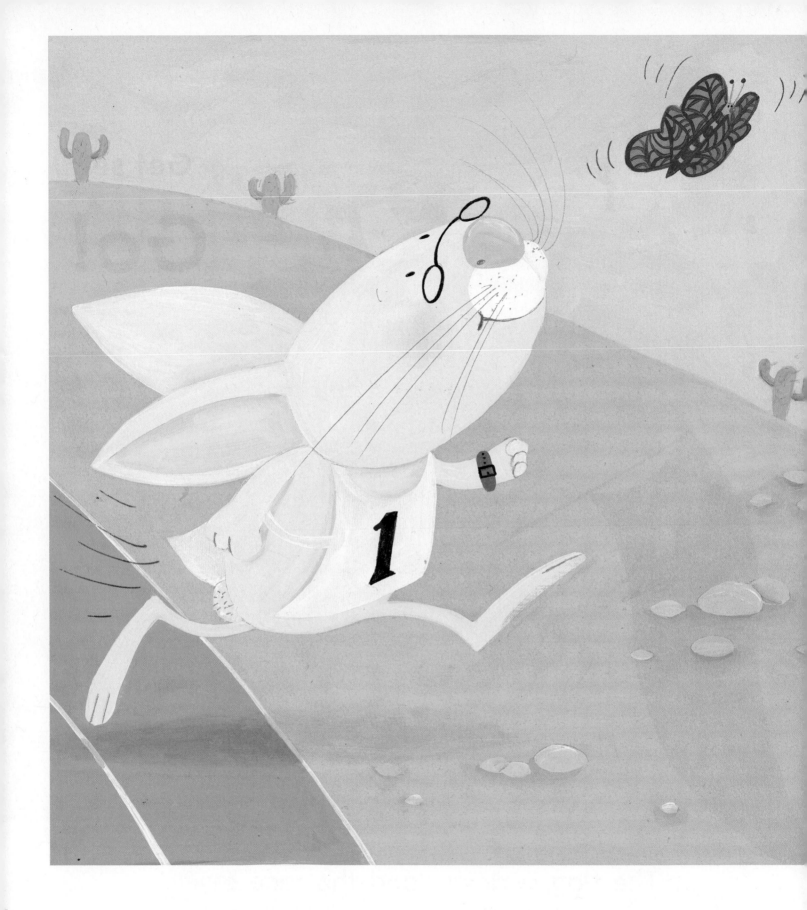

Cottontail does not get far.

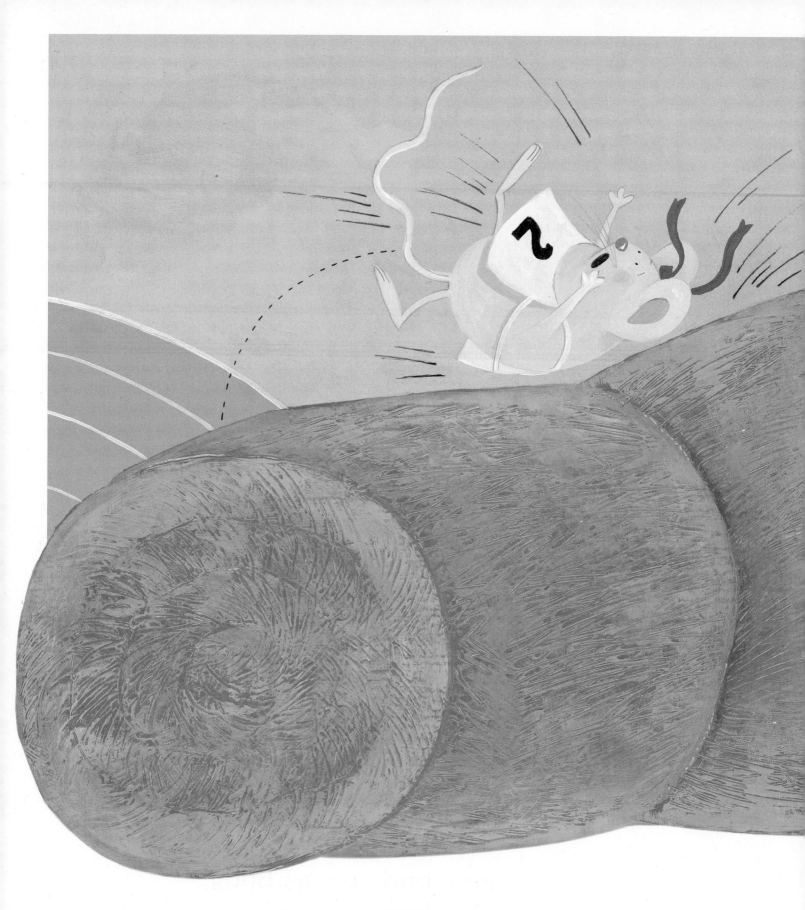

Rat falls into the hay.

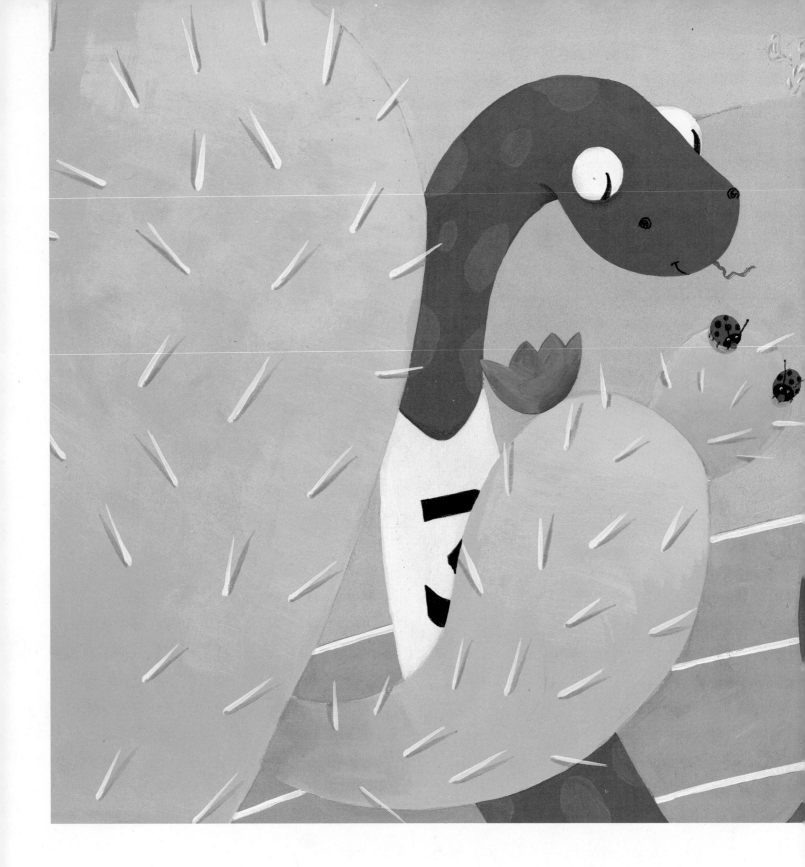

Snake stops and chases bugs.

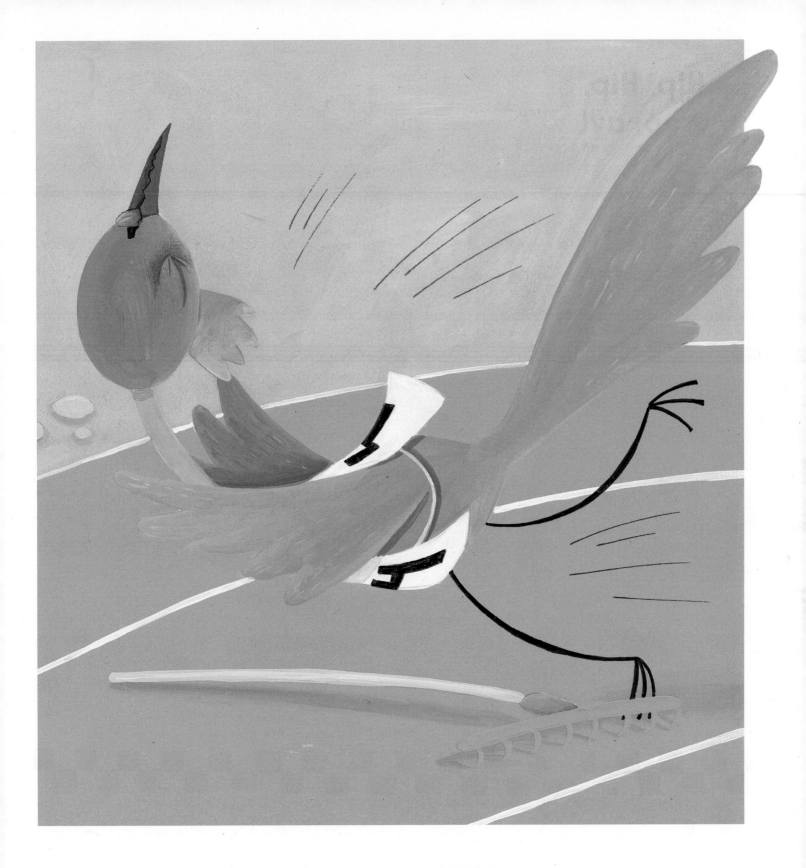

Roadrunner trips over a rake.

Who will win?

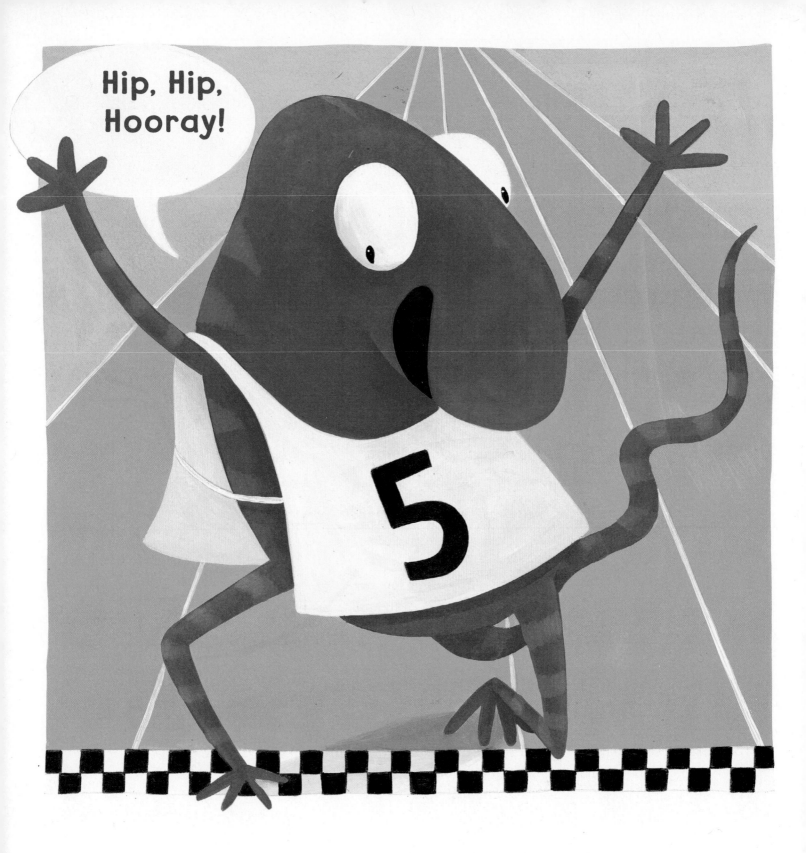

It's Red Lizard who wins!

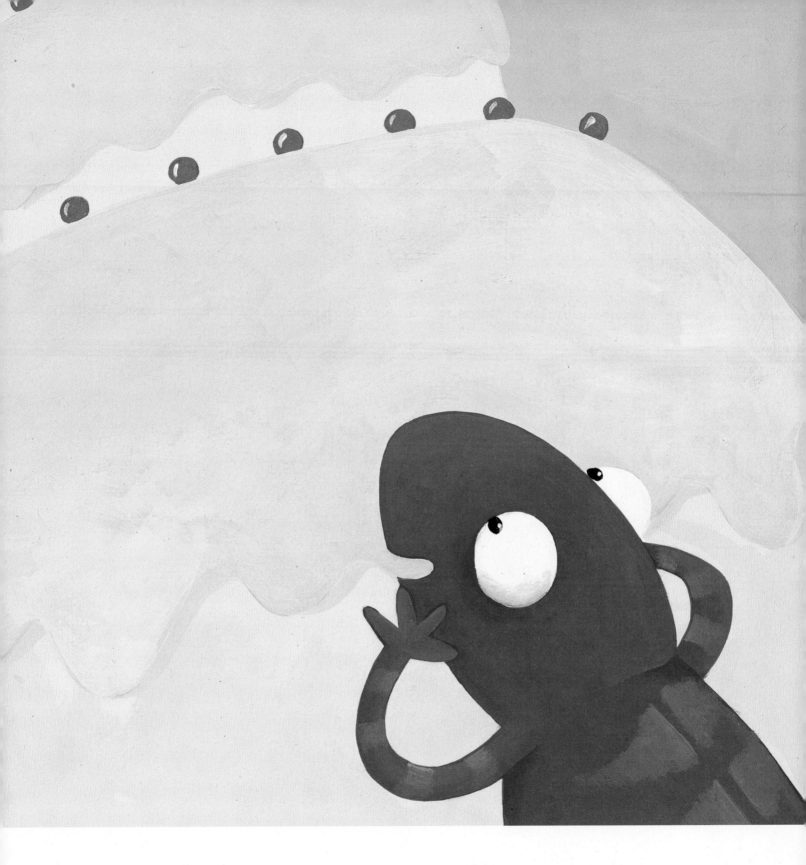

"Watch me eat this cake," he yells.
Red Lizard looks at his big cake.

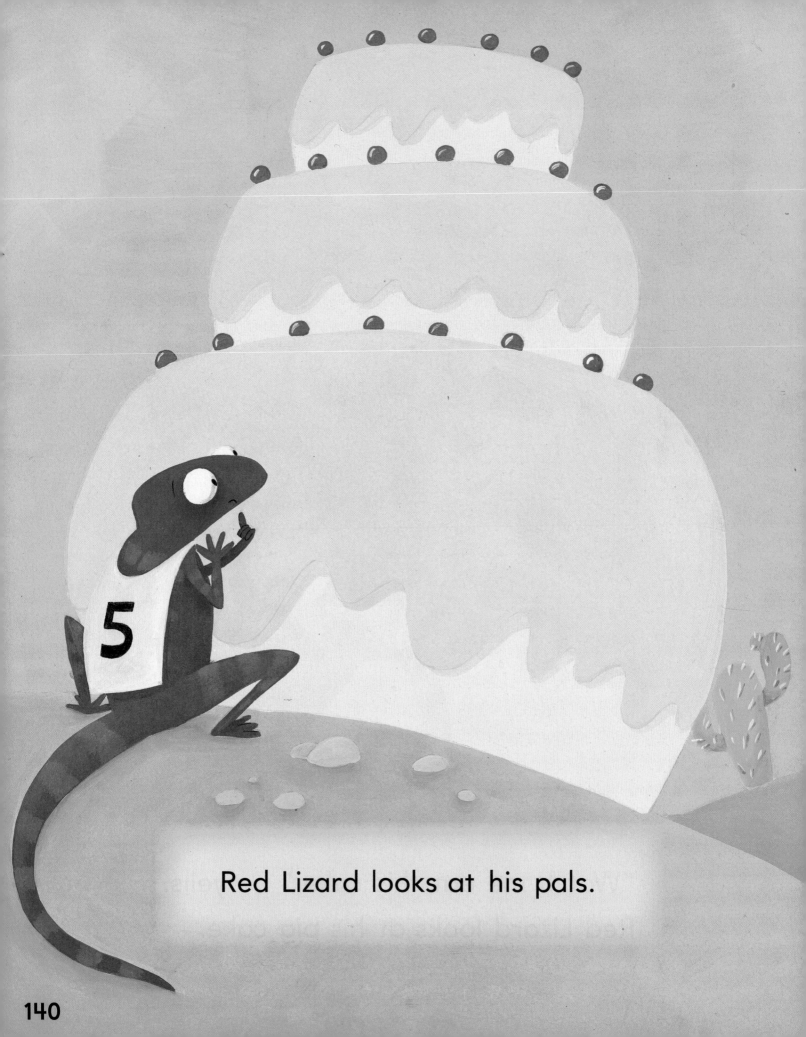

Red Lizard looks at his pals.

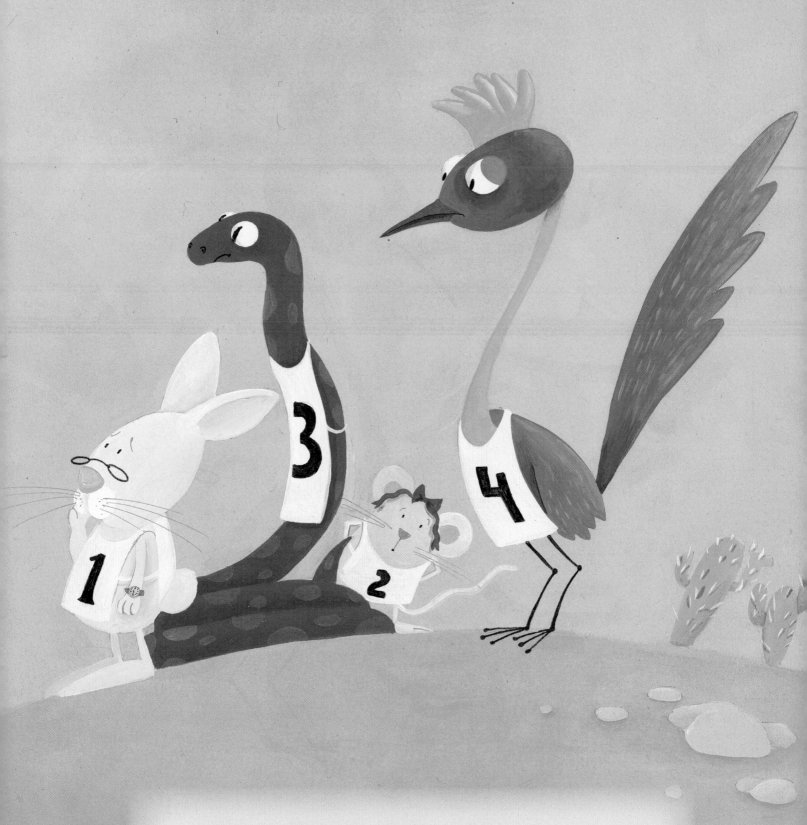

His pals like cake, too.
What will Red Lizard do now?

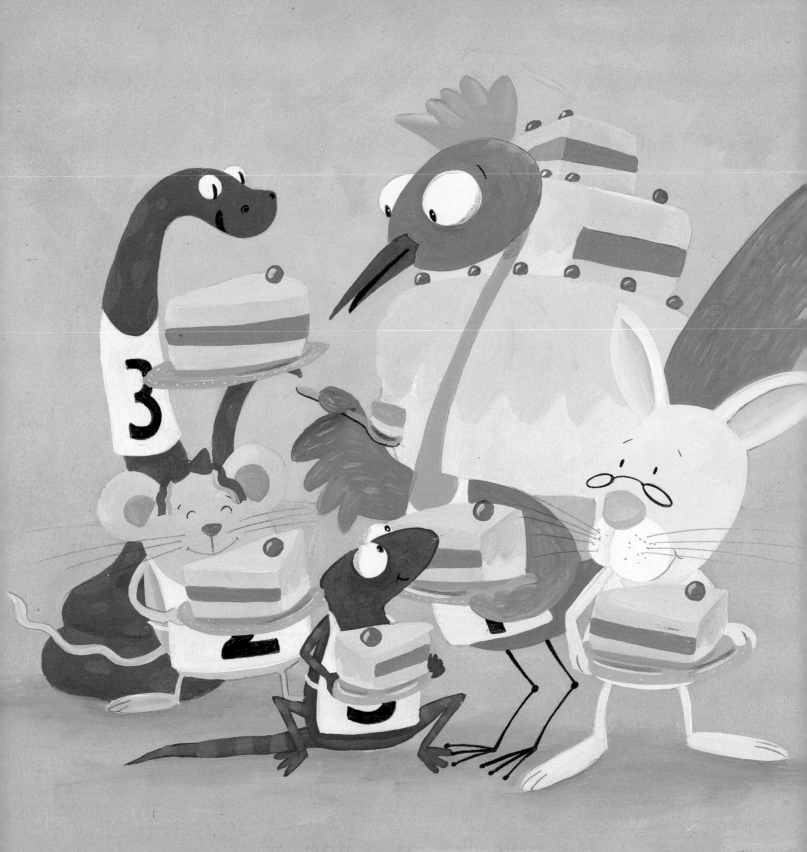

Red Lizard gets five plates.

He gets cake for his pals, too.

Hip, Hip, Hooray for Red Lizard!

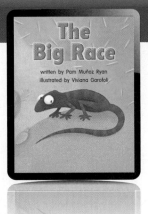

Dig Deeper

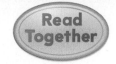

Read Together

Use Clues to Analyze the Text

Use these pages to learn about
Conclusions and Cause and Effect.
Then read **The Big Race** again.

Conclusions

You can use clues in **The Big Race** to
think about things the author does not say.
The author does not tell you why Cottontail
does not win. What do the pictures and
words show that help you make a smart
guess about why? What do you know
about races that helps you understand?
Use a chart to list clues and conclusions.

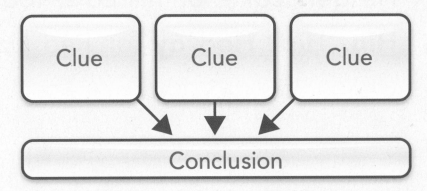

ELA RL.1.3, RL.1.7

Cause and Effect

Sometimes one event in a story causes another event to happen. As you read, ask yourself what happens and why.

In **The Big Race**, why doesn't Snake win? He does not win because he stops to chase bugs. Snake stopping is the **cause**. What happens after that? Snake loses the race. That is the **effect**.

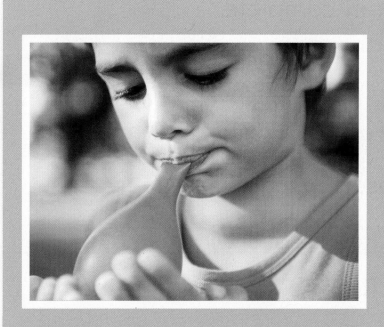 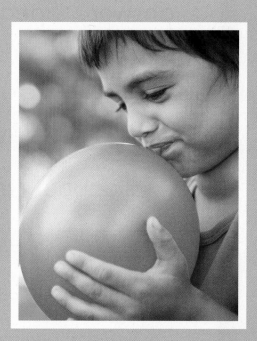

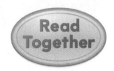

Your Turn

RETURN TO THE ESSENTIAL QUESTION

 Turn and Talk

Why is it important to have rules? Describe what happens to the animals in the story when they do not follow the rules. Use text evidence to help you answer. Speak in complete sentences.

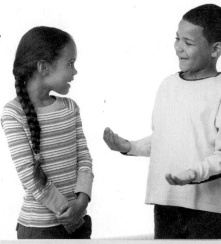

Classroom Conversation

Talk about these questions with your class.

1. Why does Red Lizard win the race?

2. How does Red Lizard feel when he wins?

3. Red Lizard shares the cake. Is this the right thing to do? Why or why not?

WRITE ABOUT READING ··············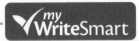

Response Choose a favorite character from **The Big Race**. Write sentences to give reasons why you like him or her. Use details from the story to explain your opinion.

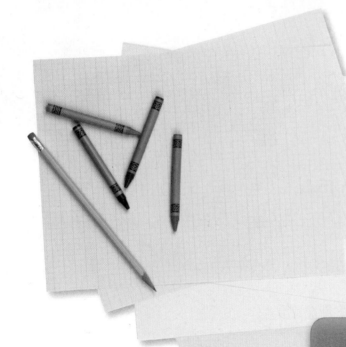

Writing Tip

Use **because** to tell why you think something is true.

INFORMATIONAL TEXT

Read Together

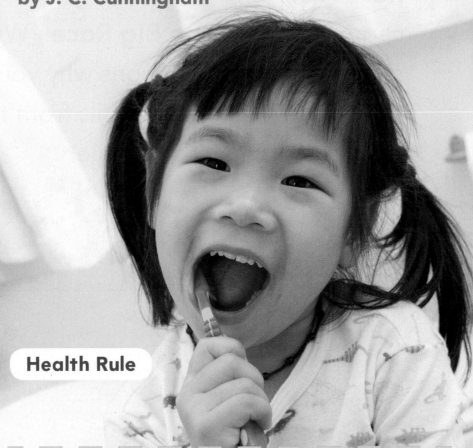

Rules and Laws

by J. C. Cunningham

Health Rule

☑ GENRE

Informational text gives facts on a topic. It can be from a textbook, article, or website. Look for facts about rules and laws as you read.

☑ TEXT FOCUS

Labels are words that tell about a picture or photo. They can name a part of a picture or the whole picture. What information do the labels in this selection give?

Rules

Who needs rules? We all do! Some rules keep us safe and healthy. Some rules help us learn. There are even rules to help us have fun!

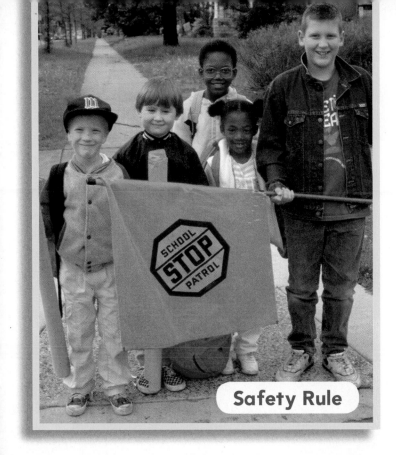

Safety Rule

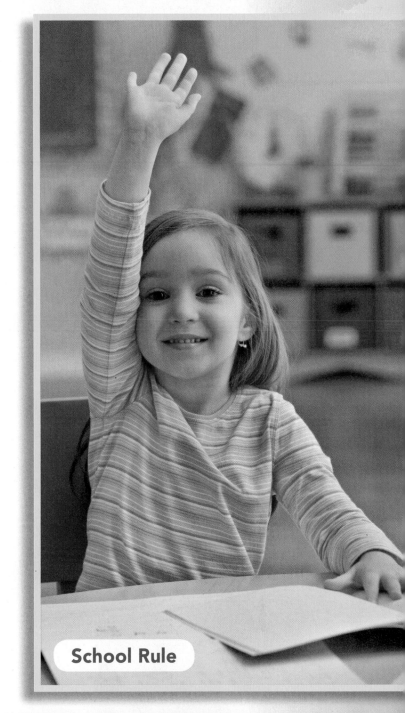

School Rule

Can you find the child following this rule?
Raise your hand to speak.
What other rules are the children following? What could happen if they did not follow the rules?

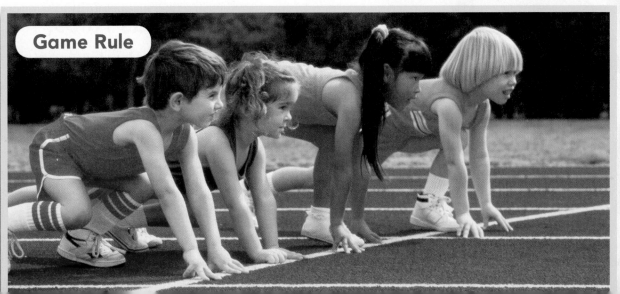

Game Rule

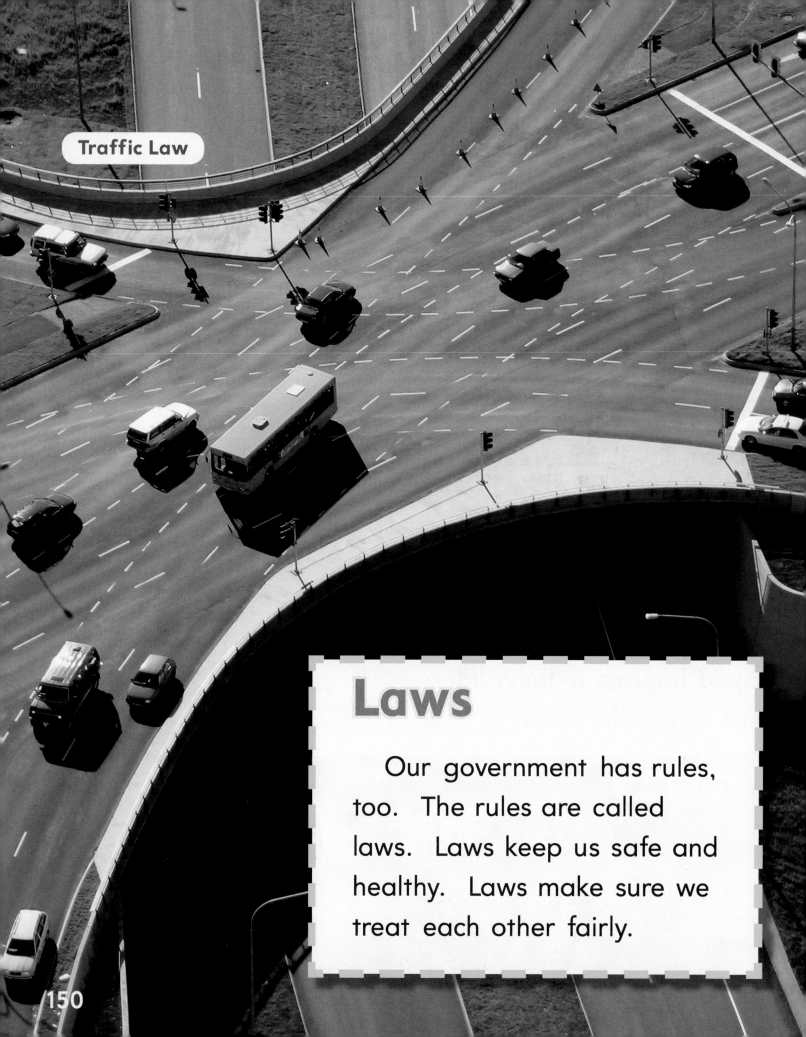

Laws

Our government has rules, too. The rules are called laws. Laws keep us safe and healthy. Laws make sure we treat each other fairly.

EMPLOYEES MUST WASH HANDS

Can you find the person who obeyed this law? Employees must wash hands. What other laws do you think the pictures show?

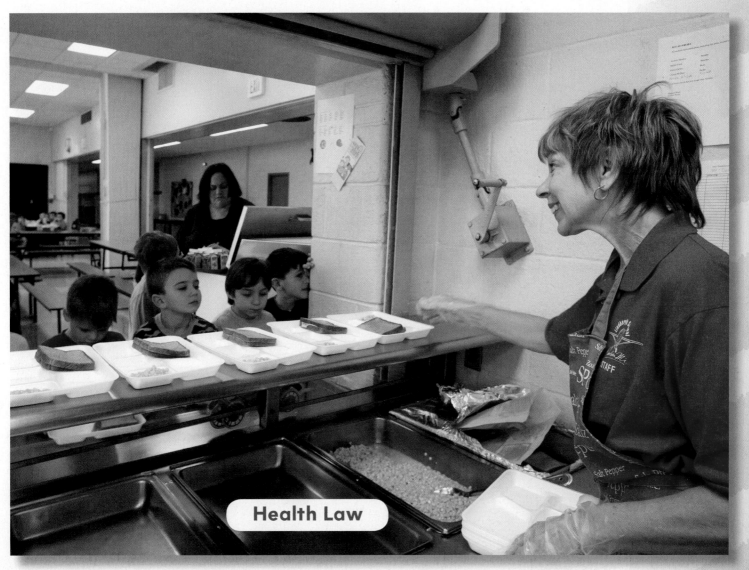

Health Law

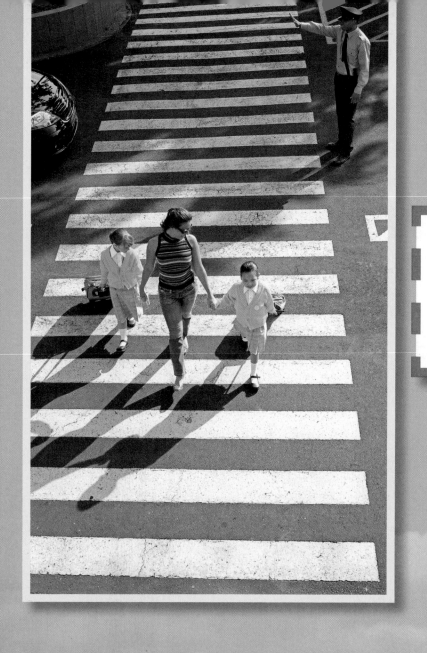

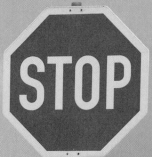

Laws help us to be good neighbors and good citizens.

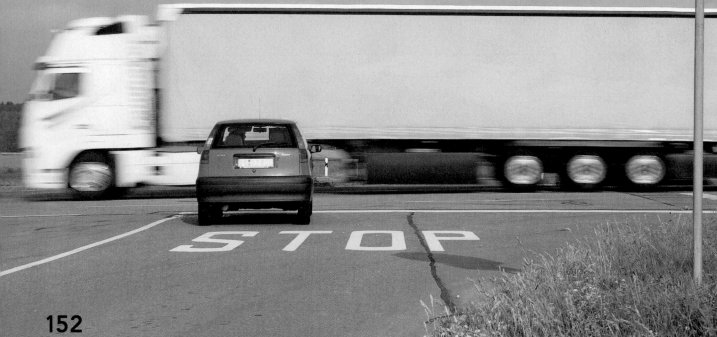

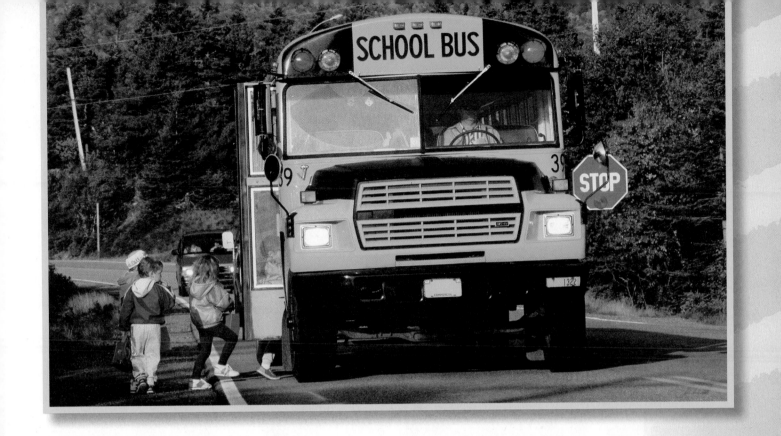

What laws do you think these people are following? How do the laws help?

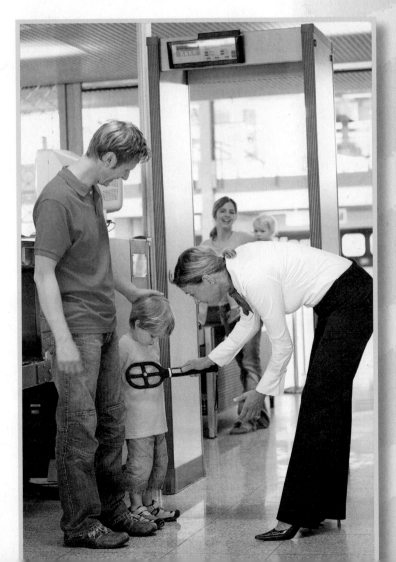

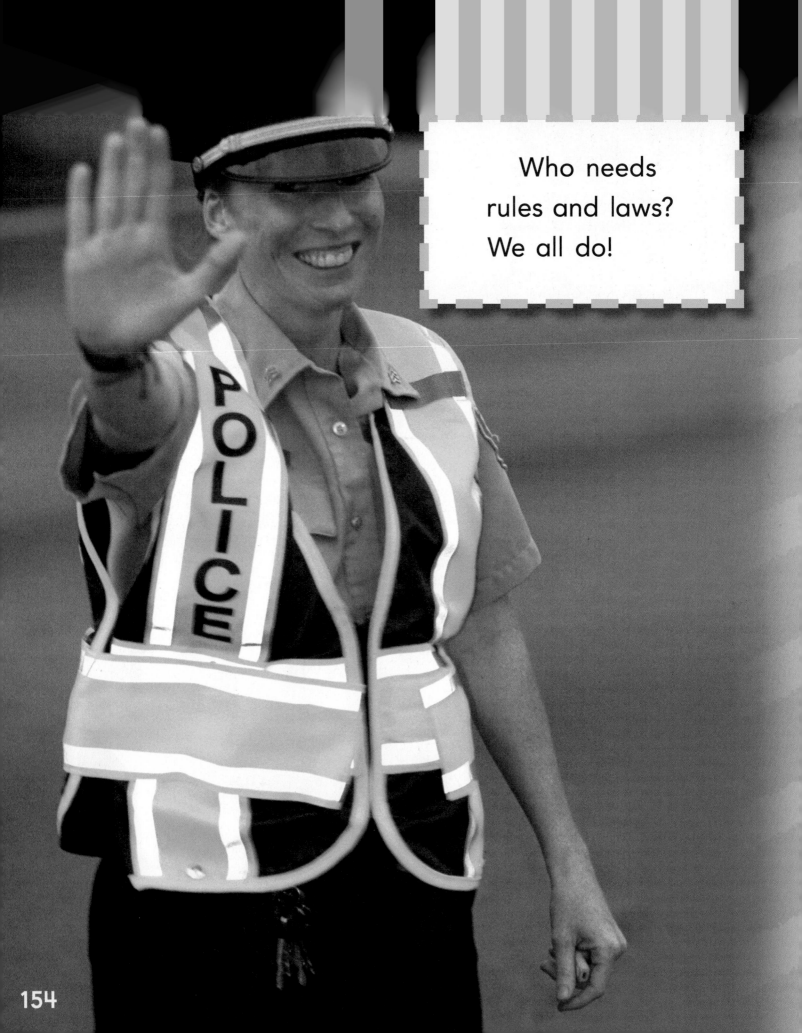

Who needs rules and laws? We all do!

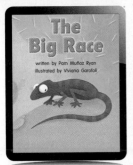
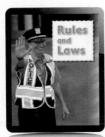

The Big Race
written by Pam Muñoz Ryan
illustrated by Viviana Garofoli

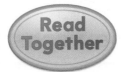

Rules and Laws

Compare Texts

Read Together

TEXT TO TEXT

Compare Stories Think about the selections. Which is real and which is make-believe? Tell how you know. Take turns sharing evidence with a partner.

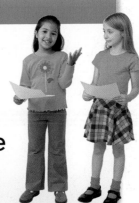

TEXT TO SELF

Write a List Write a list of rules the runners should follow in **The Big Race**. Tell why the rules make sense.

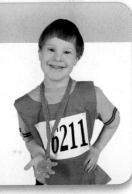

TEXT TO WORLD

Map a Race Course Pretend you will run a race through your neighborhood. Where does the race begin? Where is the finish line? Draw a map.

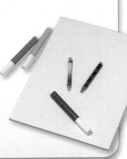

ELA RL.1.5, W.1.2, SL.1.1a, SL.1.1b

Grammar

Verbs and Time Some **verbs** tell what is happening now. Some verbs tell what happened in the past. Add **ed** to most verbs to tell about the past.

Read
Together

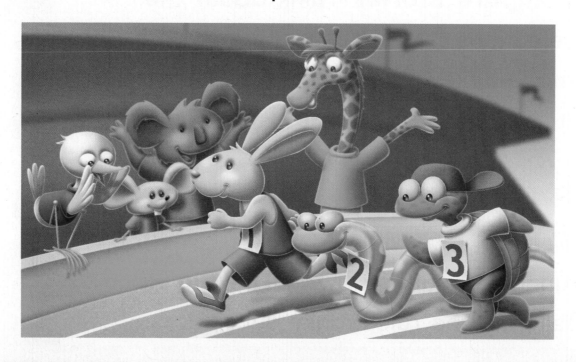

Now	In the Past
The animals **watch** the race now.	The animals **watch<u>ed</u>** the race yesterday.
They **cheer** for their friends.	They **cheer<u>ed</u>** for their friends.

156 ELA L.1.1e

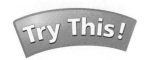

Work with a partner. One partner reads aloud a sentence. The other partner finds the verb. Together, write the verb to tell about the past. Take turns.

1. The runners look at the flag.

2. They start the race.

3. Some racers jump high.

4. They finish the race quickly.

5. The winners pick prizes.

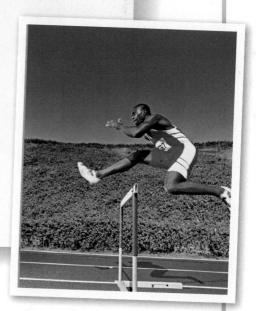

Connect Grammar to Writing

When you proofread your writing, be sure each verb tells clearly if something is happening now or in the past.

Informative Writing

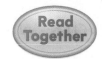

✓ **Evidence** A good **report** needs facts! Before you write, find facts to answer the question you wrote about your topic. Lena found information about lizards. She took notes to remind her of the facts.

Read Together

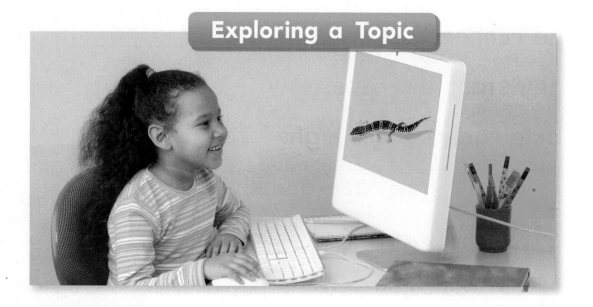

Exploring a Topic

Prewriting Checklist

✓ Did I write a good question about my topic?

✓ Will my notes help me remember the facts?

✓ Did I use good sources for information?

Look for facts in Lena's notes. Then record your own notes. Use the Checklist.

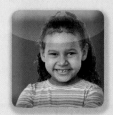

Planning Chart

My Question
What do real lizards do?

Fact 1
change color

Fact 2
run fast on back legs

Fact 3
puff up to look big

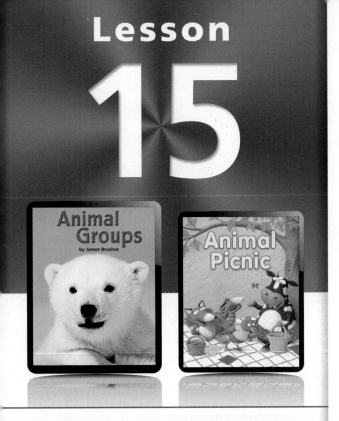

Animal Groups
by James Bruchac

Animal Picnic

🔍 LANGUAGE DETECTIVE

Talk About Words
Nouns are words that name people, animals, things, or places. Work with a partner. Find the blue words that are nouns. Use them in complete sentences. Add details to your sentences to tell more.

Words to Know

Read Together

▶ Read each **Context Card.**

▶ Ask a question that uses one of the blue words.

---

1 **bird**

An eagle is a bird with big, strong wings.

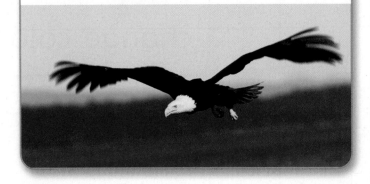

---

2 **fly**

Bats are mammals that are able to fly.

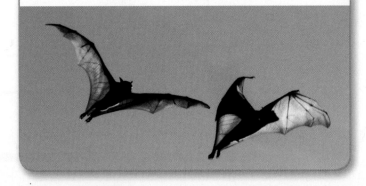

3 **both**

The lizard has **both** stripes and spots.

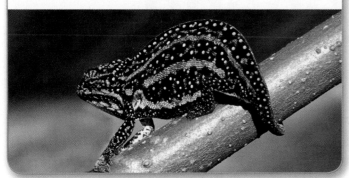

4 **long**

This kangaroo has a **long** tail.

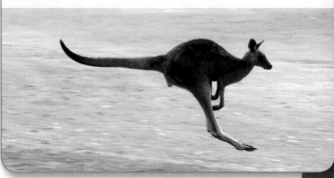

5 **eyes**

This dog has blue **eyes**.

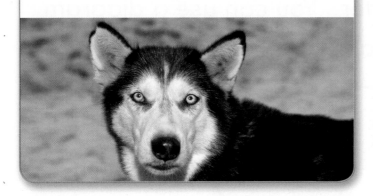

6 **or**

Ducks can either swim **or** fly.

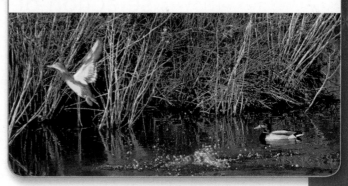

7 **those**

Those fish are not the same colors.

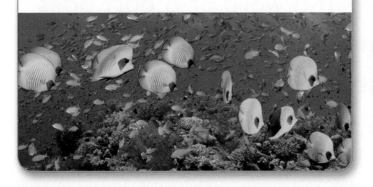

8 **walk**

The elephants **walk** together in a group.

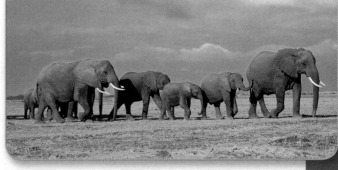

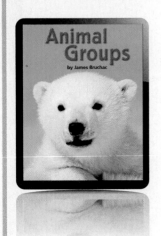

Animal Groups
by James Bruchac

Read and Comprehend

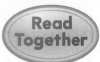

☑ **TARGET SKILL**

Compare and Contrast When you **compare**, tell how things are alike. When you **contrast**, tell how things are different. Think about how things are alike and different to understand a selection better. You can use a diagram to **compare** and **contrast** two things.

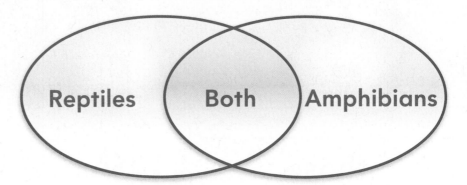

Reptiles   Both   Amphibians

☑ **TARGET STRATEGY**

Monitor/Clarify If a word or a part does not make sense, you can ask questions, reread, or use the pictures for help.

Animals

All birds have wings, but not all birds fly. Some animals have legs and some do not. Fish live in water all the time. Other animals live on land.

You will read about how animals are alike and different in **Animal Groups.**

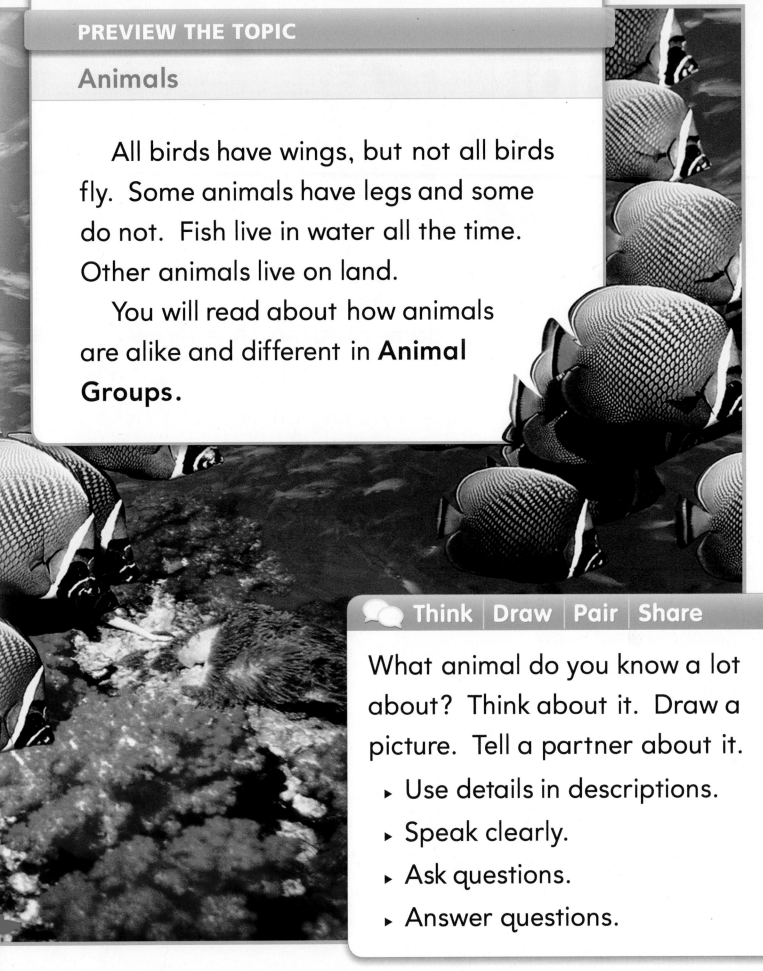

Think | Draw | Pair | Share

What animal do you know a lot about? Think about it. Draw a picture. Tell a partner about it.

- ▶ Use details in descriptions.
- ▶ Speak clearly.
- ▶ Ask questions.
- ▶ Answer questions.

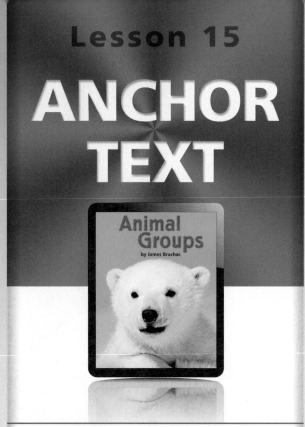

Informational text gives facts about a topic. As you read, look for:

▶ information and facts in the words

▶ photos that show the real world

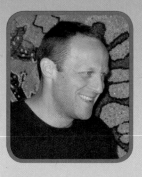

Meet the Author

James Bruchac

James Bruchac has many interests. He is a writer, a storyteller, an animal tracker, and a wilderness guide. Together with his father, Joseph Bruchac, he wrote the books **How Chipmunk Got His Stripes** and **Turtle's Race with Beaver**.

Animal Groups

written by James Bruchac

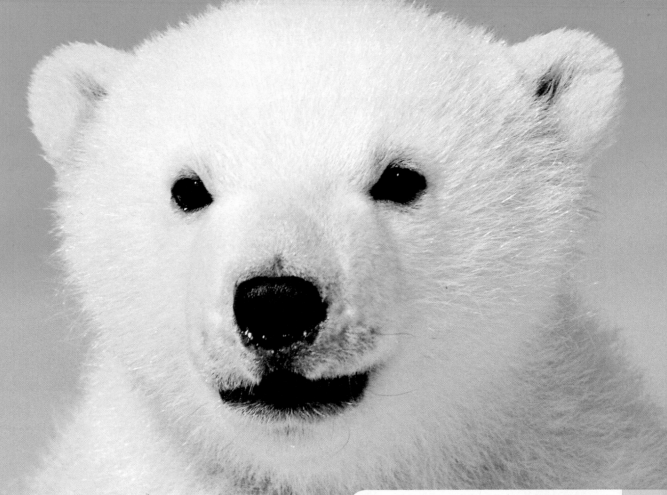

ESSENTIAL QUESTION

What makes birds different from mammals?

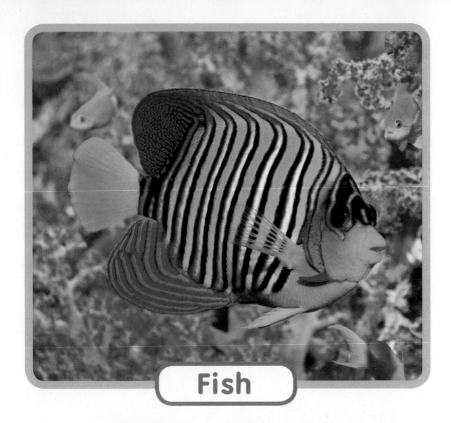

Fish

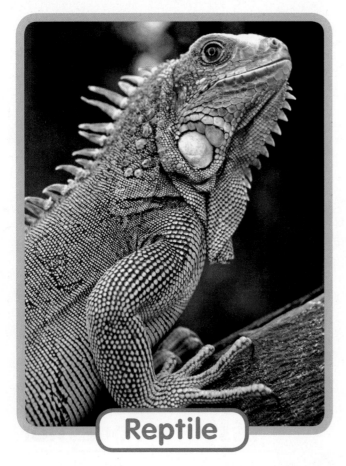

Reptile

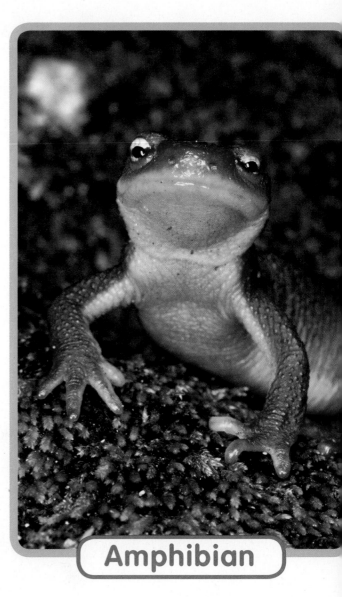

Amphibian

Let's take a look at five animal groups.

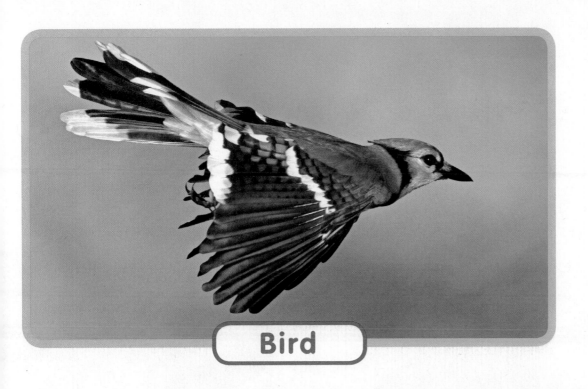

Bird

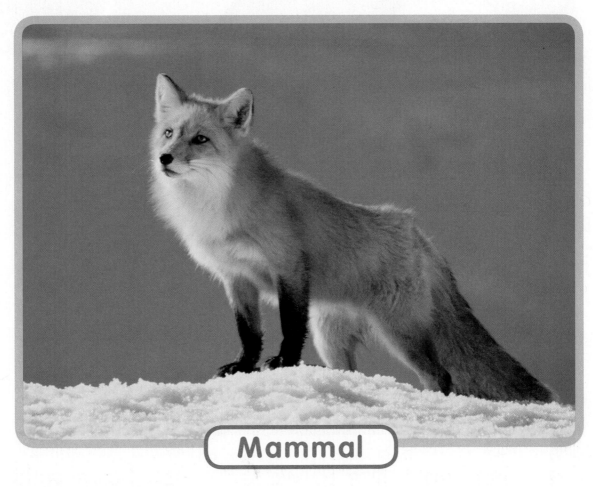

Mammal

How are animals in a group the same?

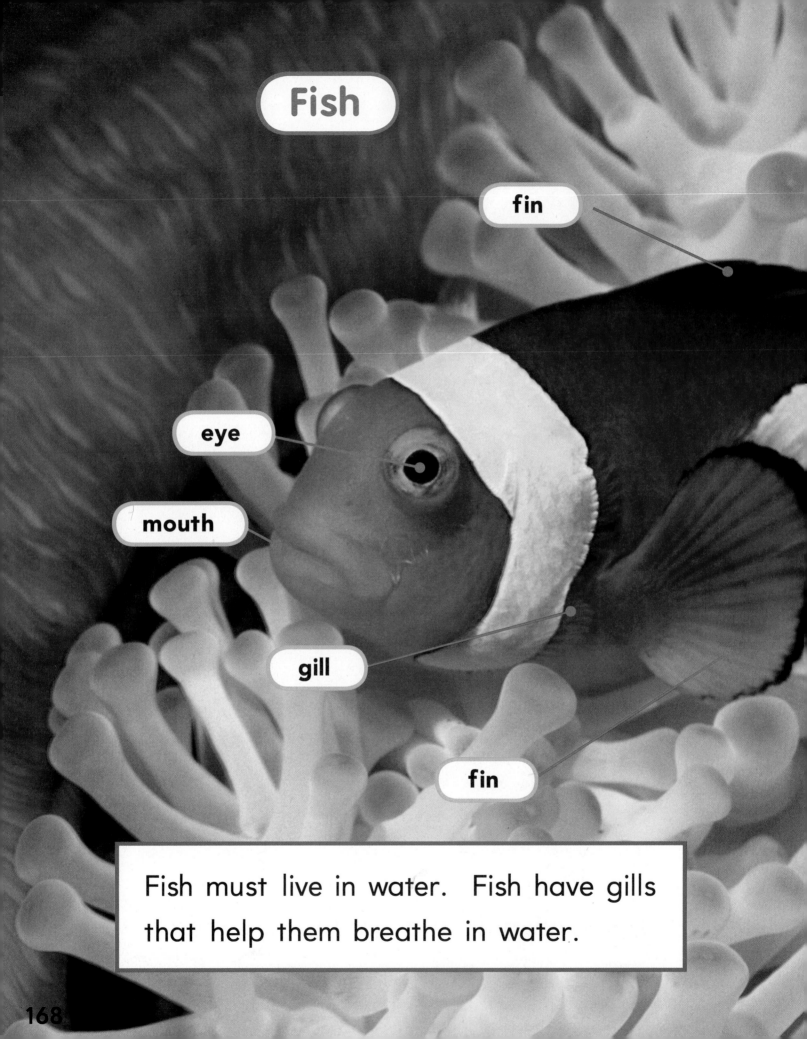

Fish

fin

eye

mouth

gill

fin

Fish must live in water. Fish have gills
that help them breathe in water.

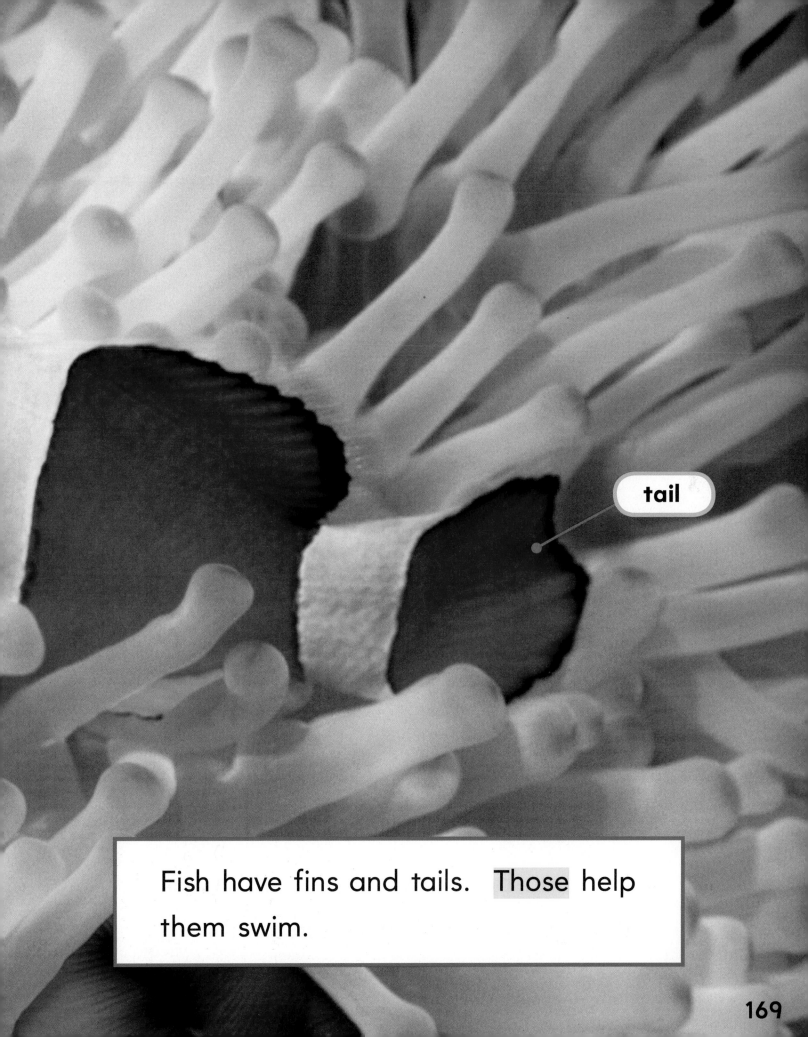

tail

Fish have fins and tails. Those help them swim.

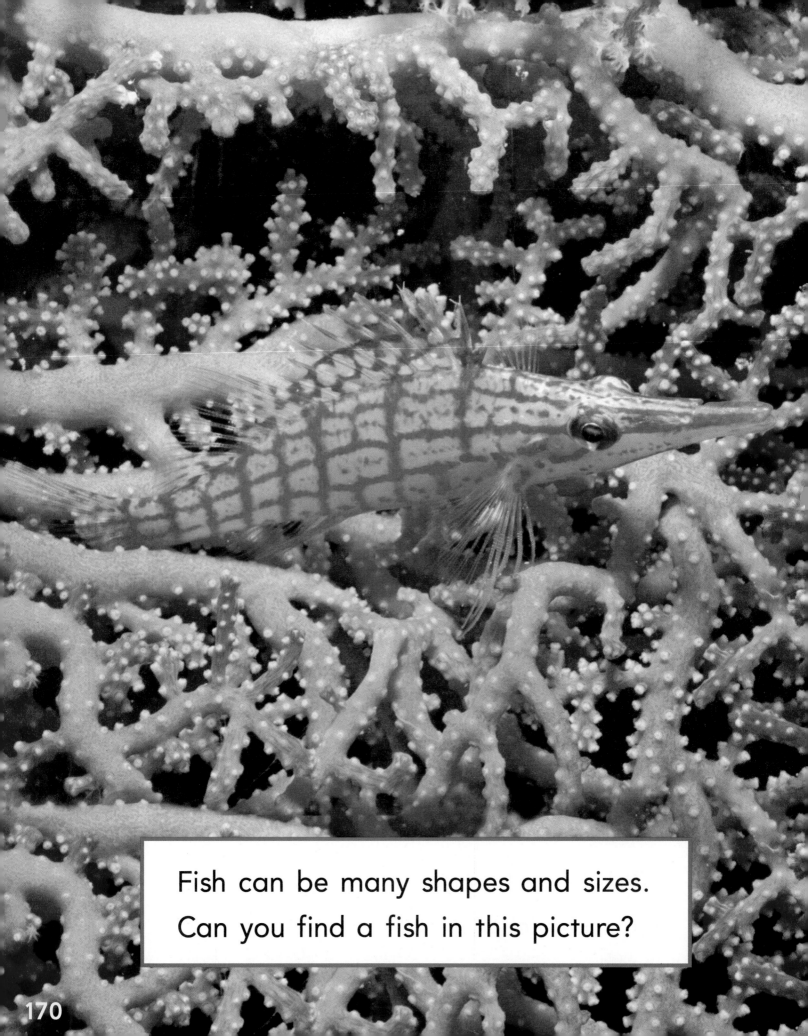

Fish can be many shapes and sizes.
Can you find a fish in this picture?

Reptiles

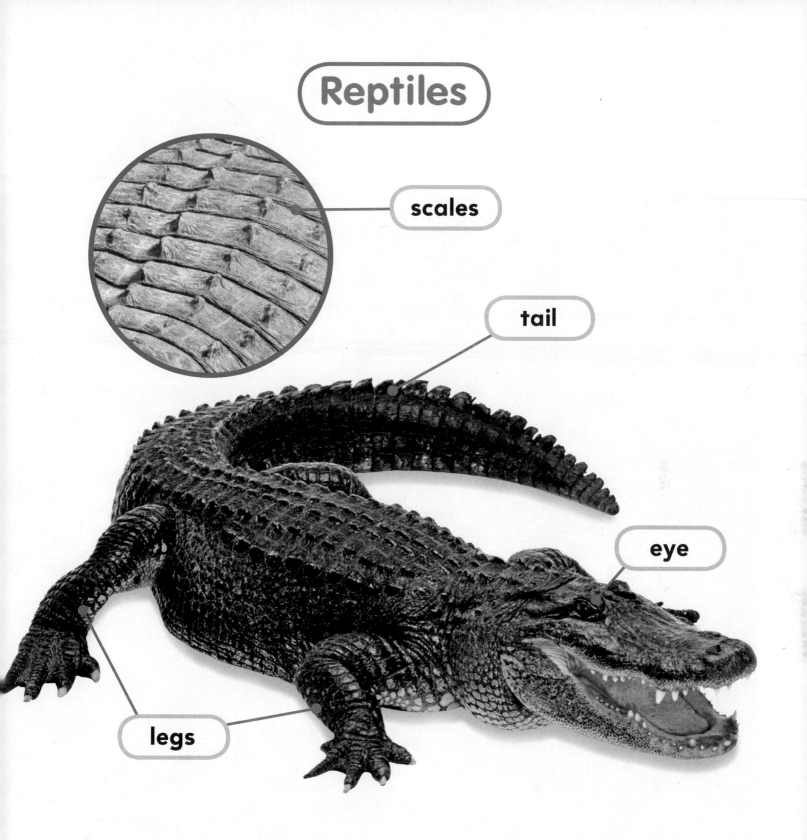

scales

tail

eye

legs

Reptiles can live on land. Some like to be in
water. Reptiles have scales on their skin.

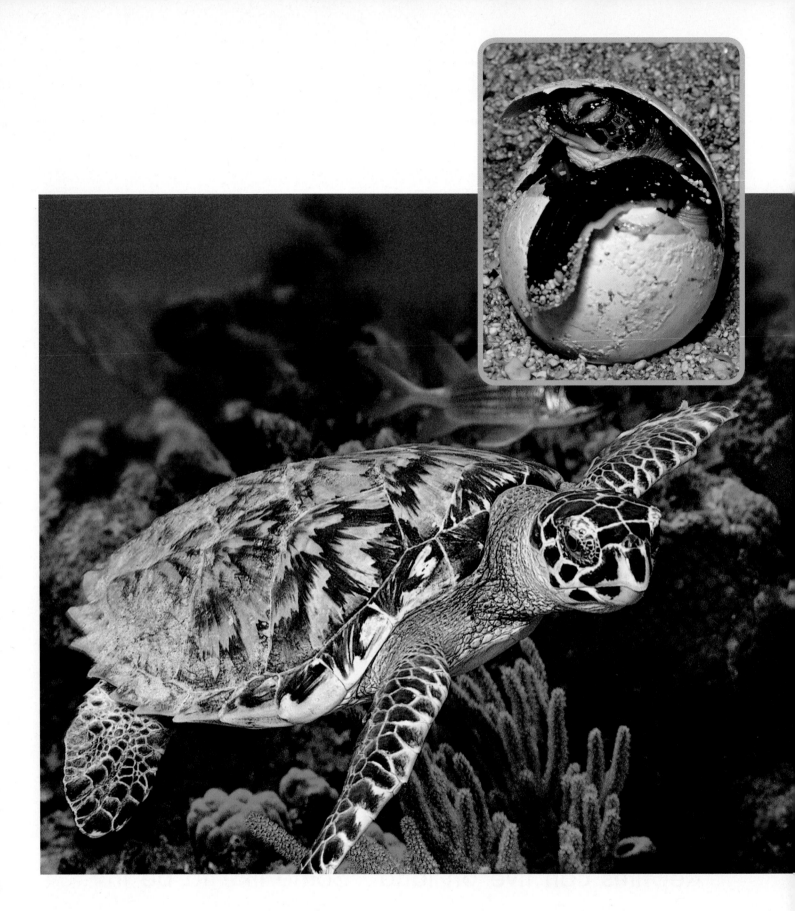

Many reptiles hatch from eggs.

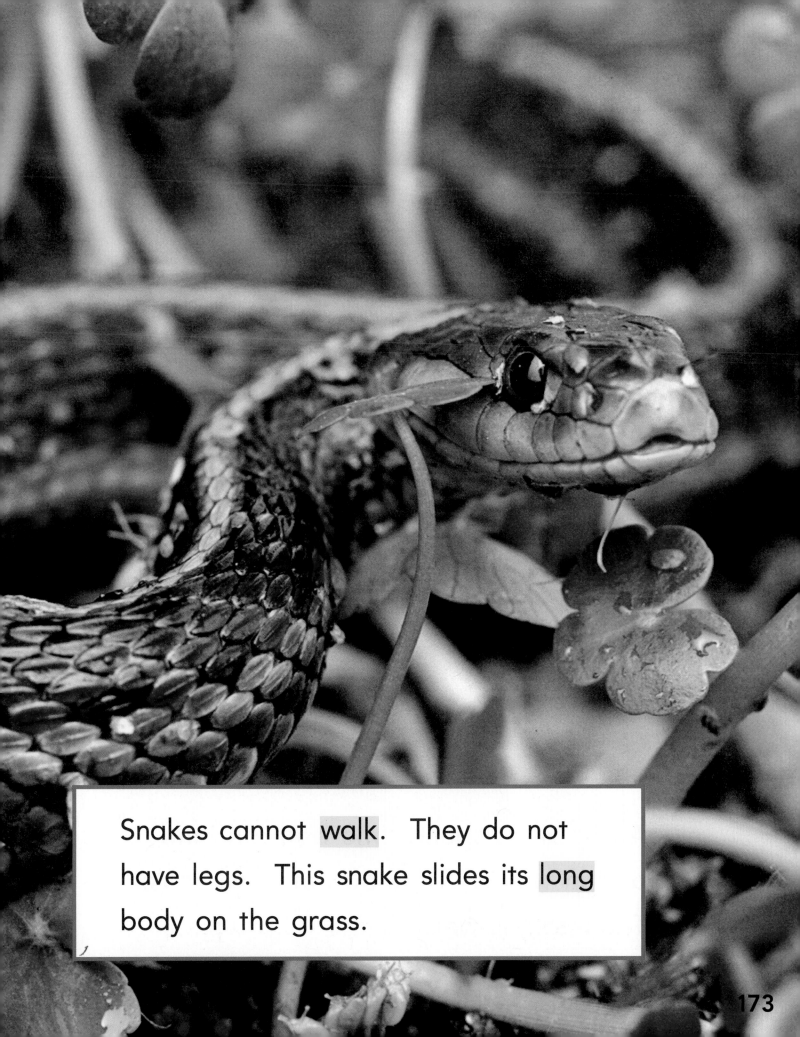

Snakes cannot walk. They do not
have legs. This snake slides its long
body on the grass.

Amphibians

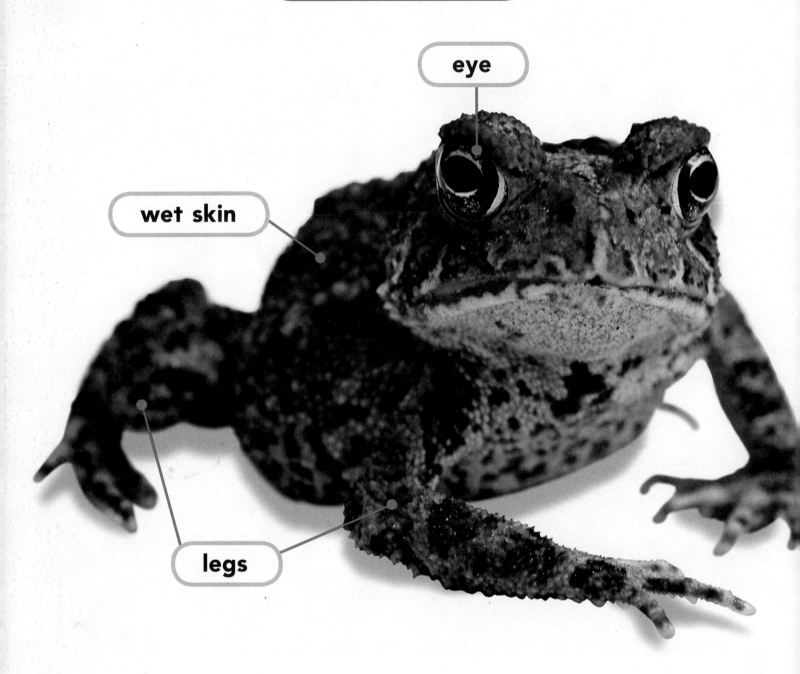

eye

wet skin

legs

Amphibians spend time both on land
and in water. They do not have scales.
Their skin is wet.

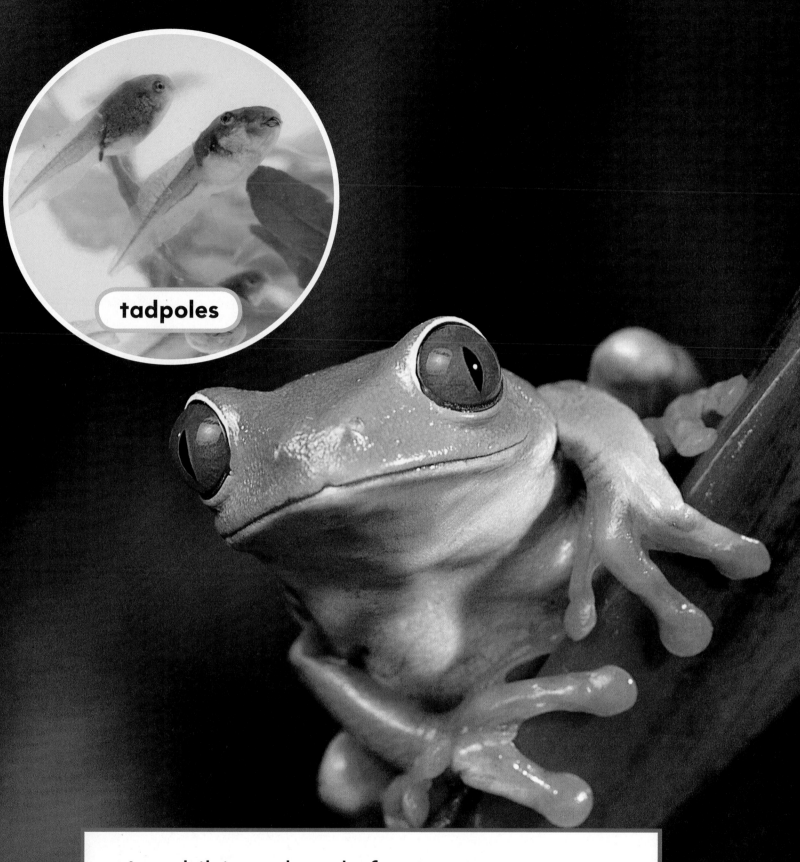

tadpoles

Amphibians hatch from eggs.
Tadpoles hatch and grow to be frogs.

Birds

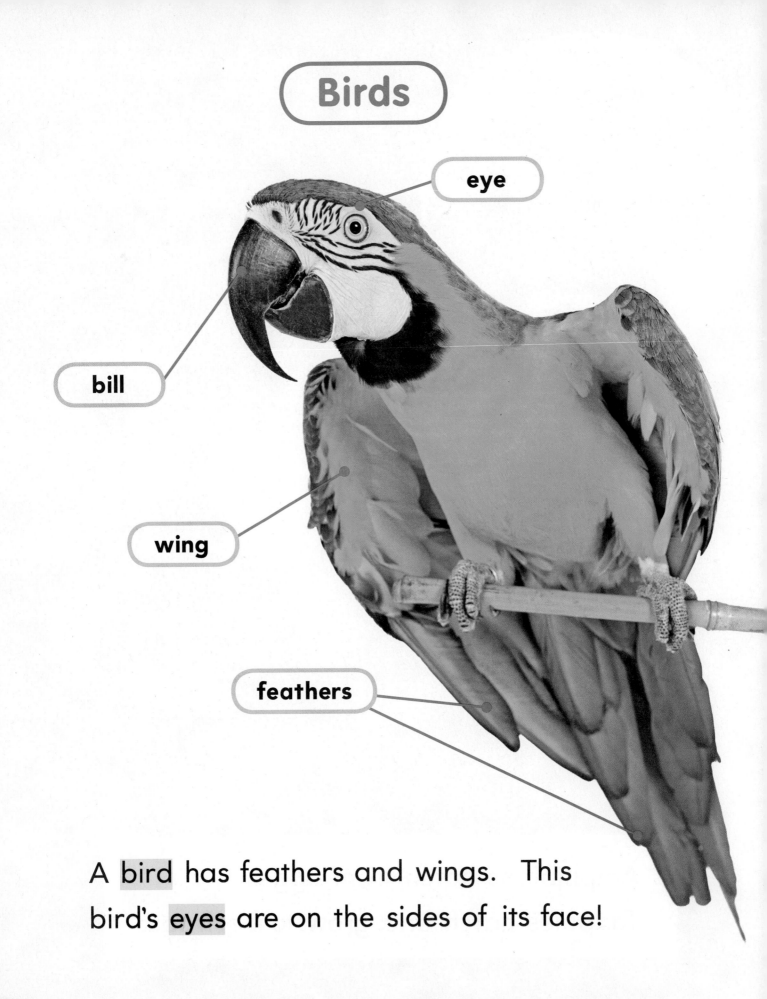

eye

bill

wing

feathers

A **bird** has feathers and wings. This bird's **eyes** are on the sides of its face!

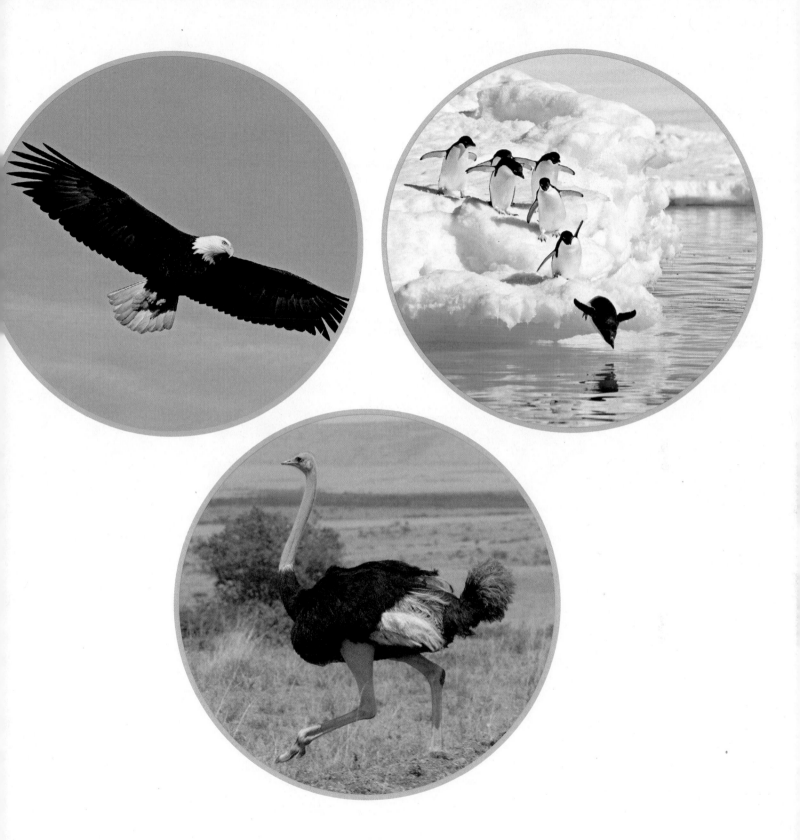

Many birds can fly. Some can run
or swim fast.

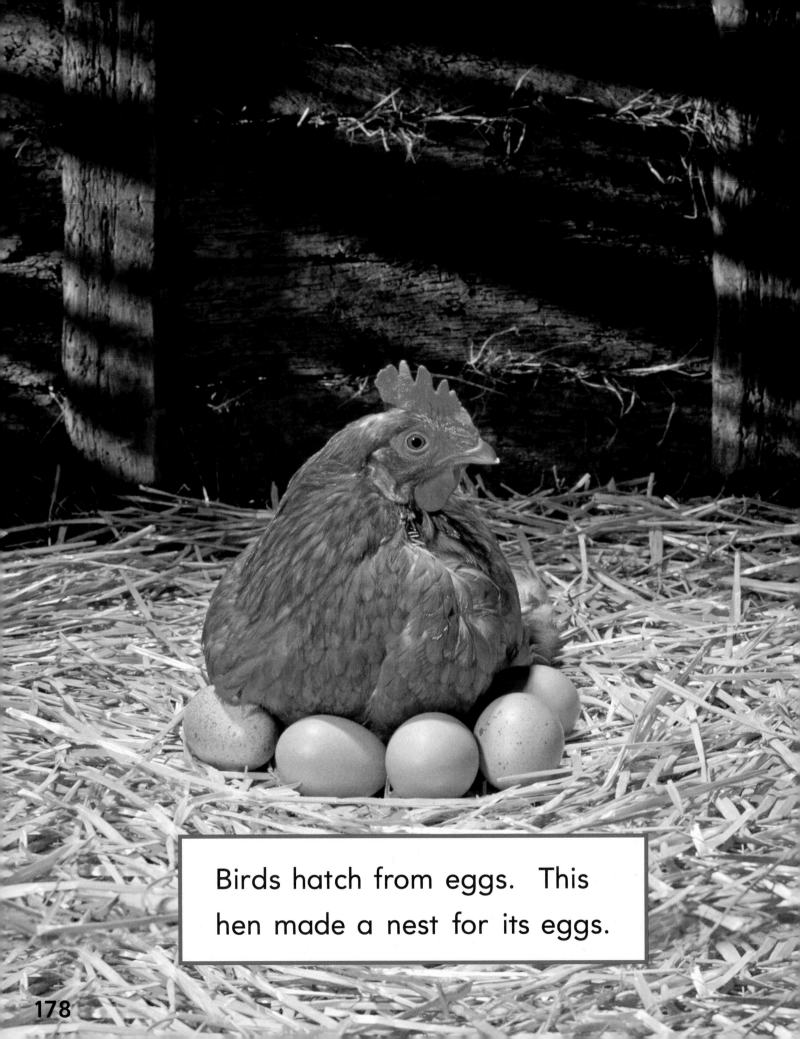

Birds hatch from eggs. This hen made a nest for its eggs.

Mammals

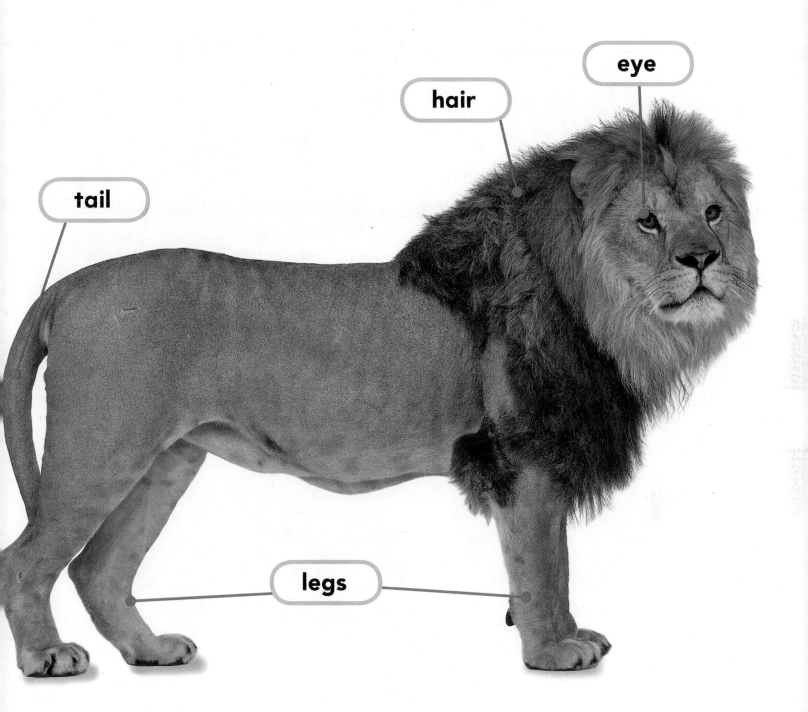

eye

hair

tail

legs

Mammals can be many shapes and sizes.
They have hair on their skin.

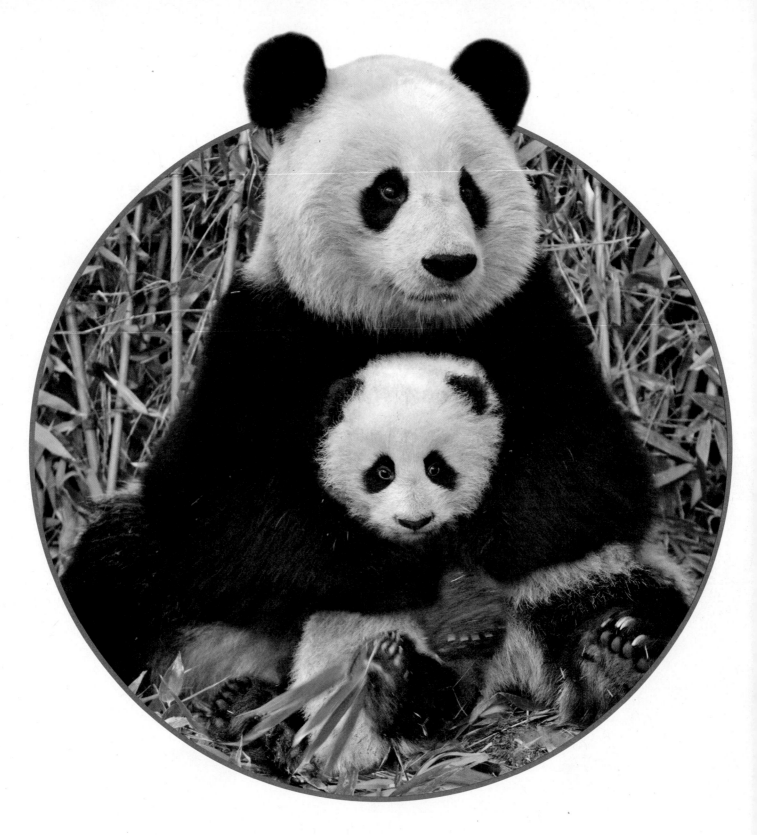

A mammal mom can
make milk for its baby.

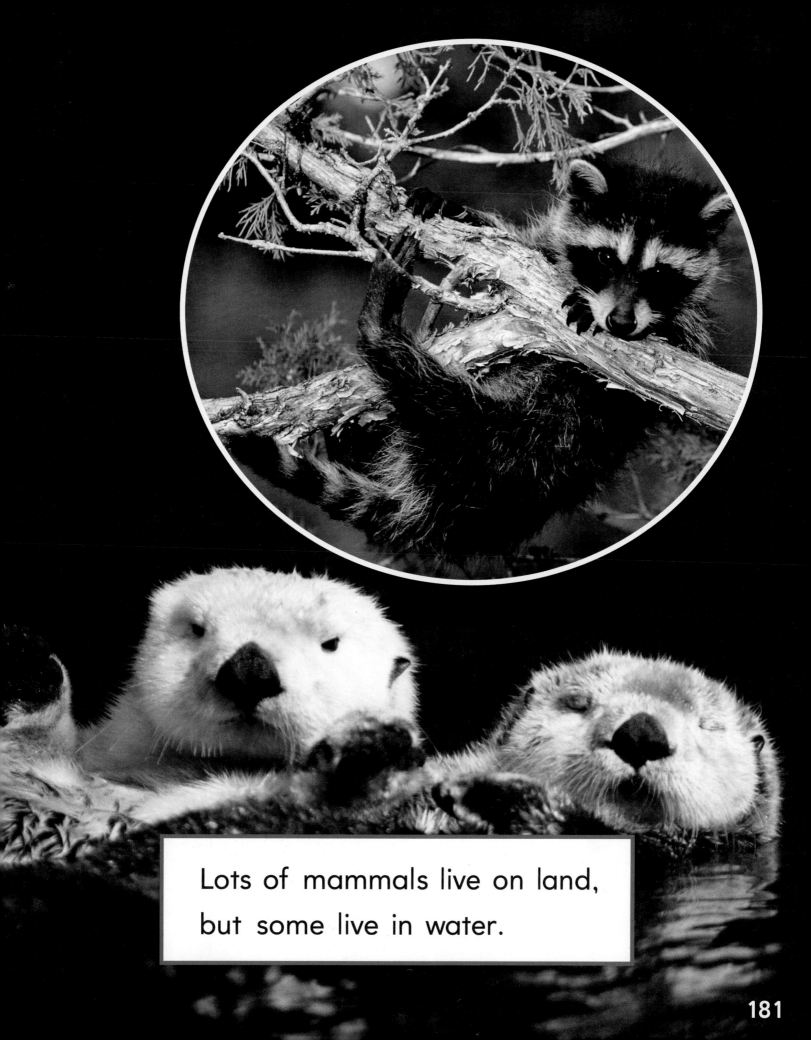

Lots of mammals live on land,
but some live in water.

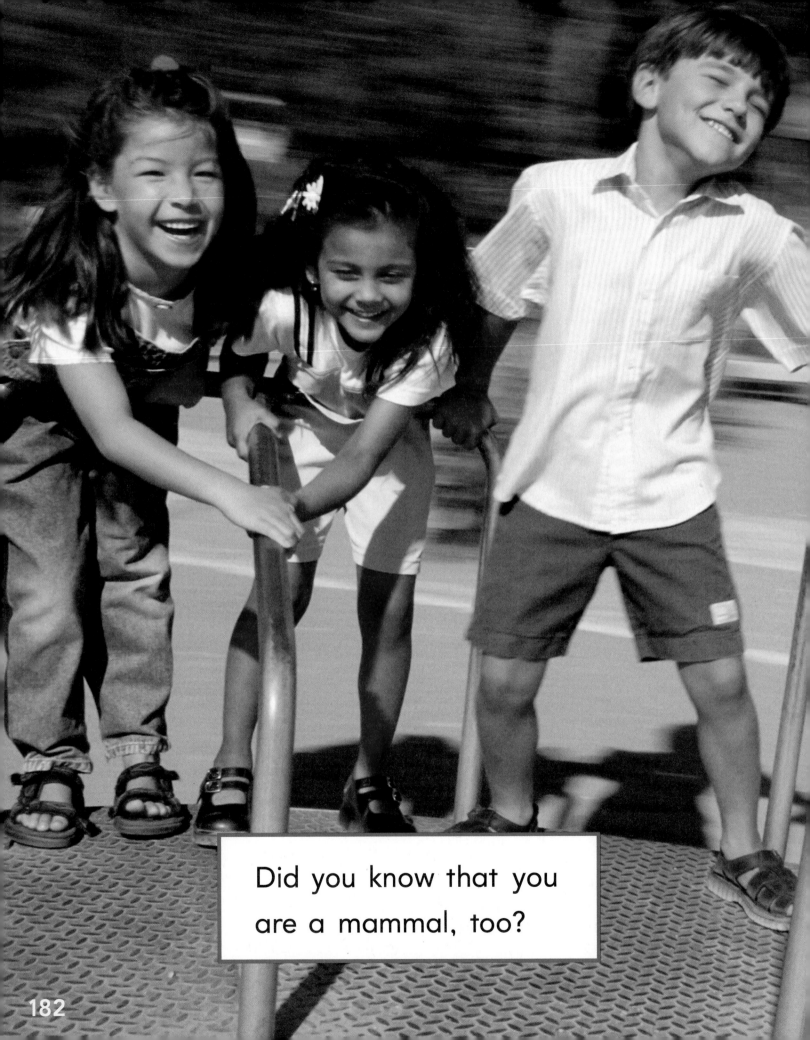

Did you know that you are a mammal, too?

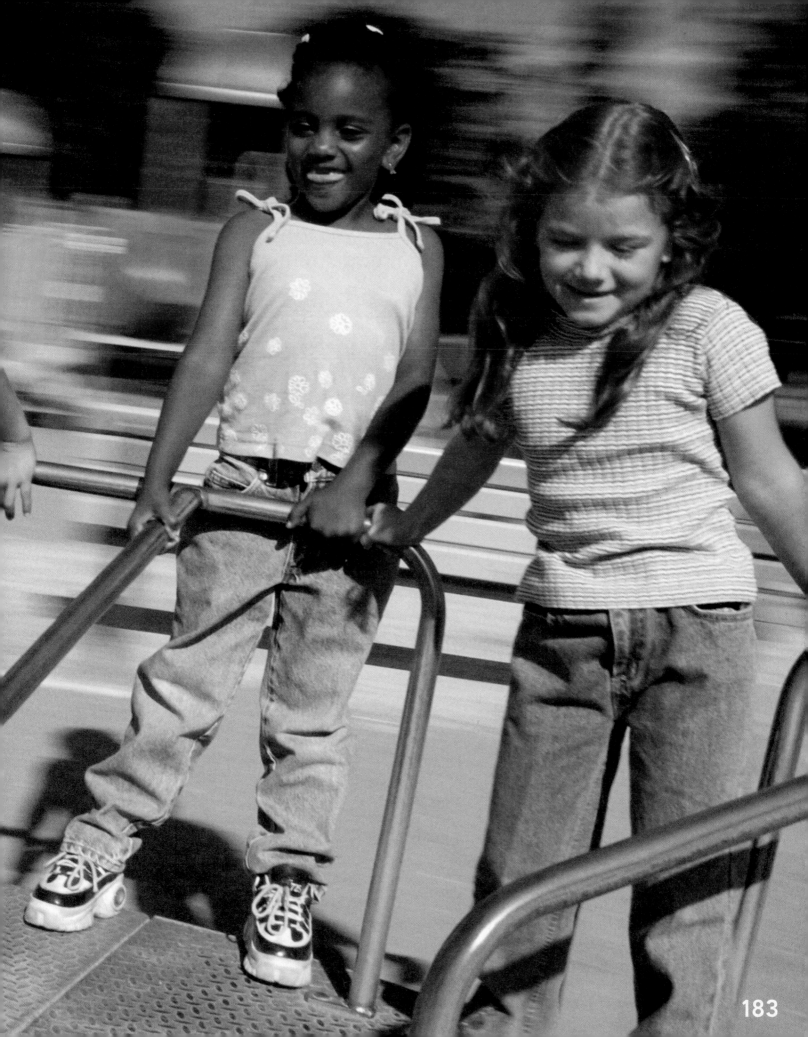

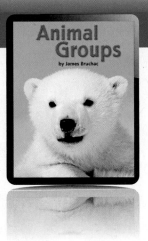

Dig Deeper

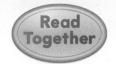
Read Together

Use Clues to Analyze the Text

Use these pages to learn about Compare and Contrast and Text and Graphic Features. Then read **Animal Groups** again.

Compare and Contrast

In **Animal Groups**, you learned what makes animals in a group the same and different. Think about reptiles and amphibians. **Compare** the groups to tell how they are alike. **Contrast** the groups to tell how they are different. Use a diagram to compare and contrast groups.

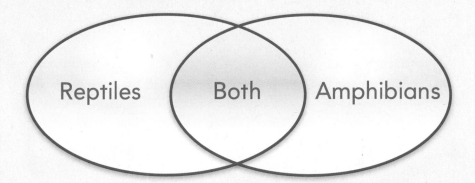

Reptiles · Both · Amphibians

Text and Graphic Features

Authors use special features to point out information. **Headings** are often at the top of a page and tell what part you are reading. **Labels** are words that give more information about details in pictures.

The heading on page 168 is **Fish**. What is this part about? There are also labels that give information. What do you learn about a fish's body?

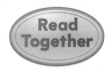

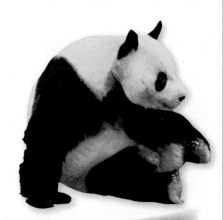

Your Turn

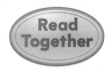
Read Together

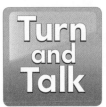

RETURN TO THE ESSENTIAL QUESTION

Turn and Talk **What makes birds different from mammals?** Choose an animal from each group. Use words and pictures from the selection to tell how the animals are alike and different. Ask questions if you do not understand your partner's ideas.

Classroom Conversation

Talk about these questions with your class.

1. How are all mammals alike?

2. How are fish different from mammals?

3. What are the five animal groups? What new things did you learn?

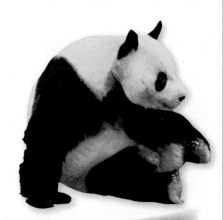

ELA RI.1.3, RI.1.7, W.1.8, SL.1.1c, SL.1.3

WRITE ABOUT READING

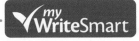

Response Use facts you learned from the selection to write a riddle about an animal. Write clues. Do not give its name. Read your riddle to a partner. Have your partner use the evidence in the clues to guess the answer.

I have gills and live in water.

Writing Tip

Use a question mark (**?**) at the end of a question.

PLAY

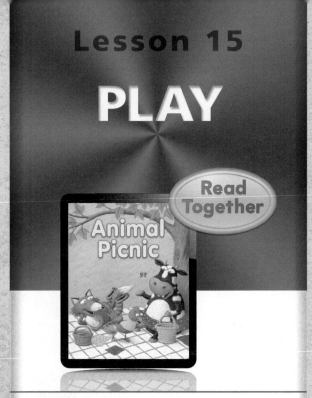

Read Together

Animal Picnic

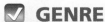
GENRE

A **play** is a story that people act out. Most of the words in a play are the words the characters say.

TEXT FOCUS

Stage directions are extra words in a play that tell about the characters and setting. They also tell what actions characters do. What are the stage directions in this play? How do you know?

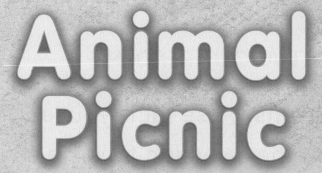

Animal Picnic

by Debbie O'Brien

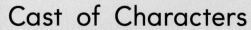

Cast of Characters

 Fox

 Cow

 Bird

 Hi, Cow and Bird. How was your trip?

 I had to walk to get here.

 I had to fly.

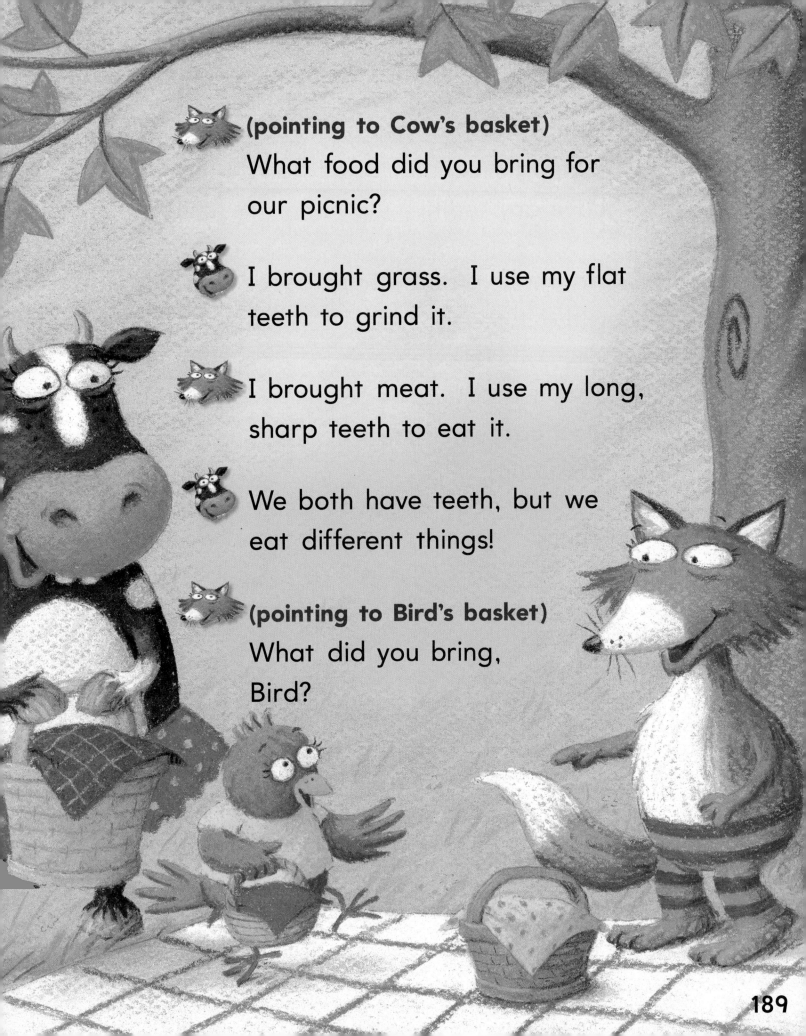

(pointing to Cow's basket)
What food did you bring for our picnic?

I brought grass. I use my flat teeth to grind it.

I brought meat. I use my long, sharp teeth to eat it.

We both have teeth, but we eat different things!

(pointing to Bird's basket)
What did you bring, Bird?

I did not bring grass or meat.
I brought seeds. Birds don't
have any teeth!

How will you eat those seeds
without teeth?

Watch this!
(Bird eats some seeds.)
Yum, yum, yum!

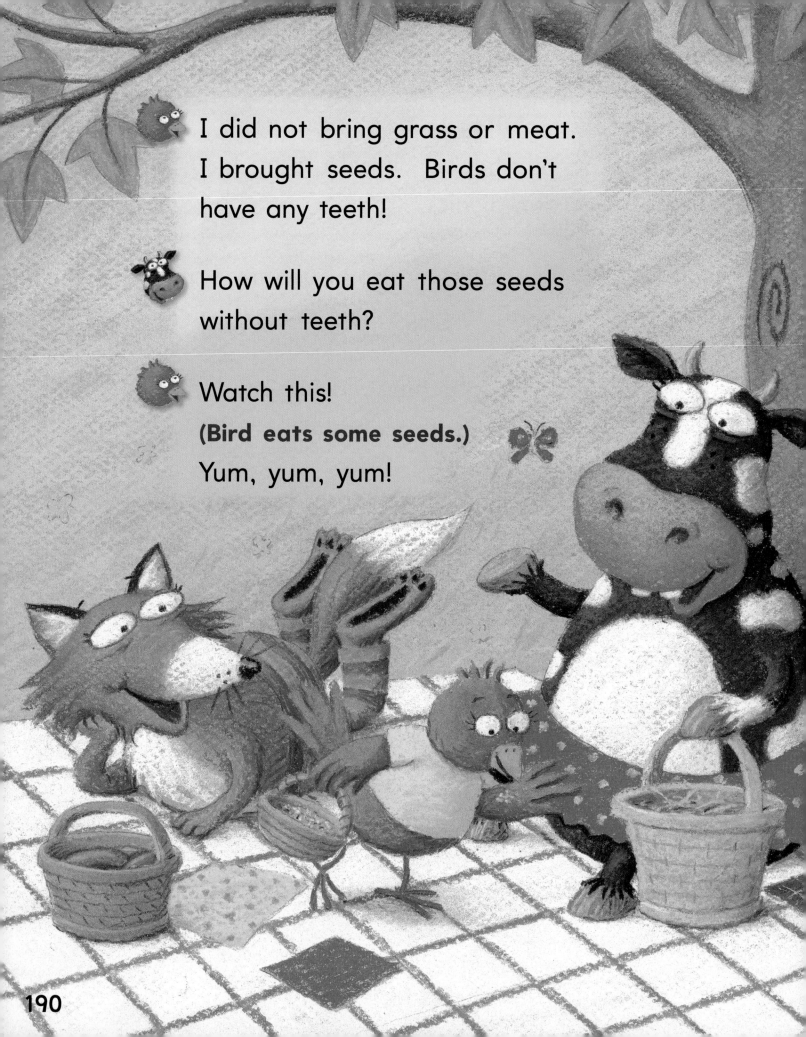

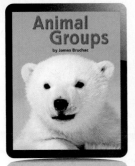
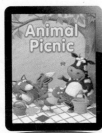
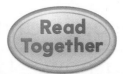

Compare Texts

Read Together

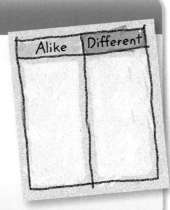

Compare Information Think about both selections. How are they alike and different? What information do you learn in each selection?

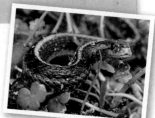

Talk About Animals Which animal group is your favorite? Talk about it with a partner. Use complete sentences.

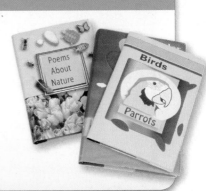

Write a Question Write a question you have about an animal in the selections. Use this book or other books to find the answer.

ELA RI.1.1, RI.1.9, W.1.8, SL.1.6

Grammar

The Verb be The verbs **is** and **are** tell what is happening now. Use **is** with a noun that names one.

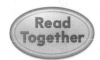

One	More Than One
This **chick** **is** small.	Two **chicks** **are** small.

The verbs **was** and **were** tell what happened in the past. Use **was** with a noun that names one.

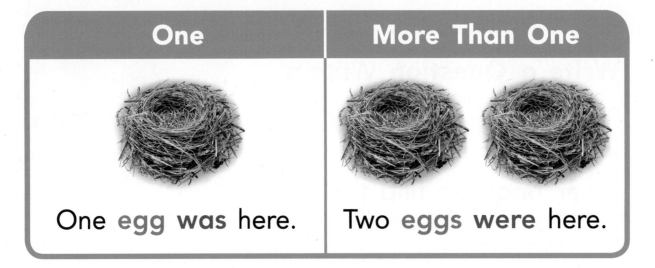

One	More Than One
One **egg** **was** here.	Two **eggs** **were** here.

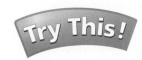

Read each sentence aloud two times, saying a different verb each time. Ask your partner to repeat the sentence with the correct verb. Then switch roles.

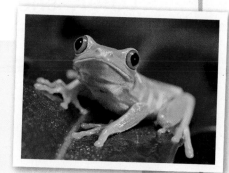

1. Animals _____**?**_____ many sizes.
         is   are

2. This frog _____**?**_____ small.
         is   are

3. A frog _____**?**_____ once a tiny tadpole.
      was   were

4. Lions _____**?**_____ little cubs.
     was   were

5. The snake _____**?**_____ long and thin.
       is   are

Connect Grammar to Writing

When you proofread your writing, be sure you have used the verbs **is**, **are**, **was**, and **were** correctly.

193

Informative Writing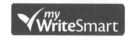

☑ **Elaboration** In a good **report**, the right words make the facts easy to understand. Lena drafted her report. Later, she wrote different words to make her meaning clear.

Revised Draft

Some lizards puff up ∧to
                    with air
bigger to an enemy.
look big.
           ∧

Revising Checklist

☑ Did I use words that make my meaning clear?

☑ Did I use correct punctuation?

☑ Did I spell words correctly?

☑ Did I write a good ending sentence?

Look for exact words in Lena's final copy. Then revise your writing. Use the Checklist.

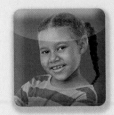

Final Copy

An Interesting Reptile

Lizards do some funny things. Some can change color quickly. Others run fast using only their back legs. Some lizards puff up with air to look bigger to an enemy. Lizards are very interesting reptiles.

Write a Report

Read Together

TASK Look at **At Home in the Ocean** and **Animal Groups.** Think about the different kinds of animals. Then write a report to explain to a friend or family member what reptiles are like.

PLAN ....

myNotebook

Use the tools in your eBook to remember facts about reptiles.

Gather Information Talk with a group about the reptiles in **Animal Groups** and the turtles in **At Home in the Ocean.** What did you learn about reptiles?

Write facts about reptiles on a chart.

- What will your report be about? This is the topic.

- How are all reptiles alike?

- Name and describe some reptiles. Tell how they move.

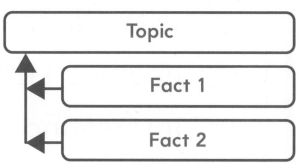

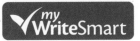

Write your draft in *my*WriteSmart.

Write Your Report   Follow these steps.

Topic Sentence

Write a topic sentence to tell the main idea of your report. Here are sentence ideas.

Reptiles are interesting because _____.

You can tell an animal is a reptile because _____.

Facts

Write sentences that tell facts about reptiles. Use your chart for ideas. Use the right verbs to go with the nouns. Add details to make your meaning clear.

All reptiles _____.

A _____ is an interesting reptile.

It has _____, _____, and _____.

It uses its _____ _____ to _____.

Ending

Write an ending for your report. Use one of these ideas or your own idea.

- Retell the main idea in different words.
- Tell the most interesting thing about reptiles.

my WriteSmart

Ask a partner to read your draft. Talk about how you can make it better.

Review Your Draft Read your writing and make it better. Use the Checklist.

☑ Did I explain what a reptile is?

☑ Does my topic sentence tell the main idea of my report?

☑ Did I use information from the texts to write my facts? Do I have examples of reptiles?

☑ Does each sentence have the correct verb?

☑ Did I spell words correctly?

PRESENT

Share Make a final copy of the report. Add pictures. Pick a way to share.

• Pretend you are on TV. Read your report.

• Glue your report to a reptile shape.

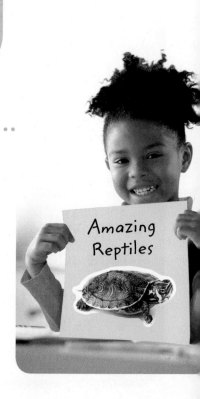

Amazing Reptiles

Words to Know

Unit 3 High-Frequency Words

⑪ At Home in the Ocean

blue	where
far	water
live	cold
little	their

⑭ The Big Race

two	over
into	four
three	five
starts	watch

⑫ How Leopard Got His Spots

brown	never
own	know
very	out
off	been

⑮ Animal Groups

bird	eyes
fly	or
both	those
long	walk

⑬ Seasons

green	fall
yellow	new
grow	down
open	goes

Glossary

A

amphibians
An **amphibian** is an animal that lives in water and on land. Frogs are **amphibians**.

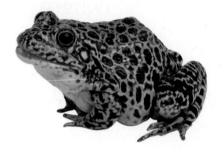

B

biggest
Something that is the **biggest** is bigger in size than anything else. The whale is the **biggest** animal in the ocean.

blow
To **blow** means to push air. The winds **blow** the cold air across the land.

body
The **body** of a person or animal is made up of the parts you can see and touch. We are learning about the parts of the **body**.

breathe

To **breathe** is to take in breaths of air. I **breathe** in the fresh air when I am outside.

C

cottontail

A **cottontail** is a kind of rabbit. That **cottontail** has a white fluffy tail.

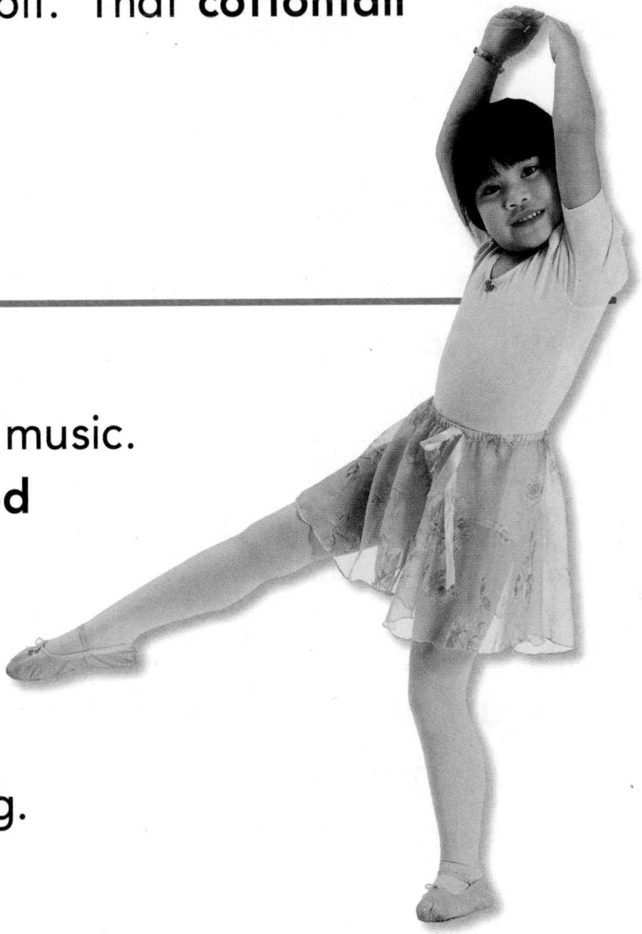

D

danced

To **dance** means to move to music. We played music and **danced** for hours.

day

A **day** is the time from one morning to the next morning. Tuesday was a sunny **day**.

F

feathers

A **feather** is a part of a bird. The bird had soft feathers.

feet

A foot is a measurement that equals 12 inches. **Feet** means more than one foot. Some trees can grow as tall as 100 **feet**.

flowers

A **flower** is a part of a plant. We planted pretty **flowers** in the garden.

G

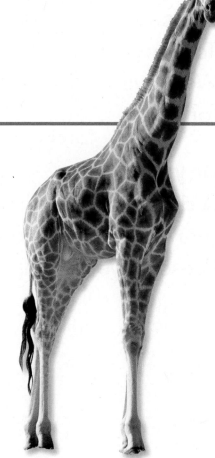

giraffe

A **giraffe** is a tall spotted animal with a long neck. The **giraffe** ate leaves from the top of the tree.

group

A **group** is a number of people or things together. A **group** of us went swimming last Saturday.

grow

When plants and animals **grow**, they get bigger and bigger. Kittens **grow** and become cats.

H

hair

Hair is what grows on your head. My dad cuts my **hair** when it gets too long.

hay

Hay is a kind of grass that has been cut and dried. My horse likes to eat **hay**.

home

A **home** is a place where people or animals live. Jellyfish make their **home** underwater.

hooray

Hooray is something people shout when they are happy. When I hit a home run, my parents yelled **hooray!**

hyena

A **hyena** is a wild animal that looks like a dog. The **hyena** is found in Africa and Asia.

L

leaves

A **leaf** is a part of a plant. In the fall, the **leaves** turn pretty colors.

leopard

A **leopard** is a wild animal that looks like a cat with spots. The **leopard** paced in its cage.

lions

A **lion** is a large wild animal that looks like a big cat. We saw a movie about **lions** in Africa.

lizard

A **lizard** is a small reptile. The **lizard** lay on the rock in the hot sun.

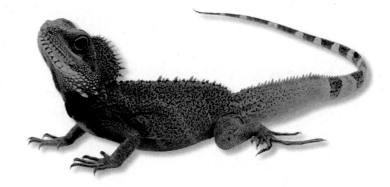

M

mammals

A **mammal** is a warm-blooded animal. Cats are **mammals**.

manatees

A **manatee** is a plant-eating animal with flippers and a flat tail that lives in warm water. When we visited Florida, we saw **manatees** swimming in the water.

O

ocean

An **ocean** is a large body of salt water. It's fun to sail on the **ocean**.

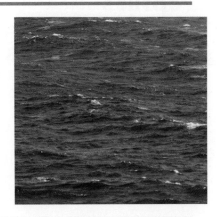

P

paint

To **paint** means to cover something with color. Aunt Carly likes to **paint** houses.

penguins

A **penguin** is a kind of bird that lives in cold places. **Penguins** keep their chicks warm.

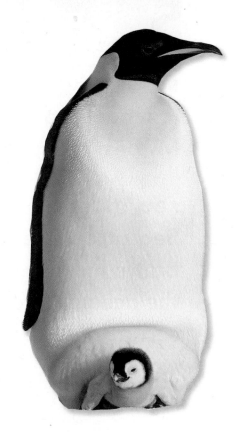

R

race

A **race** is a contest to find out who is the fastest. Selena got to the finish line first and won the **race**.

reptiles

A **reptile** is a cold-blooded animal. Snakes are **reptiles**.

roadrunner

A **roadrunner** is a very fast bird. We saw a **roadrunner** in the Arizona desert.

S

school

A **school** is a place where students learn from teachers. My best friend and I go to the same **school**.

sea otters

Sea otters are mammals with thick, brown fur that live in and by the ocean. After a swim, **sea otters** like to sit in the warm sun.

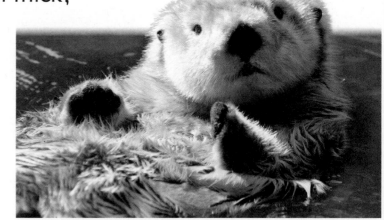

seeds

A **seed** is a part of a plant. Most plants grow from tiny little **seeds**.

snow

Snow is tiny pieces of frozen water that fall from the clouds. When we woke up, the ground was covered with **snow**.

snowman

A **snowman** looks like a person made of snow. We piled three balls of snow on top of each other and made a **snowman**.

spring

Spring is the season that comes after winter. In the **spring,** the flowers begin to bloom.

summer

Summer is the season that comes after spring. This **summer** my family will go to the beach.

T

tadpoles

A **tadpole** is a baby frog. I found **tadpoles** swimming in our pond.

tails

A **tail** is a part of some animals' bodies. Rats have long **tails**.

tall

To be **tall** is to stand high above the ground. The giraffe is very **tall**.

turtle

A **turtle** is a reptile with a shell. The **turtle** went inside its shell as soon as I touched it.

W

warm

Warm means not very hot. The tea was still **warm** after it sat for a while.

whales

A **whale** is the biggest mammal that lives in the ocean. When we went boating, we saw **whales** as big as our boat!

wings

A **wing** is a part that helps something to fly. The bird flapped its **wings** and flew away.

winter

Winter is a season that comes after fall. Last **winter** was very cold!

Z

zebra

A **zebra** is a striped animal that looks like a horse. My favorite animal is the **zebra**.

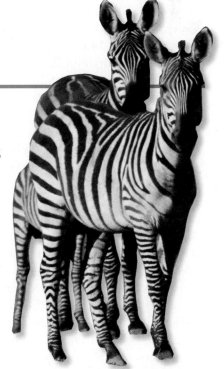

Copyright (c) 2007 by Houghton Mifflin Harcourt Publishing Company. Adapted and reproduced by permission from *The American Heritage First Dictionary* and *The American Heritage Children's Dictionary*.

Credits

Placement Key:
(r) right, (l) left, (c) center, (t) top, (b) bottom, (bg) background

Photo Credits

3 (cl) ©Photodisc/Getty Images; **3** (tl) ©Houghton Mifflin Harcourt; **3** (b) ©Melba Photo Agency/Alamy Images; **5** (tl) ©J.A. Kraulis/Masterfile; **5** (bl) ©2007 Jupiterimages; **5** (br) ©2007 PunchStock; **6** (bl) © Steve Skjold/Alamy; **7** (tl) ©Bela Baliko Photography and Publishing Inc; **7** (bl) ©blickwinkel/McPhoto/Alamy; Blind **8** ©PatrikOntkovic/Shutterstock; **9** ©belizar/Shutterstock; **10** (tr) ©Photodisc/Getty Images; **10** (br) ©Corbis; **10** (cl) ©Photodisc/Getty Images; **10** (tl) ©Houghton Mifflin Harcourt; **11** (tr) ©Corbis; **11** (tl) ©Amanda Friedman/Stone/Getty Images; **11** (cl) ©George Grall/National Geographic/Getty Images; **11** (cr) ©Stockbyte/Getty Images; **11** (bl) ©George Grall/National Geographic/Getty Images; **11** (br) ©Purestock/Getty Images; **12** © WaterFrame/Alamy; **14** ©Getty Images; **14** Courtesy of Rozanne Williams; **16** ©Brand X Pictures/Getty Images; **17** (c) Digital Vision/Getty Images; **18** David B Fleetham/Getty Images; **19** (tr) blickwinkel/Alamy; **20** (t) Science Source/Photo Researchers, Inc.; **20** Corbis; **21** (tr) Corbis; **22** Douglas Faulkner/Getty Images; **23** (tr) WaterFrame/Alamy; **24** Digital Vision/Getty Images; **25** (tr) M. Timothy O'Keefe/Alamy; **26** Mark Conlin/Alamy; **27** (tr) Mark Conlin/Alamy; **28** ©Houghton Mifflin Harcourt; **29** (tr) ©Melba Photo Agency/Alamy Images; **30** ©Houghton Mifflin Harcourt; **31** ©Photodisc/Alamy Images; **32** (tr) © Jake Hellbach/Alamy; **33** (c) Jose Luis Pelaez/Getty Images; **33** (tr) ©Houghton Mifflin Harcourt; **34** (inset) ©Lew Robertson/Getty Images; **34** (tl) ©Photodisc/Getty Images; **36** (bg) ©Photodisc/Getty Images; **36** ©Photodisc/Getty Images; **37** (cr) Photos.com/Jupiterimages/Getty Images; **37** (tr) ©Joel Simon/Digital Vision/Getty Images; **37** (tl) ©Houghton Mifflin Harcourt; **37** (tl) ©Photodisc/Getty Images; **42** (tl) © PhotoDisc/Getty Images; **42** (b) ©Alan D. Carey/Photodisc/Getty Images; **43** (tl) ©Design Pics Inc./Alamy; **43** (tr) ©Roger Tidman/CORBIS&#x0B;; **43** (bl) ©Gallo Images/Alamy; **43** (cl) ©Ann &

Steve Toon/Robert Harding World Imagery/Getty Images; **43** (bl) ©Rainer Jahns/Alamy; **43** (br) ©Tom Nebbia/Corbis; **44** Steve Bloom Images/Alamy; **45** (bg) L12: © Getty Images/Digital Vision; **65** ©stefanie van der vin/Fotolia; **67** Photodisc/Getty Images; **70** (bg) ©Tony Craddock/Photo Researchers, Inc.; **71** (cr) © Picture Partners/Alamy; **71** (br) ©Digital Vision/Getty Images; **73** ©Richard Hutchings/Photo Edit; **76** (t) ©Andrew Duke/Alamy; **76** (tl) ©J.A. Kraulis/Masterfile; **77** (tr) ©Jean Louis Bellurget/Stock Image/Jupiterimages; **77** (cl) ©Pete Turner/The Image Bank/Getty Images; **77** (bl) ©Ryan McVay/Taxi/Getty Images; **77** (bl) ©VEER Gildo Spadoni/Photonica/Getty Images; **77** (bl) ©Steve Mason/PhotoDisc/Getty Images; **78** ©HMH; **78** (tl) ©J.A. Kraulis/Masterfile; **80** ©J.A. Kraulis/Masterfile; **82** ©2007 Masterfile Corporation; **84** ©Bill Leaman/Dembinsky Photo; **85** ©Richard Hutchings/Photo Edit; **86** ©2007 Jupiterimages; **88** ©Masterfile; **89** ©2007 Masterfile Corporation; **90** ©2007 Masterfile Corporation; **92** (bg) ©Garry Black/Masterile; **93** (c) ©2007 PunchStock; **94** ©Tim Pannell/Corbis; **96** (c) ©George McCarthy/naturepl.com; **97** ©2007 PunchStock; **97** (t) ©BrandX; **98** (t) ©2007 PunchStock; **98** (bl) ©Richard Hutchings/Photo Edit; **99** (b) ©2007 PunchStock; **100** (tl) ©J.A. Kraulis/Masterfile; **101** ©Richard Hutchings/Photo Edit; **103** (tl) ©J.A. Kraulis/Masterfile; **103** (c) © willy matheisl/Alamy; **115** (br) © Cartesia/Photodisc/Getty Images; **115** (tl) ©J.A. Kraulis/Masterfile; **115** (cr) ©Jerzyworks/Masterfile; **120** (tc) © Steve Skjold/Alamy; **120** (t) ©ARCO/H Reinhard; **120** (b) © John Foxx/Stockbyte/Getty Images; **121** (tl) ©Danita Delimont/Alamy Images; **121** (tr) ©Photos.com; **121** (cl) ©Photos.com; **121** (cr) ©Jonathan Blair/Crocodile Fotos; **121** (bl) ©QT LUONG/Terra Galleria Photography; **121** (br) ©franzfoto.com/Alamy; **122** ©Alistair Berg/Getty Images; **145** (l) © PhotoAlto/Alamy; **145** (r) © PhotoAlto/Alamy; **148** (r) Big Cheese Photo LLC/Alamy; **148** (tl) © Steve Skjold/Alamy; **149** (tl) Steve Skjold/Alamy; **149** (r) Jose Luis Pelaez/Getty Images; **149** (b) Patrick LaCroix/Alamy; **150** Arctic-Images/Alamy; **151** (b) Jim West/Alamy; **151** (t) Ron Chapple Stock/Alamy; **152** (t) Superstudio/Getty Images; **152** (bg) imagebroker/Alamy; **153** (t) © Visions of America, LLC/Alamy; **153** (b) Fancy/Alamy;

154 © Steve Skjold/Alamy; **155** (tc) © Steve Skjold/Alamy; **157** (c) ©Patrik Giardino/CORBIS; **160** (b) © BRIAN ELLIOTT/Alamy; **160** (t) ©Alan and Sandy Carey/Photodisc/Getty Images; **160** (tl) ©Bela Baliko Photography and Publishing Inc; **161** (tr) ©John W Banagan/Getty Images; **161** (cr) ©Raymond Gehman/National Geographic/Getty Images; **161** (br) ©Gerry Ellis/Getty Images; **161** (bl) ©Georgette Douwma/Photographer's Choice RR/Getty Images; **161** (cl) ©Andy Thompson/Alamy; **162** ©George Grall/National Geographic/Getty Images; **162** (tl) ©Bela Baliko Photography and Publishing Inc; **164** (tl) ©Bela Baliko Photography and Publishing Inc; **165** (bg) ©Bela Baliko Photography and Publishing Inc; **166** (cr) ©Vibe Images/Jack Goldfarb/Alamy Images; **166** (tl) ©Georgette Douwma/Getty Images; **166** (bl) ©Peter Arnold, Inc./Alamy; **167** (b) © DLILLC/Corbis; **167** (t) ©Gail Shumway/Getty Images; **168** ©Photodisc/Getty Images; **170** ©Jeffrey L. Rotman/CORBIS; **171** (c) ©blickwinkel/McPhoto/Alamy; **172** (c) ©Stephen Frink/Getty Images; **172** (inset) ©Kevin Schafer/Corbis; **174** ©Yanik Chauvin/Shutterstock; **175** ©Digital Vision/Getty Images; **176** ©Masterfile; **177** (b) ©uwesMASAIMARA/Alamy Images; **177** (tr) ©John Giustina/Getty Images; **177** (tl) ©Darren Bennett/Animals Animals - Earth Scenes; **178** ©VCL/Getty Images; **179** ©Dave King/Dorling Kindersley; **180** ©Karen Su/Getty Images; **181** ©PhotoDisc/Getty Images; **181** (inset) ©Alan D. Carey/PhotoDisc/Getty Images; **183** Rommel/Masterfile; **184** (tl) ©Bela Baliko Photography and Publishing Inc; **185** David Cook/blueshiftstudios/Alamy; **187** (tr) ©Bela Baliko Photography and Publishing Inc; **191** (tl) ©Bela Baliko Photography and Publishing Inc; **192** (b) ©Steven Puetzer/Getty Images; **192** (tr) ©Photodisc/Getty Images; **192** (tl) ©Daly and Newton/Getty Images; **198** (bg) ©Houghton Mifflin Harcourt; **198** (inset) ©Przemyslaw Rzeszutko/Alamy Images; **G2** © Getty Images; **G3** © Comstock, Inc.; **G4** © Comstock, Inc./jupiter images; **G5** © Harald Sund/Brand X Pictures/JupiterImages; **G6** Getty Images/Photodisc; **G7** Getty Images; **G7** (t) ©Don Farrall/Photodisc/Getty Images; **G8** ©Exactostock/SuperStock; **G9** ©Cavan Images/Getty Images; **G10** ©Sebastian Green/Alamy Images; **G11** (b) ©Alan and Sandy Carey/Getty Images

Illustrations
Cover Jimmy Pickering; **35** Robert Schuster; **37** Ken Bowser; **41** Sally Vitsky; **46–63** Gerald McDermott; **69** Patrick Gnan; **70** Gary Antonetti; **75** Sally Vitsky; **124–143** Viviana Garafoli; **188–190** Lynn Chapman; **195** Jan Bryan-Hunt.

All other photos: Houghton Mifflin Harcourt Photo Libraries and Photographers.